MW00333273

Character Transformation through the Psychotherapeutic Relationship

Character Transformation through the Psychotherapeutic Relationship

Robert E. Hooberman

JASON ARONSON INC.
Northvale, New Jersey
London

This book was set in 11 pt. Berthold Baskerville by Pageworks and printed and bound by Book-Mart Press, Inc. of North Bergen, NJ.

Copyright © 2002 by Jason Aronson Inc.

10 9 8 7 6 5 4 3 2 1

All rights reserved. No part of this book may be used or reproduced in any manner whatsoever without written permission from Jason Aronson Inc. except in the case of brief quotations in reviews for inclusion in a magazine, newspaper, or broadcast.

Library of Congress Cataloging-in-Publication Data

Hooberman, Robert E.
    Character transformation through the psychotherapeutic relatioship / Robert E. Hooberman.
        p. ; cm.
    Includes bibliographical references and index.
    ISBN 0–7657–0353–X
        1. Personality disorders–Treatment.   2. Psychotherapy.   I. Title.
    [DNLM: 1. Personality Disorders–therapy.   2. Character.   3. Defense Mechanisms.   4. Professional-Patient Relations. WM 190 H776c 2001]
    RC480.55 .H655 2001
    616.89'14–dc21

                                        2001046170

Printed in the United States of America on acid-free paper. For information and catalog, write to Jason Aronson Inc., 230 Livingston Street, Northvale, NJ 07647–1726, or visit our website: www.aronson.com

To
Barbara

CONTENTS

PREFACE

This work took shape during my years of practice as a psychotherapist and analyst as I wondered about the mystery of change through psychoanalytic treatment. Over and over I found myself thinking about the difficulty that most experience in trying to change entrenched personality patterns. I have come to understand how crucial a sense of safety is for all and that many psychological problems represent attempts to attain that security under the press of internal and external exigencies. As I have gained experience, I have become more sympathetic to the ills of my patients, striving to understand how their attempts to be safe have created these unhappy solutions to confusing and perplexing intrapsychic and interpersonal problems. I have come to understand that it is difficult to change patterns that seem to offer a modicum of safety and satisfaction despite the pain that is experienced by the existence of the symptom. As I describe in this work, these patterns become internalized and form the patient's character structure.

I will go on to describe how this structure contains embedded conflicts and compromise formations, internalized self and other representations and reflects what I characterize as the 'family language;' the idiosyncratic way that the patient and family have learned to apprehend workings of the mind and of the world. From attempts to get my hands around the complexities of my patients' pain, I have realized that the therapy is most effective when I use the present day functioning of the patient to inform us of the elusive unconscious. Consequently, I have learned to focus on the preconscious, an aspect of which I define as the 'implicit,' that allows me a more comprehensive access to the patient's mind.

My hope is that the approach that I propose in this book will lead others to see symptoms and disorders as attempts at adaptations as opposed to pejorative psychopathological entities and to understand that an approach that looks at character structure provides a deeper and more satisfying treatment than that accorded by approaches more circumscribed.

I have been fortunate in having a number of colleagues and supervisors who have contributed greatly to my development. I am particularly grateful to four supervisors who have been clinically astute yet, more importantly, have recognized my particular talents and peculiarities and have supported and encouraged me in ways that have helped me move forward personally and professionally. F. Edward Rice, Ph.D., Linda Sherby, Ph.D., Murray Meisels, Ph.D., and Evangeline Spindler, M.D. have my gratitude. Dr. Sherby's warmth and kindness are especially appreciated. My colleagues have greatly stimulated my thinking and have moved me toward conceptualizations of behavior and personality that I could not have achieved on my own. I am lucky to be involved in an institute that values diversity and open-mindedness. Many thought provoking and enhancing conversations have occurred while traversing the hills of Ann Arbor with my good friend and running partner, David Klein, Ph.D. Karen Baker, MSW, another close friend, has demonstrated to me great courage and perseverance. Others who have been especially supportive and intellectually stimulating are: Jean Apperson, Ph.D., Marilyn Charles, Ph.D. Diane Drayson, A.M., Edward Gibeau, Ed. D., Norman Gordon, Ph.D., Bertram Karon, Ph.D., Brenda Lepisto, Psy.D., Jay Radin, Ph.D., Mark Root, M.D., Ellen Toronto, Ph.D., and Lynne Tenbusch, Ph.D. I am particularly grateful to George Greenman, M.D. of whose kindness and clinical acumen I continue to aspire. I have had the opportunity to work with an extraordinary editor, Eve Golden, M.D. who has demonstrated a remarkable ability to keep me focused and clear and to convey my point of view succinctly and without artifice. I am extremely grateful for her assistance.

My wife, Barbara, has shown great patience and understanding during the nights and weekends that have been sacrificed to this work. My children, Jessica and Josh, with their combination of bemused affection and sharp observations about their father have kept me on the righteous path of self-questioning. I am particularly grateful for the trust and kindness of my patients who have graciously allowed me entry into their lives and from whom I have learned the most.

I

◆

THE
THERAPEUTIC
EXPERIENCE

◆

Loewald (1960) once said that his interest in writing about the therapeutic interaction was to throw light on areas that he felt were not fully illuminated. My own interest is in the nature of change and transformation in psychotherapy, and I will aim my lantern at some of the darker corners of this intriguing topic, including especially the constellation of individual beliefs, habits, and psychic structures that we call character.

My goal is to look at the aspects of the therapeutic relationship that seem to me to facilitate or inhibit change, and to address some related clinical issues in this context. These are complementary endeavors; changes in clinical technique and focus reflect one's theoretical perspective, and vice versa. Like Schafer (1983), I will approach these concepts phenomenologically, and I do not intend a thorough critical analysis of the literature. This work is not designed to be exhaustive or encyclopedic, nor is it a work of psychoanalytic ideology. I do not find theoretical rigidity helpful either to therapists or to patients. On the other hand, because every clinician adopts the particular perspectives that match his or her personal worldview, it is not always possible, or desirable, to be all-inclusive.

I will focus in this exploration on the methods that individuals develop to cope with external and internal impingements: the habitual stance toward the world that we recognize as "personality." All people develop ways of dealing with the pressures of life that feel to them most safe and effective (although an outside observer might see it otherwise). These modes of *psychic survival* are first adopted at moments of stress, when they feel crucial and essential to the person who resorts to them. Even after the immediate stress subsides, however, personality configuration is shaped by these prior attempts to cope with the often overwhelming and traumatic exigencies of life. The resulting constellations of character represent *adaptive* responses that provide at least a modicum of satisfaction while at the same time affording an individual a tolerable level of safety and security.

These modes of survival are conceived and established as solutions to internal psychic difficulties, and although they may be potentially psychopathological and problematic, they must be respected as efforts to handle the underlying pain that is the impetus for their creation. They are creative solutions that represent, from the individual's perspective, the best choice available. Over time, these choices, these solutions, become the essence of the person's character structure. A characterological approach to psychotherapy implies attention to this kind of preconscious material; the subtleties of character, seldom verbalized and usually what I call "implicit," play a vital role in the success, or failure, of treatment. My own belief is that attention to such matters enriches the therapist as well as the patient, not only increasing appreciation for the integrity of the individual but also for the complexity and value of the therapeutic work.

The reader will notice that a couple of themes meander throughout the book, escaping frequently from the chapters that address them explicitly. One of these is the characterologic uses of defense, another is the pervasiveness of structural (as opposed to sexual) sadomasochism, and a third is the nature and effect of trauma. These three themes are too important and too universal to be contained or encapsulated in one or two chapters, thus I have allowed myself to expand upon them when they come up in relation to other matters. In particular this is true of early trauma, by which I mean both cataclysmic and cumulative trauma. It is important to me to make this dimension explicit because traumatic events, both large and small, have such profound effects on the development of character and its structure. Although much has been said about the effects of catastrophic trauma, it is my belief that the *subtle* effects on character development of both cumulative and catastrophic trauma have not sufficiently been described.

It would be helpful to define and to draw distinctions between cumulative and catastrophic trauma. By catastrophic or cataclysmic trauma I am referring to those experiences, such as those of Holocaust survivors, that are overwhelming to the subject's ego. Such experiences cause profound and enduring effects on the individual's psychic development. Cumulative trauma (to use a term coined by Khan, 1963) refers to ongoing assaults on the young child's ego, which individually may be tolerable, but in combination become overwhelming to the chiqľ's psyche. Greenacre (1967) and Shengold (1989), in particular with his descriptions of "soul murder," provide elaborations on cumulative trauma. I will be discussing their contributions in later chapters.

In this chapter and the two that follow I will investigate various aspects of the structure of the psychotherapeutic situation in the context of a characterological approach. Chapters IV, V, and VI deal with some important clinical manifestations of character. Chapters VII, VIII, and IX deal specifically with therapeutic (and therefore character) change.

THE BEGINNING

Most people who seek psychotherapy know very little about it, or even about the problems that bring them to the consulting room. They come because they feel pain—depression or unhappiness, a marriage on the rocks, a problem with alcohol or drug abuse, or a sense that something is just not right. It is the psychotherapist's job to educate prospective patients: on the nature the problem (*diagnosis,* or perhaps more accurately *assessment*); on what the patient can expect from treatment (*goals);* and on how these goals can be reached (*treatment methods).* In the rest of this chapter, I will elaborate on these three facets of the treatment situation, always from the point of view of the patient's experience in psychotherapy and the way that issues of character are important in establishing a constructive therapeutic milieu.

The process of psychoanalytic psychotherapy is, and sometimes remains, a mystery to many patients, despite their supposed active participation in it. One important contribution of a characterological approach to psychotherapy is that it gives patients an accessible way to understand the intricacies of personality functioning. A characterological perspective acknowledges the complexities of psychological functioning and the pervasiveness of psychological disorders, thus offering a context in which patients are better able to tolerate the rigors of intensive treatment. It also envisions psychological problems as efforts at adaptive problem solving, creating a nonpejorative atmosphere that provides additional support to already fragile, vulnerable, and self-critical new patients.

CHARACTER–THE PATIENT'S WORLDVIEW

What then must we convey to our patients to give them this extra resilience and confidence in the therapeutic undertaking? To my way of thinking, it is the characterological perspective that allows psychological problems to be seen in a broad, inclusive, and noncritical context. If this perspective is to be conveyed effectively to the patient, however, the therapist must get it in focus first.

Everyone has a characteristic way of behaving and relating in the world, which I will call a "worldview." The worldview includes belief systems about why and how people–oneself and others–operate. These beliefs are both conscious and unconscious, are very pervasive, and may cause considerable problems for the individuals who hold them, based as they so often are on childhood misconceptions, distortions, and fantasies. Yet such worldviews are not usually available for discussion, at least not early in treatment. Their roots are unconscious and their operation is preconscious, thus they are rarely articulated or even subjected to the patient's consideration. They are often ego-syntonic, in that they do not necessarily appear to derive from psychic difficulties but are felt to be intrinsic to the person's "personality," sometimes even by the person's therapist, and so may be dismissed as just personal beliefs, with no relevance to the therapeutic task.

Furthermore, implicit beliefs like this form the basis of our everyday thoughts, habits, and behaviors. We hold on to them dearly, and rightly so, because they contribute richly to our sense of individuality. This too makes them difficult to get at in therapy; the tenacious hold that some patients keep on such beliefs may be as much a matter of integrity as of resistance. For many people, the sense of individuality is a developmental accomplishment, achieved with difficulty in the face of parental attempts to dominate and subordinate. To surrender cherished beliefs may feel like failure, shame, or degradation–in short, humiliation. This is why it is so important when working with implicit belief systems to keep in mind how much people need to maintain a hard-won sense of self and to form an alliance around the exploration of such deeply built-in tendencies. Pine (1990) points out that patients strive for consistency in their sense of self, a desire for the familiar—the sense of being "home"—even at the cost of considerable self-negation and pain. To this end they may hold on to self-defeating behaviors despite "on the mark" interpretations by a sensitive analyst, unless the analyst can convey a real respect for what the maladaptive behavior has done for the patient in the past, and what it continues to mean.

CHARACTER AND CHANGE

Joseph (1992) makes this point too. From her point of view, every analyst holds in mind a "theory or theories of desirable psychic change, of what he hopes he may achieve in his work, which is his vertex. The patient consciously wishes to change, but dreads any disturbance to his sense of equilibrium, the way in which he deals with anxieties and defenses, the organization which he regards as best—this is his vertex" (p. 237). In her words, every patient tries to "maintain his psychic balance." Discordances between patient and analyst may result when an analyst tries to impose a personal sense of what the patient needs without taking into account the patient's own sense of these things. Contrariwise, when patients try to match their "vertices" to their analysts', aspects of the self that require analysis will be obscured.

 Garcia Badaracco (1992) suggests that, "The difficult patient is a specialist in non-change" (p. 210). This is a wonderful description, and I would extend it to the more global, "*All* patients are specialists in nonchange, and difficult patients are the real experts." Like most analysts, I firmly believe that psychoanalytic treatment offers the best opportunity for significant personal change and have both witnessed and participated in this process. It is an arduous and difficult process, however, and we must not delude ourselves, or our patients, that it is anything but. Psychological habits infiltrate to the deepest levels of the personality; enduring change occurs within attention to the details of thoughts, feelings, and fantasies. Each participant in the treatment brings to it an *idiosyncratic* way of seeing things. It is the coming together and separation of two individual belief systems that creates insight and change. All individuals have strong needs for a consistent and stable sense of the self and its integrity, and these needs oppose the wish for change. For this reason a certain divergence between the attitudes of patient and therapist is necessary to effect change (see chapter VII). Too much congruence means insufficient distance on the patient's character—the therapist shares the patient's own blind spots and may not recognize problems—while too much distance creates discordance and a sense of isolation. From this perspective, all analytic work is character analysis.

Another reason why assessment must be a joint and ongoing process is that people do not come to therapy with encapsulated symptoms—their symptomatic behavior and feelings are manifestations of pervasive aspects of their mental functioning. This too must be conveyed to our patients if they are to be active and informed participants in the therapeutic process. A complete view of people must include how they think about their minds, their beliefs, and their mental representations of self—and others—including their operating theories about why they (and others) behave as they do. This "theory of mind," as Fonagy (1991) calls it, "denotes the collection of intuitive ideas that all of us possess concerning mental functioning and the nature of perceptual experience, memory, beliefs, attributions, intentions, emotions and desires" (p. 640).

Fonagy calls "the capacity to conceive of conscious and unconscious mental states in oneself and others" the capacity to *mentalize* (p. 641) and recognizes it as a crucial ability. A person who has little experience of reflection and who does not really recognize the existence of separate minds cannot adequately imagine the links between cause and effect, or handle intense affect effectively. Patients, like all of us, have a "theory of mind" that reflects how they experience themselves as people, how they conceptualize causality, and consequently how they imagine others do. This "theory" is a pervasive and enduring aspect of their personality and helps define their essence. Character must be studied in analysis for this reason also; the delineation of a patient's theory of mind provides both participants with information about how events, feelings, and thoughts are processed, and about the meaning ascribed to them.

According to Fonagy (1991, see also Fonagy and Moran, 1991), problems in mentalizing result primarily from preoedipal developmental disturbances. People with *early* developmental problems that limit their ability to internalize mental representations of others are likely to lack the abilities to empathize and to see others as being separate and distinct, with minds of their own. Consequently, appropriate interventions focus on the ability to tolerate conflict. Interventions regarding forbidden thoughts and wishes are not likely to be as helpful as ones designed to help the patient understand that minds contain thoughts and volition, and thus come to an appreciation of the subjectivity of thought. This results in an increased capacity for empathy, for tolerance of affect and conflict, and in a heightened awareness of the deleterious effects of parents' externalization of their own pathology—in other words, a strengthening of ego capabilities.

However, although the distinction (Killingmo, 1989) between neurotic disorders and disorders related to developmental deficits is helpful, these two categories are not rigidly dichotomous. It is helpful to think about the ability to mentalize—to hold and consider thoughts—with all of our patients, regardless of the underlying pathology. Most people have room to become more self-reflective and thoughtful than they are, and for a deeper understanding that their behavior is motivated—as opposed to random—and that they can exert control over themselves by *thinking*.

> I had an obese patient with diabetes and other life-threatening health issues. She acted unwisely in a number of areas of her life, getting into frequent, almost violent confrontations with roommates and co-workers, for example. When we started working together, she let me know that she had seen a plethora of therapists in the past, with limited benefit. We discussed her overeating and her affect storms, and it quickly became apparent that she had never considered thinking and self-reflection as problem-solving options. At first she couldn't believe that I would suggest something as preposterous as waiting before acting. This was incompatible with her theory of mind, which was that troublesome thoughts should not be permitted to enter awareness. That recognition led to a consideration of what motivated her behavior, and with it the possibility of developing control. After one eating binge I asked her to think about what might have been bothering her prior to her overeating, and she was able to recall having had feelings of sexual arousal. Eventually she was able to understand that her eating behavior served several functions: to satisfy sexual needs while remaining apparently nonsexual, to keep her fused with overly dependent and dominating parents, and to act out her mother's hostile wishes against her.

This patient demonstrates clearly how an apparently encapsulated symptom may in fact be no such thing, and also how important it is to convey this to the patient at some point in the assessment process. Symptoms come embedded in a character structure that may not work for its owner as successfully as that person might wish. Correspondingly, the changes that patients look for are not necessarily limited to the relief of an encapsulated symptom, either. They are usually quite global and more in the nature of a kind of transformation. The stakes in modern psychotherapy are higher than they were in the days when symptoms were addressed with the interpretation of intrapsychic conflict alone. The entire personality is involved and therefore must be fully engaged; the patient and therapist both must understand this, and both must be fully and actively engaged in the assessment and goal-setting process and in the therapeutic interaction.

GOALS

As I have said, people have something in mind that they want to accomplish when they enter treatment. There is a theoretical controversy in the psychoanalytic literature, however, about the advisability of setting treatment goals or even thinking in terms of desirable outcomes (Bader, 1994). Those who advocate "goallessness" believe that the work of analysis is to analyze and that desirable outcome will follow from this; understanding is given priority over behavioral change. Too much emphasis on "cure" is viewed as potentially dangerous, both because underlying issues may be obscured by too great a focus on the external and because it can feed the narcissistic grandiosity of the therapist. Bion (1967) has said that an analyst who wishes to focus on the issue of the moment, and to provide a free and unencumbered space for their patients' exploration, must begin each session without "memory or desire." Freud supported this point of view in the Little Hans case: "Therapeutic success . . . is not our primary aim; we endeavor rather to enable the patient to obtain a conscious grasp of his unconscious wishes" (Freud, 1909, p. 120). The opposing point of view maintains that the object of therapy is also to alleviate suffering and that to ignore this is both short-sighted and dismissive of the wishes of the patient, who is seeking a "cure" of some sort.

Paradox is an essential aspect of much psychoanalytic inquiry, and so it is here; I think that both points of view are correct. "Goallessness" permits the free range of thought–free association–without which patients cannot engage their whole selves in the analytic enterprise. A curative agenda may be too limiting or encourage compliance in the patient. But patients enter treatment with *specific and concrete* goals in mind, not (usually) with the open-ended expectation of becoming more introspective and insightful. Furthermore, a therapist's assessment of a patient includes the awareness that something has gone amiss, that something needs correcting. Out of this awareness, the therapist aims interpretations in a certain direction, with a certain corrective goal in mind. Goallessness is therefore a worthwhile and essential aspect of the psychoanalytic process—but so is work toward particular ends.

How can we delineate this paradox more constructively? Sandler (1992), following Wallerstein (1965), differentiates between process and outcome goals. Process goals relate to the patient's ability to function analytically and include such phenomena as increased capacities for insight and introspection, and the expansion of ego functioning. Process goals often exist outside of the patient's awareness; people are not usually aware of the weaknesses of their own ego functioning. Outcome goals refer to improvements in the patient's situation, such as alleviation of symptoms. This is not a simple dichotomy, however. Process goals have a life impact as well, as patients internalize the analytic process as a tool for examining life events throughout treatment and continue to use it after termination. Outcome goals are, of course, influenced by the achievement of the process goals, and the desired outcome will in turn affect process goals. "If we are realistic, our view of outcome must depend on our view of what analysis can achieve in any particular patient" (Sandler, 1992, p. 192). I will explore the importance of assessment and how it informs interpretation and analytic focus in the next chapter.

I find it helpful to differentiate three different aspects of what people wish to accomplish when they come into therapy. Every patient has *explicit* goals, *implicit* goals (of which they may not be aware and which relate to their worldview and character structure) and *hidden* (unconscious fantasy) goals. Explicit goals are presented *specifically and directly* by the patient, and usually appear rational and reasonable: the relief of depression, progress in a career, resolution of marital problems. Implicit goals may be reflected in the way the patient presents to the therapist and may be reflected back by the therapist's view of the patient. For instance, consider my patient, whom I will refer to as Dr. R., who presented herself as "depressed." My evaluation led me to believe that her *explicit* complaint of depression reflected more characterological concerns in that she lacked direction and a real sense of self. I articulated this to her and suggested that this was an important area for us to address, and she agreed readily and with relief. She could not have articulated this *implicit* problem, but she recognized it as soon as I put it into words. As treatment progressed, more of her character structure became manifest, allowing her to identify and work with for the first time these hitherto unarticulated personality characteristics. Her *hidden* goal was that I would provide her with a new personality, and, because she hated being a woman, that I would refashion her into a man. Of course, neither of us was aware of such fantasies at the beginning of treatment. Nor were we aware of all of the implicit goals that needed to be addressed. When I am developing a treatment arrangement with a new patient, however, I do try to speak of the implicit goals that I *am* aware of. It helps cement the relationship, it provides a view of the patient's personality *that is less fantasy bound than the patient's own view,* and it offers a context for the work that needs to be done. (On the occasions that I do have an inkling of a hidden fantasy, I do not usually mention it; such fantasies are likely to be frightening and discouraging so early in treatment.) I feel that it is important to help patients clarify, insofar as possible, what they want to accomplish in our work. Informed consent requires that we involve patients in treatment planning as much as we can and that outcome goals should be formulated with the patient. For some patients, by far the most important goal is to be able to develop a life narrative—to be able finally to articulate feelings and concerns—and to *experience* a particular kind of relationship never before savored. To be most effective, psychoanalytic treatment must focus on implicit and hidden issues, and to add another layer of complexity, psychoanalytic clinicians must be comfortable with the paradox implicit in the very notion of defense: A behavior can both reflect simultaneously a need and a defense against that need. There are very few certainties in our business.

HOW PSYCHOTHERAPY ENABLES CHANGE

Recapitulating my theme of this chapter and pursuing it a bit further, patients who seek psychotherapy are not looking only to know how their minds work, or the "cause" of their difficulties, they seek a sort of transformation that will grant them greater security and peace of mind. *Change* is part of the desired outcome; intellectual searches for mere "understanding" are not enough. A therapeutic relationship that does not convey to the patient an *active* appreciation for the necessity of change and transformation does not sufficiently take into account the patient's needs, and therefore does not provide an adequate holding environment.

In addition, as I suggested previously, the stakes are higher now than they once were as psychodynamic psychotherapists continue to widen the scope of hoped-for therapeutic efficacy. The apparently encapsulated symptomatology of earlier days is rarely seen. When it is, careful attention is given to the personality disorders that underlie it and, as in the perspective offered here, to character structure. Countertransference manifestations continue to be used as sources of important information to the therapist-patient dyad. The therapeutic relationship is a matter of crucial importance, both as a source of diagnostic information and as a vehicle toward cure. It is such an important aspect of therapeutic success that individual psychotherapists must give considerable thought to their own ways of envisioning and using the therapeutic relationship. The more clearly one understands one's own conception of the use of the therapeutic relationship, the more effective one becomes.

The thoughts of Strachey (1934) and Loewald (1960) on the therapeutic relationship are remarkable even today in their freshness and salience. Their works are so important, so well known, and have been so much discussed that I will not summarize them extensively. Both works emphasize the importance of the therapeutic relationship in the search for change. Strachey coined the term *mutative interpretation* to describe interpretations that create change for the patient. The mutative interpretation breaks the cycle between the patient's introjected and projected hostile impulses. In essence, the analyst's benign interpretations enable the patient to introject a new object, one considerably less punitive and demanding than the old. These mutative interpretations have beneficial effects when they occur in "minute" doses, says Strachey. "The gradual nature of the changes brought about in psychoanalysis will be explained if, as I am suggesting, those changes are the result of the summation of an immense number of minute steps, each of which corresponds to a mutative interpretation" (1934, p. 144).

This comment addresses the importance of microscopic attention to the details of patients' associations, an important aspect of character-based psychotherapy, but the paper as a whole delineates the transforming nature of the therapeutic relationship. Change, according to Strachey, does not result solely from sterile interpretations of conflict and compromise formation. Psychic and behavioral change occurs within the therapeutic relationship. Loewald states, "If 'structural changes in the patient's personality' means anything, it must mean that we assume that ego-development is resumed in the therapeutic process in psychoanalysis. And this resumption of ego-development is contingent on the relationship with a new object, the analyst" (1960, p. 16).

Loewald speaks again and again of the need to attain the new object, the analyst. I, however, like most practicing therapists, believe that the necessary ego development can occur only within an atmosphere of safety, with a concerned and attentive participant and observer.

A patient in the throes of a transference storm and bemoaning her dependency on me asked why she could not do this (that is, psychotherapy) by herself. I decided to respond to her question, telling her that she needed a listener, someone to hear and to respond to her feelings and concerns, in ways that she had never experienced before. She was moved by this response.

Just as an adolescent needs someone to push against, psychotherapy patients need an alive and engaged listener, a new object with whom they can explore frightening territory safely.

The importance of the therapeutic interaction is recognized over and over again in the psychoanalytic world. It is couched in varying terms to fit different theoretical orientations, but throughout the literature, the therapist's engagement with the patient is deemed essential in effecting change. Explicitly or implicitly, all contemporary psychoanalytic models suggest a creative engagement between patient and therapist. This goes beyond the awareness and use of countertransference, beyond even the use of enactments, and embraces the larger supposition that patients—nay, people—need interpersonal engagement in order to prosper. From the characterological point of view, even symptomatic manifestations that appear to be easily identifiable as manifestations of conflict may be better seen in a larger and more inclusive context. A therapeutic approach that encompasses a creative engagement between patient and therapist is essential in drawing out those sometimes ineffable and subtle qualities of character structure.

Sandler in 1974 made an important contribution on the nature of the therapeutic interchange. "The view will be put forward that an essential element in intrapsychic conflict is what can be called the *unconscious peremptory urge*. By 'peremptory' in this context I mean that quality of compellingness and urgency, of being 'automatic,' of being driven by a force, which we usually associate with instinctual wishes or their more direct derivatives" (p. 53). These unconscious peremptory urges exist for all individuals, in wide varieties of personal and interpersonal situations. Sandler makes clear that they do not necessarily derive from instinctual wishes but may reflect unconscious aspects of the personality that include ego and superego derivatives. He urges a wider conception of human motivation than is encompassed by sex and aggression alone. For example, when a shame response has developed out of parental disapproval of assertion and independence, the most helpful therapeutic response is not always to interpret these "urges" solely in terms of conflict over the satisfaction of aggressive wishes. It may be more helpful (and more accurate) to address the patient's need to maintain a stable sense of self in the face of the onslaught of shame-filled responses. This approach exemplifies a characterological emphasis.

> Ms. T. came to me very concerned with her lack of sexual response within a new relationship. Her partner seemed more upset by this 'problem' than did she. Under the chaotic circumstances of her life, it was not surprising that she had difficulty with sexual arousal. Additionally, as we spoke it became clear to me that she had always felt unloved by men. It was further evident that she also struggled with self-disgust over her sexual feelings. She eventually was able to tell me that her father was overly strict and condemning of any emerging age-appropriate "flirtatious" behaviors. Even when she was quite little he adamantly refused to let her sit on his lap, and he warned her when she became a mother that her husband should do the same with his daughters. Thus, her need for male approval was very strong and insistent, yet the need to please gave rise to conflicts, as she could not comply at the same time with a partner's wish for a responsive sexual partner and the equally compelling prohibition against demonstrating sexual arousal.

Once I was able to clarify for the patient her internalization of her father's difficulty with his own sexual feelings, she could begin to understand the origins of her frantic need for male approval and her concern about sexual feelings and behavior. This kind of "peremptory urge" is omnipresent in psychotherapy, and it must be understood if dysphoric affects are to be alleviated. In this context it is easier to understand the elusiveness of psychic and behavioral change. People are impelled toward certain actions and persist in them despite more "realistic" perspectives, because they are rooted in unconscious concerns about safety and security and relate to the maintenance of a stable sense of self. Attempts at persuasion are usually futile until the underlying dynamics can be addressed.

THE EXPERIENCE OF PSYCHOTHERAPY

Killingmo (1995), considering patients' needs for an *experience* within the therapeutic environment, has written about the need for affirmation within psychoanalysis. *Affirmation* refers to the analyst's validation of a patient's experience: "The function of an affirmative response is to remove doubt connected to the experience or reality and thereby establish or re-establish a feeling of identity" (Killingmo, 1995, p. 508). People undergo experiences that may be breathtaking in their emotional impact but which are not necessarily appreciated as such either by the individual or by those around him.

> One patient spoke to me repeatedly about her relationship with her boss. She even mentioned a sexual relationship between them. She discussed this, however, in such a way that I did not at first understand that it was not consensual. When I finally realized this, my ability to communicate that understanding to her represented a major turning point in the treatment. She had had more than one experience in her life that had perplexed her but that had been disowned, minimized, and disavowed. Her vivid description of the rape, and my affirmation of the terribleness of the experience, allowed her to reestablish her sense of reality and to put her life in order in other areas.

Affirmation is a base from which the patient can feel safe in exploring experiences that have previously been invalidated or doubted. It demands of the therapist a nonskeptical, accepting demeanor that encourages curiosity and growth. Affirmation is not intended to uncover hidden motives but rather to help patients recapture and reintegrate experiences from whose impact they may have too greatly distanced themselves.

THE WISHED-FOR INTERACTION

Again I raise the question: What do patients look for when they seek out psychotherapeutic treatment? Sandler and Sandler (1978) speak of a "wished for interaction" within the psychotherapeutic relationship (p. 288). Explaining their movement away from the postulate of wishes without relationships, the Sandlers state, "In psychological terms, every wish involves a self representation, object representation and a representation of the interaction between these" (p. 288). The wishes to which they refer relate either to repetitions of earlier relationships or to attempts to establish a relationship that does *not* represent a repetition. Ms. T., for instance, hopes in part that she can find a way to understand herself, to explicate her hidden thoughts and feelings, without being shamed by me as she was by her father. Similarly,

As mentioned previously, Dr. R., an anesthesiologist, sought out treatment, ostensibly for depression. As the work progressed, it became quite clear that her depression reflected profound feelings of emptiness and a hollow sense of self. In Winnicott's term, she had developed a "false self." This false self was astonishingly successful, and her friends and family believed that she was happy and "well put together." She had been raised in a family that did not value openness and honesty. Her father was a tyrant, and both physically and emotionally abusive. Her mother was distant, vacant, and unattached. Her unexpressed but fervent hope was that I would provide her with a new personality through psychotherapy. She thought that I could provide her with another "false self" that would be more comfortable than the one she had developed on her own. She was also desperately afraid of being forced to expose her "secret place," which felt fragile and subject to violation.

  She could not conceive of relationships that did not represent a repetition of earlier experiences. Her only hope was to find a better version of the story, in which she was more dominant and others submissive to her will. But the central dynamic remained the same. The transference relationship was quite difficult for me at times. The falseness of her persona made it difficult for me to connect with her affectively, and this made me feel sleepy and inattentive. My only recourse was to draw her attention to her need to distance, whereupon she became more alive and connected. I believe that the treatment succeeded because my inability to tolerate her arid state of being eventually provided her with hope and a sense of aliveness. After long and arduous work, she is beginning to develop hope for a different outcome and is beginning to consider the possibility of interactions with me and with others that are healthier and less stilted than the imperious domination-submission dynamic that had pervaded her life and secretly defined how she looked at all relationships.

My invitation—my insistence—on an affectively charged relationship was the single most mutative aspect of the treatment. It was generated by an interpretation regarding her emptiness and my sense of disconnectedness, but it was the actual experience of our being together that enlivened her and allowed her to pursue her life in a more genuine way. It allowed her to recognize the futility of her fantasized sadomasochistic interactions and provided a new, potentially more satisfying model, and hope, for future relationships. Although her sadomasochistic wishes seemed to predominate, they existed within the context of a character structure in which they had been constructed not only to obtain gratification but also to maintain a stable sense of self—to maintain internalized self- and object representations and to provide a structure to her life. This is an example of the way a characterological approach recognizes conflict issues but considers them within the larger context of overall personality structure.

Wrye and Welles (1991) provide a related view in their discussion of what they call the Maternal Erotic Transference (MET): "We see the MET as rooted in mother and baby's earliest sensual contacts and manifested in concrete loving and hateful erotic wishes towards the real parts of the body of the therapist, as well as their symbolic counterparts. Its tender and sadistic expressions are typically difficult to access as they stem from preverbal life, and are also inhibited or defended against out of shame and fear of humiliation" (1993, p. 93). Within the MET, they suppose, patients hope that the therapist does not respond to their grasping, suckling, attaching, and attacking behaviors with the same disinterest, shaming, or anger that they experienced as children. Wrye and Welles suggest that some seemingly hostile and sadistic behaviors represent thwarted attachment needs, and that interpretation of such behaviors as hostile or sadistic misses the point and neglects developmental, and consequently transferential, needs. The desired interaction may be for understanding, soothing, or nurturing in the face of such unpleasant needs; it is not for shaming or accusatory responses.

This is another take on the contention I have been elaborating here that many aspects of the therapeutic relationship transcend *conflict* interpretations, as they are commonly described within an intrapsychic model. More than that, though, it is another perspective on patients' hoped for *experiences:* experiences that allow them to feel safe, understood, and without shame. Again, the mutative experience may be small in scale. It is often useful, for example, to allow patients to express their anger at the indignities suffered in every treatment without always interpreting their feelings in relation to past hurts. When a person has been forbidden this emotional reaction, the evocation of that pain in the *present* may in itself be mutative and relieving.

SAFETY, SECURITY, AND
THE THERAPEUTIC RELATIONSHIP

In sum, I believe that change in psychotherapy depends on an awareness of how clinical symptoms merge with the characterological structures that an individual has come to believe offer safety and security, and that this awareness must be shared insofar as possible with the patient. Unless respect for these solutions is conveyed within a vital therapeutic relationship, patients do not feel safe enough to divulge their intricacies fully.

This is the context in which I will develop my thesis in the rest of this study. In the following chapters, I will explore a number of clinical issues that I feel have not been given sufficient attention. I will consider them within the context of the therapeutic interaction, in the belief that this interaction provides an experience that is meaningful to both participants. It is, however, the clinician who must constantly make choices about what kind of interventions to make. Good choices and good reasons for making them are essential for maximum therapeutic benefit, and these depend upon a clear appreciation of the importance and implications of character.

II

◆

THE
PATIENT'S
WORLD

◆

Assessment does not end when treatment begins. In fact, the skills called analytic timing, tact, and sensitivity are often reflections of an ongoing assessment process.

Patients' characteristic ways of thinking, feeling, and acting, and how they fashion them, are a crucial window into the psyche. They are the result of important efforts to adapt to internal and external pressures and are essential clues to the nature of the stresses that created them. Therefore it is a wise clinician who routinely keeps a focus on assessment throughout the treatment. In this chapter, I will concentrate on various aspects of the assessment process and demonstrate how careful attention to them enables a comprehensive approach that leads toward characterological transformation. Intrapsychic conflict is one manifestation of character, but it is not the only one. Attention to the psychological themes that run through patients' lives, and to the quality of their personality organization, makes more thorough treatment possible.

THREE CASES OF "DEPRESSION"

Dr. R. entered treatment complaining of depression. Her parents had died not long before, within three weeks of each other. Some years previously she had delivered a stillborn child. At that time, she had participated in a grief recovery program sponsored by the hospital, and she had been considered quite a success; the program coordinators had asked her to talk to others in similar situations. She seemed sociable and friendly. Generally, people liked her and assumed that she was as content as she appeared, but she suffered from an abiding sense of emptiness and loneliness. It became more and more apparent, as the evaluation progressed, that a sense of dissatisfaction permeated her life and had for as long as she could remember—long predating these three losses.

Dr. R. described herself as going through life by rote—doing what was expected but with little sense of herself or the motivation behind her choices. She described her father as domineering, frightening, and abusive—he hit her so hard on the head one time that she lost her hearing temporarily. She described her mother as distant and out of touch. She herself hated being a woman, and felt like an abysmal failure. This opinion had been reinforced by her inability to give birth to a living child, but she had had similar concerns already at puberty. At that time, she had bound her breasts in an attempt to deny her femaleness and had hidden the evidence of her menses out of shame. Now, as an adult, she was a desperately unhappy person.

Mr. M., a thirty-five-year-old auto executive, also sought treatment for "depression." He had been referred by his internist, who had not been able to help him with his various psychosomatic difficulties but had recognized the patient's distress. The patient had experienced multiple significant losses as an adolescent but had always been a "good boy" growing up, never causing his parents a moment of trouble. Now, he was socially isolated, a bit of a workaholic, and had no friends or real outside interests. He acknowledged few feelings; rage was the only one he could reliably identify. He felt estranged from his wife and daughter. When his wife was away, he evinced no sense of missing her, although he did feel bereft in a general and ill-defined way. Mr. M. was not aware of my absences as significant either, although he found himself getting angry at times when I was away. He insisted that he had absolutely no feelings about me and he forgot about his sessions as soon as the door "hits me on the ass on the way out." When he began experiencing sleeplessness and panic attacks, he saw a psychiatrist for a medication evaluation and was tried on eight different antidepressants with (according to him) little perceived benefit.

Interestingly enough, however, it seemed to me that he *did* improve both within the therapy and after he began taking the antidepressants. His insistence that he received no benefit from any of our efforts represented a negative therapeutic reaction, reflecting an essentially negativistic and masochistic way of life. Consciously, he wanted to feel better but other forces held sway that kept him locked in perpetual unhappiness and isolation.

Ms. S. was referred by an infertility specialist, whom she had consulted for her failure to conceive. This was a salient aspect of her presenting picture. She treated her husband's refusal to have sex with her as a non-event instead of the real reason for her childless state. This disregard of reality was characteristic of her approach to life. Her defensive system, as is common in narcissistic and perverse patients, demonstrated a "vertical" split—she could maintain two contradictory beliefs in consciousness simultaneously (as opposed to the "horizontal" split of repression where one aspect of reality is maintained out of consciousness). She presented herself as very anxious, but this anxiety served to obscure tremendous rage and feelings of entitlement. She prided herself on being pure and (almost) virginal. When anger allowed her some semiconscious recognition of her vindictiveness, or when her "unacceptable" and "impure" sexual feelings became apparent, she got very upset. At times she was punitive and hurtful toward others. She was highly dramatic, and it seemed that she actively increased her emotional pain, gaining satisfaction from her suffering. Discomfort with her underlying issues and embarrassment over her marital problems gave Mrs. S. an abiding sense of oddness. She worried about not being just "like everyone else, normal."

After a period of interpretation of her underlying anger, her anxiety abated somewhat and she developed what she referred to as "depression." She requested a referral for antidepressant medication, and I gave her one. The psychiatrist did not feel that she fit the criteria for medication, but he gave her a trial. To me she seemed much the same on the medication, but she claimed that she felt better. She was soon weaned from it, satisfied that she was like everyone else, having been on antidepressant medication. This seemed to give her a sense of status and belonging—in the context of a medication-responsive "clinical depression," very common in her community, her marital problems and childlessness were usual and comprehensible and did not reflect oddities or character flaws.

These three individuals all saw themselves as suffering from "depression," and all three of them did experience depressive affect at times. Their problems had different etiologies, however, and, as I will show, were due less to conflict than to fundamental personality issues that required elucidation. The first patient suffered from abiding feelings of emptiness and a sense of being lost. The second had isolated himself from hurt and betrayal by staying disconnected; he was a man who destroyed meaning in his relationships. The third patient had a narcissistic and sadomasochistic personality structure. Successful treatments for the three of them were very different and had to be based upon accurate assessment of three different underlying character structures. As Guntrip (1969) has indicated, many patients are incorrectly diagnosed as depressed while suffering in fact from schizoid (personality) disorders. To attend purely to the depressive symptomatology ignores the contribution of underlying personality structures and prevents resolution of symptoms on this deeper level. Attention to character structure, on the other hand—to "implicit" qualities—provides the therapist with a sense of that person's essence; this can be conveyed to the patient in a way that allows the patient to feel understood and strengthens the therapeutic alliance.

THE INITIAL ASSESSMENT

A therapist establishes a particular treatment approach on the basis of an understanding of the patient and of that patient's dilemmas; for that reason, an accurate and adequate understanding is necessary. I will not try to offer here a detailed explication of the *techniques* of psychological assessment. Instead I will address some basic conceptual issues that I feel demand elaboration because, whether we recognize it or not, they guide the direction that the treatment will take. In this context, let me make clear at the outset that rather than trying to assess that most difficult and perhaps unfair of concepts, "treatability," I give *every* individual the opportunity to try intensive treatment I do not want to deprive any patients, of whatever stripe, of what might be their only chance to alter their lives significantly.

During the initial evaluation period, the therapist establishes a hypothesis about the factors that have created the issues presented for treatment and about the patient's personality structure. A particular treatment approach or orientation is determined, according to this hypothesis. For example, consider the common situation reflected in the previous examples: a new patient who presents as "depressed."

What kind of "depression" does that person experience? Is it the despair that may follow a loss or a death? Is it the sense of dread that arises out of a feeling of disconnectedness and emptiness? These categories are different, and they can be further delineated. To relate a sense of loss to a terminated relationship, for instance, may indicate that the individual has the ability to form attachments, but in itself it tells little about the nature of these attachments. A brooding, self-punitive depression, on the other hand, indicates the existence of a severe internalized object representation. More information about the internalized self-representation provides more information about the person's personality structure.

Mr. M.'s depressive disorder, for example, was the result of two complementary yet contrasting etiologies. To the extent that he had never worked through the losses in his adolescence, his depression reflected inadequate mourning. More salient, however, was the negativity of his character structure, and this matched that of his mother. The anger that he felt toward his loved ones and others was embedded and hidden within a characteristic negative attitude. His internalized self- and object representations reflected a particular early mother-child relationship—one with a negative attachment as its essence. Consequently, as this man went through life, he reacted to events with his and his mother's characteristic negativity and pessimism; his internalized self-representation as the lens through which he saw everything as bleak. These internalized object representations held tremendous sway and determined his character structure. Whatever ambivalent feelings he may have had toward his lost loved ones, and whatever consequent unresolved mourning, it was his negative self-structure that thoroughly imbued his personality.

Such *internal* self-representational states help to define an individual's psychological organization and are also reflected *externally,* in relationships, for example, or in the person's ability to function effectively in the world. In Mr. M.'s case, the *quality* of his depression provided information about his internal state and his consequent ability to function in the world. Psychological disorders are not isolated entities; they are a microcosm of the individual's entire psychic structure. Psychic struggles, compromises, and adaptations infuse and infiltrate the entire personality, and a broad diagnostic vision that takes this into account provides the most comprehensive view possible of the patient.

An assessment that looks *beyond* the label of "depression," therefore, raises questions about the etiology of the depression and the reasons for its continuance. These call our attention to the patient's general level of functioning, ability to maintain relationships, affective economy, possible early childhood traumas and deprivations, family issues and constellations, specific early childhood relationship patterns, ideas about parental personality issues, and so forth. Attention to these issues permits the development of a complex picture of personality structure. It creates for the therapist (and therefore eventually for the patient as well) a more holistic view of the patient. Even those so-called "neurotic" patients with putatively well-circumscribed problems provide plenty of evidence that symptoms do not exist in isolation; they tend to permeate the psyche and ramify in all areas of the patient's functioning, including cognition, affect, symptomatology, defense, and behavior.

THE EXPLICIT, THE IMPLICIT, AND THE HIDDEN

In the previous chapter, I spoke about patients' explicit, implicit, and hidden goals. To recapitulate, *explicit* issues are the "problems" the patient brings to the consulting room—depression, anxiety, marital or relationship issues, eating disorders, and so forth. These are the clinical manifestations or Axis I disorders from the DSM series. *Implicit* issues represent characterological phenomena—underlying qualities that define the person's identity. These are sometimes obvious but sometimes, even to experienced and perceptive clinicians, they are elusive and can be discovered, elucidated, and assessed only as treatment progresses. *Hidden* issues are unconscious and reach the awareness of clinician and patient through the interpretation of dreams, associations, and transference. The therapist's perception of these goals derives from the assessment process as much as diagnosis does, and assessment of goals yields valuable information and perspective on the patient's problems.

Ms. S., whose presentation I described previously, complained of intense and debilitating anxiety. When she came to treatment, these were exacerbated by serious marital difficulties. She knew that she had always felt insecure and had issues about sexual matters, but she tended to be (secretly) proud of herself for a sense of virginal purity. Beyond this, however, she had no real sense of what was bothering her. My view of these explicit issues was different from hers; I saw a high level of intense anger and a need to see herself as pure and non-sexual despite abundant evidence to the contrary. Ms. S.'s basic narcissistic personality characteristics (broadly speaking, her implicit issues) were also not very difficult to discern. She had a basic sense of entitlement, a belief in her own ultimate superiority, and a feeling of aggrievement—that life and other people treated her unfairly.

These implicit characteristics were hidden under a guise of innocence and guilelessness and had to be ferreted out of her outward personality style, although her anger and sense of vindictiveness were breathtaking on the occasions that her defensive maneuvers were stripped away. But they were also the characterological manifestation of an unconscious (hidden) wish to be sufficiently worthy to give birth to the next incarnation of God, thus gaining the pride of her parents. To do this, of course, required that she be virginal and pure. These fantasies emerged later in the treatment via dreams and waking fantasy material.

Basic personality issues (what I am calling the *implicit*) are the meat and potatoes of treatment. Because they define the individual they are often the central focuses of the treatment. In one sense "working through" represents an attempt to elucidate the personality issues that have derived from central conflicts and themes, neurotic or otherwise. The more *explicit* or conscious material lead *toward* the implicit or characterological. This in turn facilitates access to even less conscious *hidden* material, leading to still deeper and more satisfying understanding.

In Ms. S.'s case, it was the discussion of some very specific fantasies that enabled her to connect with powerful and painful memories of her sense of insignificance within the family. The treatment focused on how widely these specific and unconscious fantasies had become manifest within her personality. We also focused on how, still based on these unconscious wishes and conflicts, she derived hidden satisfaction in many subtle ways in all her relationships. Her unconscious fantasies of being as pure as the Virgin Mary came with a related belief that she would be as exalted. The unconscious transference reflected her idealization of me and the hope that I would have intercourse with her and impregnate her with the special and godly child. To this end she needed, she felt, to exorcise any feelings and thoughts that were "impure"—that is, primarily sexual and aggressive. At the same time, as a divine being she deserved to be treated in extraordinary ways and was entitled to treat others as badly as she wished.

Thus her need to feel special to maintain the illusion of omnipotence had become interwoven into her life in many ways and gave a particular flavor to her style of thinking and feeling. It greatly influenced the character of her relationships and so was directly observable within the transference. The comprehensive effort to identify these fundamental issues—in her unconscious fantasies, in her everyday life, in her daydreams, in her relationships, in her thoughts about herself, and, perhaps most potently, within the transference—eventually freed her from their maladaptive influence and allowed her to come to a reconciliation with her "ordinary"—as opposed to her wished-for "extraordinary"—life. A comprehensive treatment looks at characterological issues and at the specific fantasies and conflicts that exist *embedded* within the context of the personality structure.

LEVELS OF PSYCHIC DISTURBANCE

A clinician seeking to understand the ongoing *structural* aspects of psychic organization must also address the relative *level* of psychic organization. Some people experience preverbal traumas and deprivations that imprint upon them in ways that cannot always be accessed by language. Without the use of language, the capacity for symbolization may be impaired, resulting in concreteness, a tendency toward the literal, and a paucity of metaphoric thinking. Such patients may be prone to psychosomatic disorders, feel empty, and lack a stable sense of self. A "neurotic" patient may experience fear that his father will castrate him, but this is a different kind of fear from that experienced by a patient whose father would actually threaten or abuse or may actually have done so. Such pre- and nonverbal traumas precede and, in a sense, "trump" the development of triadic relationships and awareness of intersystemic conflicts. This is a crucial difference that must be taken into account in work with traumatized patients. Patients who have experienced physical, emotional, and/or sexual abuse at an early age often have profound ego deficits. These result in higher levels of anxiety, a lowered ability to tolerate frustration, and intense sensitivity to rejection and hurt. Transference interpretations may be experienced as accusations, and the therapist must show great patience and understanding, keeping in mind that these patients may reject, at least initially, anything other than empathic and reflective statements.

Killingmo (1989) elaborates further on the differences between patients whose pathology derives from issues related to intersystemic conflict and those whose problems develop out of developmental deficit. He suggests that therapeutic approaches will differ depending on this assessment. The former can tolerate interventions that emphasize personal responsibility. Although "neurotic" patients may have well-entrenched defensive systems, they tend less to react to a therapist's interpretations as an assault. An early traumatized patient may, initially at least, feel that any intervention that is not reflective and empathic is assaultive. The shame that has resulted from frequent humiliations causes these patients to react to certain interventions with anxiety and disorganization. "Neurotic" patients may also react strongly to particular interventions, but they often have a greater ability to observe and consider what the therapist has delivered. For these reasons, careful assessment of the patient's level of pathology can guide the therapist toward interventions that match the patient's psychic level of organization and therefore can be helpful and not cause unnecessary anxiety.

These are not hard and fast distinctions, however. People with developmental disorders may experience conflict, and those with neurotic disorders may have experienced deficits in their development. Here too a characterological approach can be helpful; it encourages a study of the patient's overall level of functioning and an effort to define and elaborate the 'implicit' structure that underlies it. This includes an intimate understanding of the childhood dynamics that provide the context from which the symptoms develop. At a cursory glance, certain patient presentations may seem similar, but they may represent, in fact, vastly different levels of functioning and underlying dynamics and thus require different types of interventions.

Consider the following examples.

In an initial evaluation session, Dr. I. indicated that he had not been able to pass his medical boards. He had taken them twice and come close to success but had failed nevertheless. His father was also a doctor, and he was expected to follow in his father's footsteps. Symptomatically, he exhibited depression, listlessness, a persistent feeling of anxiety, and a sense of social withdrawal and isolation. Yet in speaking with him, it was quickly apparent that he was a highly intelligent, cultured, and sensitive man with the ability to form meaningful and enduring relationships. He had a history of doing well in jobs and in school, but he never performed up to his potential.

My assessment indicated that Dr. I. did not have significant and serious psychological problems that greatly affected ego functioning, was capable and competent in life, and seemed able to maintain good relationships. I thought he could make good use of treatment and tolerate the frustrations of intensive therapy. From a broader perspective, it seemed clear to me that his parents, although also high-functioning, were rather secretive and surreptitiously undermining. His father had been married once before, and my patient had only recently become aware of this. He had a vague sense of what his mother did occupationally and really did not have a feel for her as a person. Dr. I. was involved with a woman of a different faith from that of his family. He had felt that she was well accepted in the family and was surprised when he realized that his mother harbored secret resentments over the liaison. He was expected to help his parents out a great deal with chores and errands around the house, as though he were a small boy and not a grown man.

As we elaborated these family relationships, it rapidly became evident that he was conflicted over his career choice and felt that he was performing 'chores' for his parents by going to medical school. This feeling of not being his own man, and the resentment of parental expectations, resulted in a sense of paralyzing confusion, and he realized that he had not really been diligent in studying for his exams.

Once aware of the underlying dynamics, he quickly passed his boards and became a practicing physician. Although he enjoyed his practice, however, he still did not feel fully content. As treatment progressed, he began coming late to his sessions and seemed to be having trouble maintaining his usual self-reflective style. Although Oedipal issues about competition and success were crucial, I did not feel that they fully explained his lassitude and lack of focus. As he spoke about his parents and their rather difficult life histories, a feeling of sadness was evident. I reached the conclusion that he had realized, in a way not very accessible to consciousness, that his parents were exceptionally needy—that they suffered from an unacknowledged sadness of their own—and that he felt reluctant to leave them by pursuing his own interests. He was not pursuing medicine solely out of his own desire and so continued to feel conflicted about his work and unsure that being a physician represented his true calling. Internal pressure from the need to please his secretly depressed parents resulted in confusion as to whose needs he was satisfying; this made it difficult to concentrate.

Issues like these demonstrated how parental dynamics had contributed to the development of his personality constellation. His parents' secretiveness and insensitivity were incorporated into his personality style such that he found it difficult to divulge his 'secret' needs and to be sensitive to his own feelings. His subjugation of his own needs reflected both (neurotic) conflicts over success and aggression and a (deficit-based) response to family dynamics. The confluence of the Oedipal concerns over success and related aggression and family concerns over his parents' unacknowledged sadness created enduring personality characteristics. These family issues could be considered to be at the preconscious level and were readily understood once pointed out, although continued work was needed to identify the extent of their influence in the many areas of his functioning. The Oedipal issues were unconscious and could be accessed most readily through the available context of the family dynamics.

Mr. H. was another patient presenting with a sense of depression and ennui. He also struggled with intense episodes of debilitating anxiety. He worked in sales, but his successes never seemed to him successful enough. As Dr. I did, he felt bewildered by his relative lack of success and was certain that he was, in some ways, thwarting himself. Mr. H., however, also felt socially isolated. He had few friends or outside activities. He had been married twice and had one son from his second marriage, but he did not have much interest in him. He had a dog that he found burdensome and tiresome.

Mr. H. sought treatment after breaking down sobbing in a movie where a character spoke of his dreadfully unhappy childhood. His past history had in fact been difficult and filled with embarrassments and humiliations. He had been abnormally close to his mother—her confidant and 'best little boy.' Having allied with his mother as both a hidden Oedipal victory and for protection from an overly aggressive father, he felt little of the kind of safety that would allow him to develop a strong sense of masculinity. He was estranged from his father, who resented his closeness with his mother. He was shamed for being a 'mama's boy,' and his slightly effeminate manner had carried over into school where he was identified as being different right from the beginning. Reluctant to grow up and move out into the world, he had been encopretic, thus expressing both his infantile wishes and helplessness and his sadism. Anxiety and panic reactions were common, and he suffered from claustrophobia on elevators and airplanes.

As Mr. H. grew up, he learned to cover up most of his symptoms and he became more adept socially. He was a good-looking man and prided himself on his romantic conquests, but he was never able to find satisfaction in them. He both searched for and feared close relationships. He became somewhat hyperactive in his flight from his thoughts and feelings, feeling this as the pressure to become a more successful salesman and the conviction that he was never reaching his potential.

Dr. I. presented with a relatively circumscribed problem that still reflected an overall personality style. Mr. H.'s presentation suggested an overall deficit in general adaptational abilities, and it was important to take note of this early on. He suffered from anxiety and depression too, but these symptoms were not focused. Rather, they represented the outer manifestations of a man overwhelmed by the pressures of life, who felt woefully overmatched. Our first order of business was to establish a working relationship that felt stable to him and safe enough that he would allow me access to his inner thoughts.

These two men, although superficially similar, were psychically organized at very different levels that required different approaches. Dr. I. had the ability to withstand the rigors of the interpretive model of conflict and compromise formation, but we still needed to pay attention to the general character structure that expressed both his neurotic constellation and the contribution from his family's dynamics. Dr. I.'s family background, whatever its problems, had given him enough sustenance to develop coping skills and ego strength.

Mr. H.'s family situation had not given him the kind of support to enable him to confront life with vigor and enthusiasm. Mr. H. needed to feel safe before he could be able to look more deeply at himself. Once that sense of safety was achieved, we could look at and address compromise formations and other conflicts and elucidate how the fear of, and need for, connection pervaded his entire personality structure.

FAMILY IDENTIFICATIONS

From the beginning, children are inculcated with family identifications. In the process of development, they internalize representations of self and object, and the eventual inner sense of self that results from this process reflects the way the particular child represented the significant people in his or her life (typically the parents) and the perceived relationship between these objects. From an object relations point of view, the child's personality is based on these internalized representations. This is not necessarily a straightforward process, however. In all children this process of internalization is subject to distortion due to the immaturity of the ego. Furthermore, it is important to apprehend the *entire* representational world as internalized. A patient abused as a child will internalize representations of both the abused and the abuser and will often feel in conflict among these differing aspects. It is important for a therapist to be aware of the complexity of these internalizations. Mr. H. identified with his absent and hostile father both by his lack of interest in his own child and his hostility toward his own internal sense of vulnerability. Being in psychotherapy put him in mind of his previously helpless self and made him feel panicky. This in turn interfered with thought processes and created a sense of void between sessions. On the other hand, his passivity, his lack of real ambition, and his depressive demeanor maintained a sense of identity with his mother. His desperate search for comfort and safety caused him to vacillate between these two identifications, with never any opportunity for a peaceable reconciliation between them. A previous treatment that had focused on his inability to form commitments had not helped him gain the understanding of his complex hidden identifications and their effect on the development of his personality structure.

The handing down of traumatic unresolved complexes from parent to child is much more common than usually ascribed. These situations afford ample opportunities for the perpetuation and embedding of specific conflicts. The sadness with which Dr. I. struggled represented an intergenerational transmission of unresolved mourning (Shabad, 1993). His parents' unresolved sadness kept him from knowing his own mind and his own motivations and interfered with his clarity of purpose. These effects were used in the service of Oedipal concerns, by preventing him from attaining a level of success that might put him at odds with his father and create uncomfortable competitive and rivalrous feelings.

The more patients understand their family dynamics and the roles that they play in their family dramas, the more freedom of choice they ultimately can achieve. Yet strong anxiety is aroused when patients look for alternatives to their accustomed ways of being. Identifications represent a sense of familiarity and safety, however maladaptive they may be.

THEMES

Painful, frightening, and disorganizing experiences of early childhood tend to become established over time into major defining themes or "organizing strands" (Klein, 1998). These themes often reflect actual occurrences from childhood that later, through condensation and concretization, organize other confusing and bewildering experiences. Furthermore, even in the absence of unusual emotional stress, the inevitable distortions created or perceived by immature egos may remain unconsciously present as unrealistic fears and fantasies. Such distortions tend to gain a life of their own as symptoms, because they represent efforts to contain overwhelming thoughts and feelings while at the same time providing the individual with some sense of control and satisfaction. They become psychological constructs that organize experience and, though often anxiety-arousing and distressing in their own right, they are perpetuated because they bind greater anxieties, thus making them more tolerable.

Mr. R. was a fifty-year-old teacher, whose two-year-old brother had drowned when the patient was five. Mr. R. was witness to the attempted resuscitation. His upbringing prior to this tragedy had been unfortunate too; he had a mother who was unresponsive and hostile to his needs and a father who was strict and physically abusive. His way of adapting to these privations was to become extremely efficient and self-directed. He felt that he had failed his brother by not saving him, even though he had not at the time had the capability to do so. Every task subsequently became a test, and every failure became a new failure to save his brother—or to save himself, because he interpreted his brother's death as proof of his parents' homicidal wishes toward him and, by displacement, toward himself.

Treatment was a torture to him. It also represented a test, and he often wondered whether he would get out of it alive. Every aspect of his life was imbued consciously and unconsciously with the trauma of his brother's death. Attachment issues reflected concerns-about being attached to a homicidal parent. The normal issues of Oedipal rivalry developed even greater urgency because of the very real death experience of his childhood. He desired closeness, yet feared it, as too close an attachment represented to him the loss of the sense of self, conceptualized as drowning. His "unconscious peremptory urge" (Sandler, 1974) drove him frantically to succeed, lest he meet his brother's fate. When he became upset with someone else, his identification with his hostile parents left him extremely anxious about homicidal wishes. Because his family never discussed the tragedy and got furious if he broached it, he had come to believe that it was forbidden to discuss his many secrets.

This is a clear example of how trauma can infuse a life and become part and parcel of a personality. This patient's sense of himself was based on the traumas of his early life. They affected attachment and dependency issues, infected normal aggressive and competitive strivings, and created strong guilty feelings over success. Hidden anger and fears of rejection resulted in an isolated and coldly perfectionistic life. Mr. R. did gain some gratification from this painful state of affairs, however—a sense of superiority about his intense need to succeed and the feeling that he could "run circles" around others, including me. Most of what happened in his life and in his therapy reflected the attempted solutions to the psychic dilemmas engendered by his disturbed family relationships and the death of his brother. These solutions transcended intrapsychic conflict and had urgently to do with concern for his psychic and physical survival. A perceived criticism from me felt to him as if I wanted him dead and vice versa.

Yet it was paradoxically the "building in" of this terrible trauma that made it a vehicle by which we could eventually look at and discuss his issues in a less threatening way. The transference became intolerable for him at times, and he often could deal with here-and-now issues more comfortably in displacement onto the traumas of his past. He could work through his own annihilation fears without feeling too fragmented by discussing his fantasies about what had happened to his brother.

Organizing strands like this condense many different conflicts and developmental difficulties into a cohesive narrative that helps patients grapple with preverbal sensations and ineffable and evanescent thoughts. Pulling apart the "strands," so to speak, allows disavowed, out-of-consciousness aspects of the self to be recaptured and condensed and displaced conflicts to be worked through. These strands or 'themes' represent many components that go into making up the character structure. Family identifications, family conflicts, intergenerational issues, intrapsychic conflicts, and various attempts to fashion satisfaction out of internal and external pressures combine to become an individual's psychological self. This is what I mean when I speak about how conflicts become embedded within the family identifications. I don't feel that conflict interpretations are not useful or essential; only that they are limited. Themes may emerge over and over in a variety of contexts, enabling therapist and patient to address salient issues from many different perspectives. The identification and elucidation of these themes strongly contributes to the development of a stable sense of self.

QUALITY OF PERSONALITY ORGANIZATION

At different points in treatment, the therapist may want to address particular aspects of a patient from different angles. To be able to make such choices, it is necessary to understand the *quality* of the patient's personality organization, by which I mean the particular internalizations and identifications that have formed the patient's personality structure. These are preconscious, implicit, and often reflective of family ways of thinking and behaving. In a sense, they represent the "language" of the family of origin. This nonverbal aspect of the patient often must be intuited, *and then conveyed back to the patient,* so that these characteristic ways of thinking can be identified and understood.

> One patient, dangerously obese, became enraged when a public utility truck parked in a spot that was unmarked but was known to her to be reserved for my patients and me. She blocked the truck in, chastised the driver for parking in a spot where he did not belong, and then came to our session feeling upset and overwhelmed. As we explored her behavior and feelings, I realized that she was furious that he had violated a rule, "broken a law." In this context, many of her self-destructive, outrageous, and unhappy aspects became comprehensible. Despite the poor choices that she often made, from her perspective she was merely following family rules of behavior. To act like a calm and reasonable person, watch her diet sensibly, and respond to others with respect—all these violated family rules of be-

havior and challenged her identifications. Asking her to alter her self-injurious and provocative behavior was tantamount to asking her to go against intense family prohibitions.

The prohibitions themselves were known to her, of course, but had not been identified as rules that must never be broken for fear of great punishment. As I verbalized this insight to her, she became calmer and began herself to understand some of her previously incomprehensible behavior.

Once internalizations have been identified and a dynamic and structural sense of the patient emerges, the astute therapist begins to be able to understand the patient intuitively. Therapeutic intuition is not magic but is based, as are so many of the other issues of timing and tact that I have discussed here, on the understanding that comes with ongoing assessment. The therapist learns to understand the logic of the patient's psychic system and functioning and begins to have a sense of what to expect—and also of what is unexpected and therefore particularly worthy of notice. Out of all the patient's associations, the therapist must make decisions about what to address. An intimate understanding of the patient's characteristic way of thinking and world view leads to the issues that are hidden or embedded within the patient's implicit thought processes. A patient may be well versed in a family language and yet not know that their family perspectives may very well be based on pathological beliefs.

Just as spoken languages have rules of grammar, so do family 'languages' operate with logic and consistency. Characteristic ways of feeling, acting, and behaving become familiar within the treatment relationship, and deviations from the characteristic are often indicative of material to be explored. A sudden shift in demeanor can lead the therapist to material that requires identification. Furthermore, knowledge of the patient's history leads to an understanding of the dynamic issues that are likely to emerge in the treatment. These historical experiences, along with family identifications, contribute to the formation of a character structure.

Ms. G. seemed very close to her mother, and the two women shared a number of interests and attitudes. Ms. G. had followed her mother into the teaching profession, and they spent considerable time together. She entered treatment complaining of a bewildering sense of something not being quite right and occasional bouts of panic. As we examined her history, it became apparent that she greatly idealized her domineering father while degrading her mother for not being as successful and (outwardly) capable as he. Her idealization of the father necessarily included an identification with him and a secret disaffiliation with the mother. As the treatment progressed, it became clear that she herself had her own technique of domination and that, although it was hidden, it was pervasive. Each day in the beginning of her therapy she would greet me, asking me how I was. If I did not return the courtesy, she would become silent with unacknowledged rage and then masochistically self-punitive. Eventually I began to understand the unverbalized way in which she processed disappointment; it was reminiscent of her father's behavior, although not so obvious.

Often only the self-abasement was visible, as if her primary identification was with the debased mother. Secretly, however, she was punishing me by trying to make me feel uncomfortable for her unhappiness. Her anger and need for control were hidden. They were identified only as I became aware of her family history and with it her family identifications and the skillful use of their family language. Her need to repeat the family dynamics by making me into her disrespected yet disobedient mother was intense, because she needed to see one of us as subservient. Whenever I rescheduled an appointment she would invariably want her usual appointment to be rescheduled into that new, supposedly temporary time.

Although she could not generally articulate her reason for these requests, as I learned her family 'language' I began to understand that she felt she deserved some control and consideration because she had done me a 'favor.' In her family, no desire ever was simply satisfied without a required payback. Her wish for the new appointment also reflected her conviction that what she did not have was always more valuable than anything she already possessed. Obviously, she was continuously discontented and consumed by envy, although the envy was hidden under a cloak of self-abasement. I began to understand that unhappiness really obscured a sense of being cheated and underscored her sense of entitlement. At the same time, it was very difficult for her to accept these insights because acknowledging her dominant desires put her at odds with the internalized father imago that demanded obeisance. The patient had internalized a representation of father that was frightful. Her real and actual father was old and decrepit, but she still felt the need to portray herself to me and others as helpless and incompetent. She feared that I would try to dominate and control her should I know of her wishes to dominate and control me. Her defense was to present herself in a masochistic, self-punitive manner to hide her dominating needs, which hid her assertive strivings from her internalized father imago.

To know such aspects of a patient directs the therapist to issues that reside in the preconscious and that need to be made conscious. Such direction is an important aid, as it is not always possible to wait for the patient to verbalize these issues. Some patients are not able to put such subtle identifications into words, especially because they represent self-descriptions that have been kept secret by necessity.

PSYCHIC ANNIHILATION

Mr. F. was in treatment with me for a number of years. He described himself as filled with insecurity and feelings of inadequacy. He was extremely passive and socially fearful and would venture out only if invited by others. He spent considerable time fantasizing relationships with the women with whom he worked, but he never asked anyone out. While he was in college he had imagined a secret relationship with another student, imagining that she had toward him the feelings he had toward her despite their never having spoken.

He had four older sisters, a dominant mother, and a passive, uninvolved father. Two of his sisters remained at home as adults, two others were married, and one of these was estranged from the family. Neither sister at home worked. He had been referred for treatment by the therapist of a woman whom he had managed to get involved with, but who tired of his passivity. The treatment was difficult and only moderately successful. Mr. J.'s concern about criticism rendered me nearly ineffective. Almost anything I said was perceived as a judgment, even if it only reflected something he himself had said. He held many things against me, including the fact that at our first meeting I did not tell him where to put his coat.

I viewed him as someone whose mother and father had not read his needs correctly and had consequently left him feeling out of tune with the world. His relationship with me replicated that feeling. Furthermore, he suffered from what appeared to me to be intense castration anxiety—so intense that well nigh any action terrified him with the threat of retribution. Even more, though, he was terrified of psychic annihilation. His sisters and mother so overwhelmed him that he existed under constant fear of his sense of identity and personal boundary being intruded upon and similarly viewed our relationship as a constant threat to the integrity of his self. Consequently, he felt the need to battle with me, to render me as impotent as he felt. Although he never acknowledged any improvement, he did become more sociable and less depressed over his time with me. Certainly his basic issues were not significantly altered.

Some patients who have been so traumatized and intruded upon are unable to form a therapeutic relationship. Their anxiety is about the survival of their psychological self. As with this patient, they fear *psychic annihilation,* and this fear is often combined with severe castration anxiety. Here, too, comprehensive assessment of the patient facilitates more accurate understanding of the anxieties that motivate particular symptoms and behaviors. Issues about psychic survival typically infuse the personality broadly, and are strongly compelling in the formation of "nameless dread."

THE PRESENT AND THE PAST UNCONSCIOUS

The therapist listening to a patient's associations must make decisions as to what type of intervention to make and when. Killingmo (1989) has made a distinction between statements that emphasize the validation of the patient's perspective and meaning and the interpretive approach that emphasizes hidden motives and the explication of *hidden* meaning. Sandler (1992) differentiates between *reconstruction* and *construction.* He uses the former in the common sense of an attempted historical exegesis of the patient's past aimed at understanding the forces that formed the psyche. Construction, as used by Sandler, refers to an explication of the patient's mental processing in the present (implicit goals and issues). Sandler and Sandler (1978) also suggest an orientation that concentrates on the "present unconscious" as opposed to the "past unconscious." The "present unconscious" reflects present concerns, including transference concerns, but has an intimate tie with past unconscious issues. This approach encourages exploration of underlying character structure and is accessible, affectively meaningful, and relevant to the patient.

It is not clear where the dividing line lies between unconscious and preconscious. It may be that what the Sandlers call the "present unconscious" corresponds to what I am calling the "preconscious." The most helpful interpretations are made from preconscious material; once identified, the patient recognizes it easily. More deeply unconscious material requires a "leap of faith" if the patient is to accept it and this, as I will discuss next, is not always possible.

THE CAPACITY TO KNOW

The capacities to solve problems, establish therapeutic relationships, and delay gratification are all attributes commonly thought to be necessary for a traditional conflict-oriented psychoanalytic treatment. Because of the abuse and deprivations that contribute to the formation of severe personality disorders, however, these attributes may well be missing in the more disturbed. It is helpful for the therapist to be able to identify their presence or absence so as to be able to approach the patient appropriately (Fonagy, 1991; Fonagy and Moran, 1991). Reality is painful for such individuals with their histories of trauma and neglect, and when sufficiently stressed they may endeavor to alter or ignore intolerable aspects of reality to maintain as much psychic equanimity as possible. Such denials of reality, however, require an "attack" on thoughtfulness, because thought represents painful connections as well as comfortable ones (Bion, 1957; McDougall, 1995; Chasseguet-Smirgel, 1988). The afteraffects of trauma are profound and far reaching, and I will discuss how trauma helps to create a personality constellation where the need to "not know" conflicts with self-knowledge that is the essence of psychotherapeutic cure. I will provide some preliminary thoughts on these matters here from the assessment perspective, and I will deal with these issues more fully in Chapter IV.

Curiosity suffers as well from the need not to know. The therapist's goal to help the patient to "know," in fact, may run counter to the patient's desires. When "knowing" for a patient is equivalent to acknowledging an overwhelmingly painful experience, that patient and the therapist are not going to be working toward the same ends. In fact, to try to get such a patient to "know" something, if the something is painful enough, can very much feel like an attack. Most therapists believe that "knowledge is power," and that the more one can understand, the more control one has over one's destiny. In the abstract this may be true but is not true pragmatically for a person struggling for everyday survival within an intolerable reality. The fantasy of a symbiotic relationship with the mother, unsullied by and unshared with the father and where psychic pain is vanquished (Chasseguet-Smirgel, 1988), is a profoundly enticing one for disturbed patients. It feels essential to them. Independent thought implies separation from mother, which becomes unbearably painful.

Disturbed patients often have memory problems arising from ego deficits; this creates a frightening sense of disconnectedness and sometimes feelings of panic. Chasseguet-Smirgel suggests that patients mired in this "archaic matrix of the Oedipus Complex" respond better to lengthier interpretations, presumably because they are less able to destroy a larger quantity of meaning. Patients who are organized at a neurotic level benefit more from rather short interpretations; they can use their own thoughts to make connections, and too lengthy interpretations may be unnecessary and intrusive. More disturbed patients require more thorough explications. It is my sense that they relish the sound of the analyst's voice, which may be a soothing contrast to those of their external and internal objects.

In my experience, effective therapists have an "uncanny" way of making interpretations that capture the essence of the patient's struggles of the moment. Here too such qualities of tact and timing often reflect unacknowledged accurate assessments of how immediate concerns are reflecting larger issues of personality structure. Assessment occurs both on macro and on micro levels. An overall sense of the patient drives and structures the treatment, assists the therapist in listening to associations from a certain perspective, and enables the therapist to help the patient formulate goals both implicit and explicit. On a more immediate level, accurate assessment assists in maintaining a sense of continuity for the patient, puts the everyday struggles within the larger context of personality structure, and gives the patient a present-day sense of understanding.

I feel most effective when I can help patients develop narratives of their lives—who they are, why they feel as they do, and how they have come to certain solutions to internal and external problems. Narratives like this give people a profound understanding of their nature and create a strong sense of self. In my experience, these narratives are developed primarily through attention to the patient's present-day functioning, with reference to the past when necessary for further elaboration, or through the patient's spontaneous recall. Painful realities from the past often do need to be explicated, as patients often have little sense of the antecedents of their problems. An understanding of the past also enables patients to understand aspects of their psychology that derive from internalized and introjected objects. It is best, however, when exploration of the past occurs within the context of the patient's character structure, in relation to the present-day material that has brought the past into focus. Effective therapists move back and forth among these venues, using them as appropriate according to the specific issues being addressed and the patient's immediate strength in dealing with painful material. The characterological approach looks at the whole patient and encourages the use of multiple approaches so the most comprehensive treatment possible may occur.

Throughout a treatment a therapist must make many decisions: when to emphasize the here-and-now and when the transference; when to develop a narrative; when to work with conflict and compromise formations; when to concentrate on the reconstruction of the past. The most important factor in determining the thrust of treatment is to follow the affective vector. Staying with the patient's emotions, trying to understand why, *in the moment,* particular thoughts and feelings are being experienced, seems to be the way to offer a treatment that is most accessible and comprehensible to the patient. In thinking about the patient and what form an intervention should take, I find it most useful to maintain a clear picture of the patient's associations in the context of the whole character structure within present-day struggles. In this way, the therapist can help the patient establish the concept of a person operating within a context—one in which a stable sense of self is possible, and one in which it is possible to feel more grounded and secure. This approach does not negate the importance of intrapsychic functioning but keeps it in the context of character structure.

III

◆

THE
TREATMENT
STRUCTURE

◆

As I have said, patients perplexed by their behavior, thoughts, and feelings are relieved to learn that these are not so perplexing to their therapists; they are not mysteries but reflections of the patient's attempts to cope with life's demands and anxieties. The therapeutic encounter and the therapeutic relationship are structured to further the analysis and elucidation of these reflections.

When therapists decide how to structure a treatment to accomplish the goals (explicit, implicit, and hidden) that the initial evaluation has just identified, however, their decisions are made not simply on the basis of the patient's perceived needs. They are influenced also by their own varying visions of the psychotherapeutic enterprise, visions that are a conflation of theoretical leanings, experiences in training, and personal proclivities. In this sense, all clinicians, like all families, have individual "languages." These develop through identifications and compromise formations that include both family and professional influences, and they are passed on to patients as family languages are. As patient and therapist develop a relationship, a *mutual* language begins to form. This bridges the gap between their two separate experiences and differing perspectives and helps them to understand each other. They come to the work with their own visions, though, and these visions influence the way the work proceeds.

In short, just as the patient inevitably comes to the work of therapy with an established character—and the language, the visible and invisible traits, and the worldview that comes with it—so does the therapist. Everything I have just said about the development, establishment, and inscrutability of character traits in the patient applies equally to the other party in the therapeutic encounter, and where it shows the most is in the therapist's way of structuring and conducting therapy. Every decision made about or within the therapeutic framework is informed by the therapist's own particular conception of the nature of the psychotherapeutic enterprise, and just as our patients' experience of therapy is enriched by attention to the way "character" infiltrates life, so is our experience enriched by attention to the way our characters influence our practice.

This is a topic with endless ramifications, but I will content myself with addressing several of the large and pressing structural decisions made by psychotherapists early in treatment and some aspects of the context in which they are made. In particular, I will explore how therapists' idiosyncratic proclivities lead them to different therapeutic positions and how these do and do not facilitate the analysis of character. I will illustrate with case material and with some references to the literature how the worldview of the therapist—sometimes consciously articulated and sometimes not—is reflected in working choices, and how awareness of this can further the therapeutic process.

THE THERAPEUTIC RELATIONSHIP

The first goal in treatment is the establishment of a therapeutic relationship. Like any other relationship, this requires time and nurturing, and like any other relationship it is shaped by the fears, desires, and expectations of the people involved—ours as well as our patients'. It is important to remember, for example, that although we feel ourselves to be trustworthy and reliable, we are essentially strangers to our patients, and only with experience will they come to agree (or not!) with us. There is nothing necessarily defensive or pathological in a patient's wariness; on the contrary, the very rapid development of confidence in the therapist may not be a good prognostic sign, reflecting as it sometimes does a pathological dependency and a naïve grasp of relationship. Different therapists will understand such variations differently, depending, for instance, on how much they tend to grant patients the right to do things their own way, or how much they feel that good patients should be able to recognize and trust "benign" authority. So the way the patient settles in is a valuable source of information about the patient and the patient's internalized object relationships—and about the therapist's. Like the characterological traits discussed previously, these are aspects of functioning that may not be directly accessible or readily verbalized, but they may be seen through the therapist-patient interaction, in both directions.

> Ms. S. entered treatment in the throes of divorce. She developed an intense erotized transference (Blum 1974) almost immediately. She began calling me frequently with "emergencies," developed elaborate fantasies about me, and engaged in constant mental dialogues with me, so intensely that she became confused sometimes about what she had actually told me versus what she imagined I knew. Because often I was not in fact privy to these internal discussions, I frequently felt adrift. This was a reflection of a general difficulty in her life. Her family had not treated her as a real person. They had had great expectations of her, but these did not take into account her own inclinations and proclivities. That was how Ms. S. treated me—as a nonperson who existed only as a projection, to satisfy all her needs. This treatment created countertransference reactions in me, leaving me feeling alternatively bored and irritated. I, however, took solace in understanding that her attempt to merge our identities was reflective of her own experience as a child, and that it was helping to educate me about her underlying character structure. Another therapist might have felt, for instance, that her need to treat me like this represented hidden castration fantasies and that rendering me impotent matched her feeling about herself and could be taken as an attempt to make me into her similarly imagined disfigured state.

Still, Ms. S. took well to my approach to treatment. She began to examine her psychic workings as I repeatedly interpreted her wish to change her relationship with me from therapeutic to need-gratifying. As she became curious about herself and her psychology, the psychoanalytic work became satisfying in its own right.

As patients gain more control over their lives and begin to understand the workings of the mind, real pleasure in the work becomes possible. An interactive therapeutic approach models for the patient a sense of assertion and active involvement. This is another extremely important way that the analyst's attitudes influence the work. Psychoanalysis and psychodynamic psychotherapy must be taught and demonstrated. Therapists learn to be effective therapists by identifying with their own therapists, and patients incorporate the self-reflective analytic functions modeled by their clinicians. To some extent the patient's identification with the therapist brings their two disparate worldviews into accord; still, it is important for both participants to recognize that worldviews, like all character-based issues, are constructions and not representations of some impossible "veridical" reality.

THE WORK OF PSYCHOANALYSIS

The work and the setting of psychodynamic psychotherapy are unfamiliar at first to most patients. Some find introspection easy and take to the process quickly. Others need help developing the skills for psychodynamic work, and here again the therapist's vision of the therapeutic enterprise determines how this help is (or is not) delivered. For example, a patient's initial clumsiness in therapy may reflect ignorance as much as defense or resistance. Some patients require more information about their therapist than is commonly provided in the classical model, which sometimes gives rise to struggles over the "rules" of anonymity and neutrality. Some naïve patients expect advice. Very few understand much about their own psychological disturbance. Attention to the patient's underlying personality structure and day-to-day preoccupations can guide the therapist to an appropriate level of disclosure. Furthermore, discussion of the reasons for not answering questions (or of any other peculiarities of the therapeutic process) furthers a cooperative attitude in this most difficult of undertakings. By the same token, open discussion of the patient's problems from a characterological perspective gives the patient a working model of psychological functioning that goes beyond symptom and expands understanding.

Showing patients how their difficulties emerge out of their "implicit" level of functioning is comprehensible, palatable, and useful, keeping the processes of therapy or the internal dynamic processes mysterious is not. To do so may result in a demoralizing idealization of the therapist and an increase in the sense of helplessness with which most people approach therapy. Open discussion of the patient's problems, and the therapist's ideas about them, enables the patient to understand them more directly, with less reliance on rationalization. Some patients have established explanations for their difficulties that they expect the therapist to confirm; these tend to be compromise formations that lessen shame and painful self-awareness. These explanations usually correspond to family rationales about people, and how and why they function as they do. Helping patients to see both the intricacies and the comprehensiveness of their problems eases the way into more intensive treatment. Obviously, cruel confrontations with unpalatable and heavily defended-against wishes are not helpful, but it is both possible and important to convey to patients enough of a sense of how their disorders work that they can understand the rationale of treatment.

Psychoanalytic inquiry is a process of joint discovery—therapist and patient work *together* in an ongoing exploration. Many aspects of the patient are hidden from both participants, and the pleasure (and the likelihood) of analytic discovery diminishes when certainty replaces curiosity. Still, it reassures patients to have some sense of where their problems come from, and to be able to understand the proposed treatment in that context. Psychoanalytic treatment helps the patient to establish connections among present-day functioning, life history, and enduring personality characteristics. As these become clear, the patient feels understood, the analytic process makes sense, and the structure and experience of treatment look less overwhelming, less frightening, and less mysterious. The use of the therapeutic relationship both as a model of the patient's intrapsychic and object relational representations, and as a new object for identification, provides a potent tool for personality development.

Dr. R., mentioned earlier, sought treatment because she was depressed. She had had some previous psychotherapy, but hadn't gained much from it—she didn't even remember much about it. She did know that her therapist had told her that she had low self-esteem and that she needed to be more assertive in her daily life; this, of course, was true, but no help to Dr. R. She continued to feel empty and isolated, and found little meaning in her life. She could not even articulate the feelings of emptiness and meaninglessness that were the crux of her unhappiness, or recognize them as such. It wasn't until I pointed them out to her that she became able to identify them to herself: to give words to something previously ineffable. This new capacity intrigued and relieved her; she was fascinated by the prospect of getting to know more about these issues and figuring out how to achieve some sense of meaning and fullness in life. I was able to show her how these difficulties were not discrete entities, but were interwoven into her personality in a manner that she could so far not see, and that her life was to that extent being governed by unconscious processes. That was why, I told her, I recommended analysis; it was a process designed to help her articulate her unknown thoughts and to work through unconscious conflicts and belief systems so that she could begin to understand herself in a new way. She appreciated this suggestion and agreed to begin analysis. Her conscious acceptance of this plan did not, of course, mean that the road would be easy. As treatment progressed many issues came up about frequency of visits, the nature of the psychoanalytic process (she often expected me to tell her what to do), transference issues, and goals of treatment (she had not told me that she expected me to provide her with a new personality!). Nevertheless, these less conscious issues were grist for the mill, and we were proceeding consciously and conjointly according to an explicitly identified therapeutic contract while we dealt with them.

The development of this explicit model of the psychotherapeutic enterprise greatly enhanced her immediate sense of being "held" and contributed to her belief that I could understand her and help her. As time went on, implicit aspects of the therapeutic process, which can only be experienced and not explicitly taught, became more obvious and were more fully internalized.

FREQUENCY

Frequency of visits is sometimes seen as a function of psychological health, and not always in consistent ways. Some clinicians believe that only neurotic patients can tolerate the stress of frequent sessions without becoming unglued; others believe that it is the fragmented and disorganized patient who needs the ego support and holding environment of everyday meetings. It has been my experience, however, that most patients welcome the opportunity for intensive work if the proposal is framed properly in the context of a shared assessment.

When Dr. R. came into treatment she felt unfocused about what was wrong with her. She was relieved when I told her that I thought her problems had more to do with underlying personality issues than with the diagnostic label of "depression." She had never before had a context that made sense of her past and present feelings and behaviors. She relished the opportunity to become engaged in the process, and although she was a bit hesitant at first, she agreed to come four times weekly.

My explanation to patients about how psychological problems become entwined and interwoven with people's personalities usually meets with recognition and relief. They also help make clear why therapy requires careful attention to detail and why frequent sessions are important; complicated interweavings must be elucidated, and details may be lost when sessions are scheduled with lesser frequency. To identify the ephemeral and nonverbalized requires intimate knowledge, and intimate knowledge requires frequent meetings; so, as I will describe shortly, does the acquisition of fluency in the patient's language.

Rothstein (1995) suggests that resistance to the therapist's recommendations regarding treatment frequency is just that, a resistance. "I have conceptualized these patients' initial objections as *enactment resistances*. These symptomatic enactments often have a transference significance and derive from unconscious fantasies that are best understood as compromise formations" (p. 4). He goes on to suggest that treatment prior to the acceptance of the analyst's recommendations can be considered a "modified analysis," because it means that patients agree at least to consider the possibility that their reluctance to commit to four sessions weekly represents a defensive posture. Rothstein's approach shows some flexibility, because he recognizes that some patients may require a modified analytic framework before they can become engaged in a formal analysis.

Nevertheless, patients may be reluctant to commit to intensive treatment for a variety of reasons. A patient with a sexual abuse history may experience such interpretations of "resistance" to frequency of treatment as assaultive and accusatory. People with issues about shame may fear the notion of an "uncovering" treatment and need to keep it at some distance; years of preparatory work designed to shore up a fragile ego or work through fears of humiliation may be necessary before such a patient agrees to more intensive work.

Here, as in other structural decisions, the therapist's worldview profoundly influences his or her understanding of the patient's behavior and how that behavior is dealt with. The patient may *never* agree to more intensive work—and respect for the patient, at least in my worldview, requires that the therapist not pathologize on principle every point of disagreement (see the section on analytic authority following). The patient is free to make the choice about frequency, so long as I can comfortably work with that patient within those parameters. Reluctance to accept the frequency prescribed by the therapist may reflect unconscious resistance related to compromise formation, as Rothstein asserts, but it may also reflect many other issues integral to the identity of the patient, and the integrity of the patient must be maintained. Reluctance to accede to the therapist's wishes may represent a crucial need for autonomy and separateness; I once told a patient that I understood that he needed to say "no" before he could say "yes," and this statement allowed him to acknowledge the need for more sessions.

AUTHORITY WITHIN THE THERAPY SETTING

Every therapist, deliberately or not, also takes a position on certain aspects of power within the therapeutic relationship, an important one of these is the extent to which the therapist can claim authority as the ultimate arbiter of reality. The therapist's attitude toward this question will contribute largely to the shape the treatment ultimately takes, and like all other aspects of therapeutic structure, it relates as much to the therapist's own implicit functioning, or worldview, as it does to conscious conviction. The therapist's characteristic attitudes, wherever they lie on the authority spectrum, are conveyed to the patient, influencing both therapeutic process and outcome.

Briefly, the spectrum can be described like this. Some therapists believe that they are less emotionally involved than the patient and so less subject to transference distortions; these therapists tend to see themselves as possessing an authoritative viewpoint on questions of material versus psychic reality. Others believe that both participants are emotionally involved, and therefore both susceptible to distortion. Either way, implicitly or not, the belief is transmitted to the patient, and it affects the tone of the treatment and the kind of material produced, as patients learn very rapidly to understand their therapist's "language." They also try, not always knowingly, to cooperate, structuring associations, dreams, and behaviors to adhere to their therapist's preferences.

PSYCHIC REALITY

The way in which a given therapist conceptualizes 'authority' within the psychotherapeutic setting is related to his or her position on the nature of reality, psychic vs. external. A complete discussion of the controversial and important issues surrounding the question of psychic reality vs. external reality is far beyond the scope of this work. It seems clear, however, that what we *feel* to be true is usually more important to us than any verifiable, veridical reality. Patients, like all of us, sometimes distort what they perceive, and to assist them in understanding these distortions is very valuable. My own worldview does not require me to call upon the august authority of the analyst to "verify" reality, when one can often call instead upon patients' own vision of reality to help them to identify distortions (Renik, 1998; Grossman, 1996).

A patient became very concerned about whether a person she had frequently seen in my building was an associate of mine and whether I might have been transmitting confidential information. I certainly could have insisted upon my innocence but I thought it better, for the moment at least, to defer such protestations. This enabled further discussion that allowed the patient to recognize how concerned she was that some thefts of hers might become known.

In my view, to insist on the therapist's version of reality is counterproductive. An open discussion of possibilities of alternative explanations, and continued emphasis on associations, can often result in new understandings. The patient's psychic reality provides a window into the patient's inner world (Fonagy and Target, 1996; Target and Fonagy, 1996). To understand the patient's characteristic way of looking at internal and external life, to identify family identifications, and to learn the "language" of the patient are far more useful than fruitless and alienating conflicts over whose version of "reality" is correct. Ultimately, respect for the integrity of the patient requires of the therapist an open and inquiring mind, and an acknowledgement that the patient is the ultimate authority on how he or she will configure reality, internal and external. A clinician who *insists* that one perspective is correct without trying to understand the patient's point of view may miss alternative (and probably more complex and meaningful) possibilities, which may very well include contributions from the countertransference.

Furthermore, it can be extraordinarily useful at times to sit back and listen to the patient as he or she tries to understand his or her history *without* reference to the transference. In good therapy patients begin to be able to understand how pathological responses to everyday events may be related to childhood difficulties and the distortions engendered by trauma, an immature ego, or family identifications. Such autonomous understanding of personality structure are invaluable. Therapists who can muster the grace to cede control and authority to their patients promote independence and help in the necessary deidealization process. Individuals who can use their own minds to explicate previously confusing experiences feel more in control of their lives and less dependent on others to do this work for them. They are on the road to being able to carry out the therapeutic process on their own, which is perhaps its ultimate goal.

THE NATURE OF THE
PSYCHOTHERAPEUTIC ENCOUNTER

This is not a simple issue, however, and given its complications it is not surprising that different therapists see the matter of authority and reality differently. The nature of the treatment relationship is such that the patient is identified as being the one with the psychological disorder, and the trained and treated therapist as the one who can see the surround in a more objective and less emotionally tinged way. Patients are encouraged to regress, to develop transference reactions—to distort—and otherwise to bring their pathology out into the open. Therapists are expected to be more in control of themselves, and, by virtue of their training, to be able to offer their patients an expanded perspective. Consequently, while at any given moment the analyst's position may not be "privileged" over the patient's, still there is an expectation on both parties' parts that the analyst is capable of an objectivity that the patient is not. Schafer (1983) speaks of the "second self" of the analyst, which can function in ways that transcend personal pathology and be "healthier" than one really is.

These questions about the therapist's authority relate closely to important current theoretical discussions about the nature of the therapeutic encounter and controversies about whether a concrete, objective view of reality is possible. Renik (1995) thinks that the analyst's point of view must not be given more weight than the patient's. Although most analysts in theory agree with this laudable sentiment, it has been my experience that it is a very difficult perspective to maintain. The fact that an analyst or therapist subscribes to one particular theoretical orientation or another suggests in itself a preferred (implicit) way of looking at the patient and at life. These are conveyed to the patient by the nature of the analyst's attention to associative material. Thus the clinician structures the therapeutic encounter according to his or her worldview, setting a particular *type* of stage on which the patient's life drama will be acted out and elucidated.

Patients, through subtle cues, orient to their therapists' mode of communication and adapt to it, as children learn the language of the community in which they are raised. Even clinicians who deeply embrace the ideal of a free flow of ideas and prefer a nonauthoritarian approach have very specific ideas about the nature of the therapeutic encounter, and these ideals are communicated to the patient. However they may strive to maintain their dedication to the subjective, all therapists possess an "objective" (to them) belief system that defines the manner in which they practice. Every analyst or therapist has therefore a tremendous influence on the nature of the encounter, whether this is desired or not.

Therapists who advocate a two-person, relational, intersubjective perspective, for example, (Mitchell, 1998; Hoffman, 1996, among many others) believe that the emphasis in psychoanalysis should be on the interactive matrix between therapist and patient, and that attempts to reconstruct the past as if it were a buried treasure, existing in a finite and concrete way, is misguided, unhelpful, and impossible. They suggest that because the past is known mostly through the present, there can be no veridical elucidation of the past; reality is unknowable and impossible to ascertain. They emphasize the inherent subjectivity of both participants and suggest that what *is* knowable is that which occurs between them. Furthermore, this perspective encourages a personal and interactive relationship between therapist and patient. "Stated succinctly, and summarizing the movement from the beginning until now, we have traversed the distance from analysis as *solitary reflection* to analysis *as relational struggle*. In the latter, against the backdrop of the ritualized asymmetry of the psychoanalytic situation from which we draw special moral power, we participate as intimate partners with our patients as they wrestle with conflict and as they choose from among, and struggle to realize, their multiple potentials for intimacy and autonomy, for identification and individuality, for work and play, and for continuity and change" (Hoffman,

1996, p.133). He suggests that the attainment of a sense of evenness of status within the therapeutic relationship is salutary in and of itself.

Proponents of this point of view believe that the relationship with the therapist is a new relationship, and therefore transference manifestations are not necessarily repetitions of the past; they may, however, be new occurrences based on the unique characteristics of the two participants. The focus is on the participation of the therapist. "Those of us, especially, who have turned away from an objectivist view of the analyst's role and replaced it with the view that the patient's experience is partially constituted interactively in the analytic situation, in other words, those of us who have been trying to work out a 'constructivist' view of the analytic process are faced with the necessity of coming to grips with the full implications of that perspective for the role of the analyst in the patient's life" (Hoffman, 1996, p. 110). This approach emphasizes a search for meaning and understanding that helps the patient to develop a narrative sense of his or her life.

The contrary position focuses upon the patient (one person) and sees the therapist's involvement as more interpretive and less interactive and experiential. This is exemplified by Brenner (1996) and Kernberg (1996), who hold the analyst to be by training and experience an authority on the normal psyche and on psychopathology, and suggests that change in psychoanalysis occurs through elucidation of the patient's intrapsychic conflicts as they become manifest within the transference. Brenner and Kernberg emphasize relatively little the analyst's emotional involvement and see the resolution of conflicts that originated in the past as a central focus. "My own conclusion from the data available to me is that patients' symptoms are pathological compromise formations due to conflicts over sexual and aggressive wishes of childhood origin" (Brenner, 1996, p. 22). Considerable attention is paid to helping patients adjust to and accept the unpleasant realities of life, and to understanding defensive needs to distort reality. Uncovering hidden desires and fears and the resulting compromise formations are the focus of this orientation.

Winnicott (1969) and Kohut (1971, 1984), on the other hand, take the patient's viewpoint as the privileged one. Both of these theorists, who emphasize helping patients to develop and strengthen their sense of self, are exquisitely sensitive to the salience of the patient's psychic reality and are little concerned with issues about verifiable external reality. Although they believe in the efficacy of the therapeutic experience, Winnicott and Kohut are not interactive in the same way as are the intersubjective and relational theorists. They believe that the therapeutic relationship is beneficial in and of itself, provided that it is used in ways that counteract imbalances from childhood. They believe that early environmental failure provides the greatest contribution to psychological disturbance in children and adults.

Kohut has emphasized the narcissistic disorders, but his theories are increasingly applied to other disorders as well. He believes that it is the therapist's failure to empathically understand the patient that leads toward positive change. "Each optimal (nontraumatic) failure will be followed by an increase in the patient's resilience vis-à-vis empathy failures both inside and outside the analytic situation: that is, after each, optimal new self structures will be acquired and existing ones will be firmed" (1984, p. 69, parentheses added). In Kohut's framework, the patient's sense of self has been damaged by narcissistically damaging experiences in childhood. The therapeutic alternation of empathic failure and correction addresses past narcissistic blows and leads to enhanced self-esteem. Noninterpretive techniques such as idealization and mirroring contribute to psychic change. The therapist is used as a self-object, a sort of auxiliary self, who supports and enhances a self too vulnerable to manage to maintain itself on its own. The process of treatment is not to analyze defense and resistance. Disorders of the self create symptoms that, according to Kohut, are mistakenly ascribed to intrapsychic conflict. The therapist is not the definer of reality and does not look for distortions that emanate from pathological compromise formations. Misunderstandings between the participants are seen as the responsibility of the therapist. "If there is one lesson that I have learned during my life as an analyst, it is the lesson that what my patients tell me is likely to be true—that many times when I believed that I was right and my patients were wrong, it turned out, though often only after a prolonged search, that *my* rightness was superficial whereas *their* rightness was profound" (1984, pp. 93–94).

Similarly, Winnicott (1969, 1963b) holds that environmental inadequacies—an inadequate "holding environment"—presages psychological disturbance. "Arising out of failure in this area of the facilitating environment can be seen the whole subject of the development of character disorders associated with the setting up of various kinds of false self, these representing failures of self-establishment and self-discovery" (1969, p. 711). Although Winnicott makes many allusions to interpretation, his main emphasis is on providing a particular kind of therapeutic experience for the patient. Enabling the patient to experience being 'held,' tolerating the patient's aggression, acknowledging the patient's attempts at reparation, are all noninterpretative experiences that Winnicott deems curative. Winnicott clearly states his feelings about interpretation and about privileging the patient's view. "It appalls me to think how much deep change I have prevented or delayed in patients *in a certain classification category* by my personal need to interpret. If only we can wait, the patient arrives at an understanding creatively and with immense joy, and I now enjoy this joy more than I used to enjoy the sense of having been clever. I think that I interpret mainly to let the patient know the limits of my understanding. The principle is that it is the patient and only the patient who has the answers. We may or may not enable him or her to be able to encompass what is known or become aware of it with acceptance" (1969, p. 711). Winnicott has suggested that his noninterpretative methods are most applicable to the character and psychotic disorders, but his approach, like Kohut's, has been applied across the whole psychopathological spectrum.

All of these theories is to some extent limited by the worldview of the theorist. The constructivists may not attend sufficiently to intrapsychic conflict; the "classical" analyst may ignore the contribution of countertransference influence to a patient's behavior in therapy. Kohut, I believe, does not sufficiently recognize the intricacy of the psychological structures that are built up over years of coping with the exigencies of life. These structures have a life of their own and do not collapse and disappear when a patient's self-structure is bolstered. Winnicott focuses in theory on the resolution of aggression, although criticism has been leveled at him for failing to address it in therapy (Hopkins, 1998). I wonder whether sufficient attention is given to the need to analyze, as opposed to just tolerate, aggression.

Let me illustrate how the worldviews expressed in theory can manifest themselves in practice and in the structuring of treatment. Any given psychoanalytic encounter can highlight the proclivities of that particular therapist. Consider a case described by Renik (1998). A patient describes having a cold and expresses reluctance to attend a friend's Seder for fear of spreading her germs to the other guests. Renik lets the patient know that he wonders about her decision: "Does Margaret feel that I should cancel appointments when I have a cold or the flu? Because, I tell her, I don't. Does that seem irresponsible?" (p. 567). He and the patient link her self-abnegating attitude to an identification with a cold and withdrawing mother. In subsequent sessions Renik points out to Margaret some aspects of reality that she might not have considered in the interpretations that she has come to about important events in her life. "I encouraged her to consider whether certain of her expressed ideas were realistic, and I presented her with certain of my own ideas about reality for consideration" (p. 573).

Renik believes that the analyst should not try to impose a view of reality (that is, an analyst's "privileged" view) on the patient but should give the patient the opportunity to make up his or her own mind. Although the sessions described were sensitive, helpful, and reflective of Renik's comfort with self-disclosure, however, they do indicate that Renik follows one particular view of this patient, as opposed to the many other ones possible. Another analyst might have wondered what hidden anger and resentment might be expressed in the patient's fear of spreading germs. A third might notice the patient's strong masochistic tendencies. I myself would hope to pursue both avenues with this patient—the hidden aggressive and self-destructive conflictual issues along with such implicit, characterological ones as masochism. Every therapist influences treatment in subtle and not so subtle ways, and it behooves all therapists to keep aware that the material produced in their consulting rooms is being produced, at least in part, in conformity to their own language.

In another mode, we can look at a case presented by Brenner (1996). He tells of a time at the beginning of his career when he was convinced that the patient's lack of progress "expressed both her wish to render me impotent and her consequent, unconscious guilt and need to punish herself, but my interpretations to that effect seemed useless, however well supported they were by dreams and other analytic material" (p. 27). After months of struggle, Brenner came to believe that perhaps the patient was right and that he was wrong: that it would be best for her to terminate treatment. The patient, feeling that she had "won at last," was triumphant (p. 27). To Brenner this example demonstrates that the analyst's view is more likely to be "right" than the patient's. That is a reflection of his worldview. I myself wonder instead what might have been missed in the way this analyst articulated to his patient her supposed intransigence. She is free to come and go at will; why is there even an argument about whether she continue or not? Perhaps the disagreement reflects the patient's unstated rebellion against the dogmatism of Brenner's attitude, which may convey to her a need to be right.

And there are ways to imagine a situation like this that transcend the question of who is right. Feinsilver (1999) suggests that many such impasses reflect the unacknowledged counteridentification by the analyst with conflicts of which the patient is struggling, at the moment. The analyst unknowingly, through concordant identification (Racker 1957) tries to, "do back to the patient what the analyst feels is being done to him/her" (Feinsilver, 1999, p. 275). From this point of view, Brenner could be seen as identifying with the patient's aggression and turning it back against her, rather than helping the patient understand her *characteristic* way of functioning within relationships. Her behavior, not just a matter of attempting to render her analyst impotent, represents an elaboration of what have likely been the defining relationships in her life, and her *own* sense of impotence. Awareness of this possibility might have transformed the impasse into a discussion of these characterological issues and could have included an elucidation of her need to dominate the analyst as she had felt dominated. Further discussion might have ensued of the guilt created by her needs to dominate. My point here, as in the Renik example previously, is not to support or dismiss any particular analytic approach but to indicate how much influence the analyst has, knowingly or not, on the structure of the treatment, and by extension how important it is for analysts to remain aware of this.

COLLABORATION

The roles of therapist and patient, like their worldviews, are also subject to expectations and distortions, explicit, implicit, and hidden, by both participants. The therapist envisions his or her role, like other aspects of therapeutic structure, based upon personal proclivities, professional experiences, hidden needs, and more generally on an "implicit" worldview.

In "role" I include the level of activity taken by the participants, their ways of cooperating and collaborating, their ideas about relative status, and their expectations of each other—like whether the therapist has "answers," and what the patient should contribute. Role beliefs generally reflect attitudes that are not directly discussed; they operate like background music. These "implicit" attitudes can hide issues and conflicts that are better identified and explicated.

Some therapists envision a collaborative effort, where each participant is expected to be a relatively full partner in carrying the responsibility for the success of the enterprise. Others imagine a more authoritarian approach where doctor-patient lines are clearly drawn and where the therapist is expected to make concrete suggestions or at least offer definitive interpretations. Therapist personality constellations make significant contributions to the type of approach taken and greatly affect the nature of the therapeutic relationship. Therapists need to be cognizant, therefore, of how their preferences for one particular stance or other affects the therapy. Brenner's approach in the previous situation, for example, may have exacerbated already existing issues within the patient about her own competency, potency, and adequacy. Implicit role expectations that are not verbalized and discussed may have iatrogenic effects.

Patients, too, have conscious and unconscious expectations of the roles that they and their therapists should play. Explicitly, for instance, Dr. R. was quite willing to cooperate in the psychotherapeutic process as I described it—to free associate and be a forthright, active participant. She had along with these conscious but unarticulated expectations that I would take an authoritarian and privileged stance; preconsciously, she also expected that I would provide her with a new and improved personality—that is, make her a totally new person. Because she believed, unconsciously of course, that gender was alterable, she expected that she would have the opportunity to become a man if she so desired.

Her underlying expectation of the therapeutic process, therefore, was not one of exploration and collaboration, but these role expectations were informative of her general character structure. Because character imbues the patient's life, it makes its presence known in transference and in areas that are often not explicitly addressed in therapy—like the respective roles and responsibilities of the participants.

Consciously, Dr. R. wished to feel better and more in control of her life. She hoped for a clearer sense of herself. Unconsciously, she had impossible fantasies that she hoped would remove her feelings of desperation. Her preferred position was that I was an authority and thus a possessor of the power to right the wrongs that she had suffered. She did not see herself as an active participant in the process, and in fact it was the way she understood the psychotherapeutic process that informed us of her internal authoritarian state of mind. Her transference fantasy of the godlike therapist was an indication of her internal object representations, and her hidden goal was for me to transform her into a similar omnipotent being. One aspect of the treatment was to identify and understand the roots of this hidden goal and to help her to become more collaborative in life and in our work. Taking into account her sadomasochistic characterological issues helped me to understand the paradoxical wish that I be authoritarian, both as a potential identificatory object and as one that she could strive to overthrow.

In this case, sensitivity to these issues, particularly the need to view all patients as active participants, helped me to minimize enactments; specifically it helped to keep me from being drawn into Dr. R.'s provocations, and from becoming punitive and domineering. This experience (I hope!) will provide her with an identification to challenge her more pathological characteristic, one of domination and submission.

Bohm (1999) writes convincingly that the·analyst is best served who follows three precepts: "Not to discard what we do not understand, not to know more than the analysand and not to have a prepared programme" (p. 503). Certainly there is no need to argue with this. All clinicians have preferred ways of looking at patients, at life, and at the manner in which we view mutative interventions. It is impossible to deny this subjectivity, which includes the false belief in some absolute or perfect openness.

The wish to understand patients ever more completely may be a laudable goal, but it is one that is more important in the seeking than in the accomplishment. All therapists are limited by their worldview, by their personal shortcomings, by the intractability of certain psychological disorders, by our incomplete understanding of psychic processes, and by the complex nature of personality. All of the current psychodynamic approaches have something to offer. I myself am most sympathetic to the interactive approach, but I recognize that it has a downside too, failing as it sometimes does to recognize certain transference manifestations as indicative of underlying negativistic and sadomasochistic *structural* personality characteristics (Kernberg, 1996). Patients have destructive thoughts and wishes, and these need to be recognized and addressed. When therapists see their patients as victims of forces beyond their control, little attention is given to their negativistic, sadomasochistic, and destructive sides. A therapist who insists upon some version of a patient's essential goodness dominates the patient as much as a therapist who sees destructiveness at every turn, and thus perpetuates the patient's dynamic of control and domination.

We do our patients no favors by denying the reality of their destructiveness, or any of their other realities, whether we do it out of theory or in an unwitting denial of our own primitive rage. The result is that a crucial aspect of the patient is not analyzed. An effective and caring clinician must address the less pleasant aspects of our patients and, by association, of ourselves. This is best accomplished by attention to character structure, the awareness that pathological responses develop out of the patient's need to adapt and adjust to overwhelming situations, and·the knowledge that symptomatology is part of the larger picture of character structure.

The scope of therapeutic inquiry is expanding, to the enrichment of the field, but the elucidation of unconscious material suffers when attention is given only to the interactive domain or to the domain of conflict. It is attention to the preconscious, "implicit" level of functioning that provides signposts to the unconscious. Approaches that emphasize the past within the present, the unconscious within the conscious, and the internal within the transference provide patients with a strong sense of their overall functioning and its relationship to their personality structure.

CLINICAL MATERIAL IN CONTEXT

Another way therapists structure the therapeutic encounter has to do with how they view the material presented in a given session. Some clinicians, following Bion's lead, approach every session "without memory or desire," preferring to see it as an entity unto itself and a new opportunity to capture the unconscious. Others see the material of each session within a context—the patient's current life situation, the prevailing character structure that informs it, current transference material—all with an eye toward explication of unconscious material. To my mind, this approach, with its emphasis on the here-and-now, makes for the liveliest treatment and the one most relevant to the patient's everyday life. Furthermore, it emphasizes the adaptive aspect of symptomatic behavior, thus diminishing the stigma of "pathology." It also encourages a sense of continuity and provides a discernible direction, heartening the patient who may often feel lost and confused. Approaching the patient's associations in the context of current issues both within and outside of the treatment leads to an increasing sense of the continuity between past and present, between internal and external, and between preconscious and unconscious.

CENTRAL ADAPTIVE CONTEXT

Langs's (1976) concept of the "central adaptive context" is a useful way of viewing each session. His position is that patients come to their sessions with an issue or central idea that they want to work on. These are not always accessible to consciousness, and when they aren't they must be inferred from the patient's associations. Generally, I have found, these issues relate to relatively circumscribed concerns and so give the session focus. They may relate to the patient's external life, thoughts, feelings or behavior, or transference issues. The patient, of course, is not always aware of the specifics of this concern, and so the major task of any given session may simply be to identify it. Making the preconscious conscious is the first course of action, and then to explain it, if possible.

Langs's concept is useful for the therapist trying to tease out issues embedded in the patient's character structure. It can help to structure the treatment, and it can be very helpful with patients whose associations seem chaotic and frantic. It can be reassuring to the therapist, too; when one is flooded with patient angst, it is helpful to be able to pick out one salient message as the source of psychic and transferential pressure. The use of Langs's technique enables patients to observe the workings of their own minds and to see how conflict and defense operate in the real world. It makes clear to the patient that the work of the treatment has a specific goal and that psychotherapy is not just a meandering exploration with no end in mind. As time goes on, patterns emerge out of these foci, and some of the central issues demanding attention become identifiable. Furthermore, they can be placed in the context of the patient's general personality structure. The "central adaptive context" also keeps the treatment firmly anchored in the present, maintains an experience-near feel, and provides real life examples for the patient to grasp. Connections to past events (reconstruction) can be made as needed, as can allusions to the patient's typical fashion of functioning.

FREE ASSOCIATION

Free association has been viewed, correctly, as a major source of psychoanalytic data. However, clinicians do not always feel that the material that comes up in treatment is presented all that "freely." Patients assent readily enough to the suggestion that they say everything that comes to mind, but consciously or unconsciously, many have no intention of doing so. I asked one patient about his reluctance to say whatever came to mind even after quite a long time in treatment, and he responded, "I know that you asked me to do that, but did you really mean *everything?*" In the rest of his experience, people did not really mean what they said. His hesitation to speak freely had defensive underpinnings as well, because anything he found uncomfortable could be suppressed in the rationalization that I probably did not *really* want to hear about some particular embarrassing thought, memory, or fantasy.

Patients usually respond to the suggestion that they free associate with some discomfort, and we know that the ability to associate freely is a goal and not a rapidly or easily acquired skill. Furthermore, interferences in free association represent important areas for further exploration (Busch, 1995). Still, like many of the other aspects of the therapeutic setting, the way a therapist thinks about free association and resistances to it reflects a particular worldview. An authoritarian analyst may scold or withdraw when a patient violates the "fundamental rule." A more forgiving but perhaps less probing analyst may ignore significant lapses in association out of the intention not to make demands and to provide a free and open space.

Kris (1996) and Busch (1995, 1997), representatives of the ego psychology tradition, emphasize the importance of breaks in the flow of associations. These discontinuities, they believe, represent areas of conflict, and attention to them yields information about the patient's problems and characteristic defensive posture. Busch (1997) emphasizes the importance of attending to the patient's associations as stated, rather than making interpretations about hidden meanings. For Kris, the goal of psychoanalysis is to facilitate the flow and continuity of free associations. If that goal is achieved, other goals—such as the attainment of insight, reduction of symptoms, improvements in relationships, and so on—will necessarily follow. Consequently, both of these writers emphasize the importance of resistance analysis, both to help the patient resolve conflicts in the here and now and to elucidate the workings of their minds. They suggest that resistance analysis enlarges self-knowledge and the capacity to confront and deal with the demands of reality. This approach, particularly as expounded by Busch (1997), searches out hidden motives and places a premium on the exploration of the ego and of ego defenses. Exploring unconscious fantasies and drive derivatives are not a primary focus, nor is explication of disowned or disavowed aspects of the self.

The approach exemplified by Ogden (1996a) contrasts with this one. Although Kris believes that the goal of psychoanalysis is to facilitate continuity of associations, and Renik (1995) emphasizes the goal of increased self-awareness, Ogden suggests that the ultimate goal of psychoanalytic treatment is "to enhance the analysand's capacity to be alive as a human being" (p. 888). He emphasizes the importance of reverie in the analytic process and feels that facilitation of that capacity enhances attainment of the patient's goals. From Ogden's point of view, both patient and analyst need to be able to use *reverie* in order to comfortably live in the world, whether within or outside the treatment. The patient therefore is seen as having a choice—an inalienable right—about whether to speak or to remain silent.

This contrasts with the slightly authoritarian quality of the foregoing approach, where "resistance" implies almost a willful disregard to a fundamental "rule." Ogden suggests that the need for privacy is crucial and that to favor the outward expression of thoughts over silence violates the integrity of the individual. He says to his patients, "I view our meetings as a time for you to say what you want to say, when you want to say it, and for me to respond in my own way. At the same time, there must always be a place for privacy for both of us" (p. 890). Winnicott has said that the center of a healthy personality "never communicates with the world of perceived objects, and that the individual person knows that it must never be communicated with or influenced by external reality. . . . Although healthy persons communicate and enjoy communicating, the other fact is equally true, that *each individual is an isolate, permanently noncommunicating, permanently unknown, in fact unfound*" (1963b, p. 187). A silent patient, therefore, is not necessarily a resistant patient, but perhaps one struggling with issues about being known or not known, communicative or silent: issues about *being* in the world.

It is clear that a patient would have a considerably different experience of analysis in these two different frameworks. Kris and Busch emphasize understanding of the hidden workings of the patient's mind within the here and now; Ogden looks more toward an understanding of the patient's unconscious through the formation of the analytic relationship via the analytic third (the joint analytic space created by patient and analyst). Is it possible to reconcile these two very different, but important and valuable, views? Freud (1940) said, "What we want to hear from our patient is not only what he knows and conceals from other people; he is to tell us too what he does not know" (p. 170).

This suggests that the patient, despite his good intentions, is not able to indicate to us directly what we need to know to help him; he does not know. Well versed though he may be in his family "language" (identifications), he does not have enough distance to be able to describe it or to articulate its rules and etiology. Without an effort at free association, therefore, treatment may remain superficial and fail to touch upon the underlying defensive apparatus that protects the patient from knowledge of the implicit and hidden workings of his mind. Free association gives the analyst a picture of those workings. Along with nonverbal cues, transference and countertransference manifestations, dreams, and a knowledge of the patient's external world, it adds immeasurably to awareness of the internal workings of the patient's mind.

Of course, the very idea of a "rule" in psychoanalysis runs contrary to some notions of the psychoanalytic method, and to insist that a patient "must" say all that comes to mind is authoritarian and often unproductive. Patients disclose *when* and *if* they feel comfortable. It is true that patients can use this freedom to avoid discussing painful things, and may use the treatment to further their pathological modes of functioning, but that is equally true of everything in analysis. In the end, analysts approach their patients from their own personal and professional perspectives; some feel more comfortable in the arena of resistance analysis, while others live more comfortably in the realm of the patient's unconscious. Still others feel that elucidation of the transference yields best results. Each approach has strengths and liabilities, and different patients may benefit more from one than from another. Although it is naïve to imagine that every clinician can feel comfortable in all modalities, it does not seem unrealistic to imagine we can all adapt our approaches to some extent based upon particular patients' needs. The best solution therefore seems to me to strive to hold in our minds the alternative possibilities of perspective offered by competing approaches.

Some examples might illuminate these issues further.

Ms. S. began her treatment with endless narratives of incidents in her life that had no discernible relevance to anything. They seemed to obscure more than to illuminate. She spoke breathlessly, quickly, and with apparently great intensity, full of anger at injustices that had been perpetrated upon her. I found myself feeling a bit bored and annoyed. She was quite taken by the therapeutic process, however, and had quickly formed an intense transference, erotic in nature. I came to understand that her manner of speaking was a result of several factors. First, she had feelings of sexual arousal so intense that she tried to distract herself by becoming angry. Second, she had no serious intention, at that point anyway, of telling me about these. She felt equally unsafe about disclosing other painful and self-critical notions. Finally, her early life experience had taught her that one was better off not disclosing inner truths. Both consciously and unconsciously she believed that a false self was preferable.

As we addressed these issues, she became more forthcoming, but evasion remained her stock in trade. Hardly a session went by without an assertion from her that she had nothing to *talk* about, and I would often ask her what she was *thinking* about. She would laugh and tell me that she had had a fantasy or a dream, but then not disclose it, saying if pressed that she "forgot." Gradually I realized that she was engaging me in seductive behavior, luring me into chasing after her associations the way a lover pursues a coquettish ingenue.

Mrs. J., through many years of a very long analysis, did not speak when she first lay down on the couch—often five or ten minutes would go by before she said anything. Sometimes she had the wish to remain completely silent throughout the session. I tried resistance interpretations, suggesting that there was content that she might be avoiding. Sometimes she agreed that this was true, but from her point of view, she was mostly going over in her mind what to talk about. She might be thinking about what was bothering her, she might be ordering discussion topics in her mind, she might be trying to get her emotions under control (because she viewed them as messy), or she might be trying to obliterate me by pretending I wasn't there. Any suggestion that communicating her thoughts might be helpful was met with agreement but little change. In her worldview, silence was the better option, and speaking about her difficulties took great effort. In one illustrative incident, she had uncharacteristically forgotten a business meeting, inconveniencing a number of people. We explored this event after the fact, from a number of vantage points. It became clear to me that she was sifting through her thoughts and not speaking extemporaneously. I pointed this out to her and indicated that if she been able to speak more freely *before* the forgotten meeting, we might have had access to the unacknowledged feelings that motivated the memory lapse.

This was illuminating to her, but disclosing to me the specifics of her life remained sufficiently distasteful that she still found it hard to be spontaneous. She wished to get better by expanding her self-understanding, but a more intense wish was to get better by attaining a nirvana-like state in which she could be absolutely even-tempered, experiencing no feelings except contentment. She believed that she was better off pushing unpleasant thoughts and feelings out of her mind, as she had done before coming to treatment, and the dysphoric effects evoked by talking in her sessions increased her reluctance to come.

Her trouble associating freely was defensive in the sense that content was being unconsciously avoided. But in front of this, so to speak, other safety issues existed. The expectation that she would free associate was felt as a compelling demand; this was counterproductive, as it stressed her to the point that she could not contemplate anything freely. I finally suggested that she not worry about "free associating" but rather just talk or not talk according to her preference, and that we would be content with that. This did relieve the pressure to the extent that she became able to speak more freely. The major focus of the treatment was to help her become comfortable enough with herself to be able to divulge what was going on in her mind and thus eventually give us access to more hidden material. I also wished to increase her openness enough to investigate the inner workings of her mind (conflict and defense). Her goal of becoming "perfect" by having no untoward thoughts or feelings was antithetical to the goals of psychoanalysis.

A third patient was often disparaging of her husband for reasons that seemed to me to be both reasonable and not. Although she could superficially acknowledge her "unreasonableness," her feelings did not really make sense to her. One day she spoke about distrusting her husband's driving. I asked her about this, and she acknowledged that he was really a good driver. She then disclosed that she had become uncomfortable with his driving some years before, when he had driven them home several hundred miles in an ice storm. She was perplexed about this, because he had clearly driven well under very difficult circumstances. She mentioned that they had been with another couple. I knew that these people had once suggested that they try mate-swapping, and I wondered aloud if that suggestion had been made on this trip. This was indeed the case, and we began to see that it was not her husband that she felt uncomfortable with, but her friend. This opened up an important area of discussion concerning her hysteric-like disavowal of aspects of others that were upsetting to her.

The first case illustrates a patient who superficially agrees to the "fundamental rule" but has no particular inclination to follow it. That fact alone was informative and important. It highlighted personality characteristics that could not be directly talked about but that were demonstrated by the quality of her interaction with me. Her relationships with others were filled with these kinds of dishonest interactions, even though she characterized herself as open and honest. The interpretive approach of elucidating heretofore unacknowledged but characteristic ways of thinking and feeling yielded good results, and over time this woman became more able to speak freely and honestly.

Ms. J., on the other hand, was not particularly responsive to interpretation. Encouraging her to speak more freely was a waste of time and not to the point. She rarely spoke spontaneously—only when she felt sufficiently safe. Although I am sure that there was specific content that she felt uncomfortable divulging, it is more salient that she viewed *any* content as potentially dangerous, having been raised by sadistic and abusive parents. She was a woman who needed the kind of approach exemplified by Ogden. She responded angrily to any pressure and needed to develop the capacity for reverie that would eventually enable her to communicate with me about those aspects of herself that made her so uncomfortable, but she needed to feel the freedom of not having to communicate before she could do so.

The third patient made good use of the free associative method to identify causative factors in her difficulties with her husband. She allowed her mind to open up and said what came into it without censure; this resulted in the clarification of some important marital and personality issues. The interactive approach can work against the formation of this kind of analytic encounter, because the therapist's involvement may preclude the kind of thoughtful meanderings that can help patients recapture denied or disallowed aspects of themselves.

These examples show three of the many responses that individuals may have to the free-associative process. Reverie allows the patient a safe space from which to contemplate inner states of being. Furthermore, the process of reverie furthers free association, as the patient has the opportunity to speak without feeling pressured. On the other hand, some patients, as exemplified by Ms. S., use whatever modes are available to avoid painful feelings. At times this behavior is consciously deceptive, and to ignore these deceptions is to collude with them. It is important to address resistances in a manner that is accepting and nonaccusatory, but it is necessary to address them. To do otherwise ignores the reality of the aggressive psychopathology that some patients present.

Free association allows access to patients' minds as nothing else does. I do not present it as a rule, and I recognize that gaps in the associative flow are as important as the content. I recognize that the request to free associate makes a demand on some patients that they cannot fulfill, and that ultimately patients need to feel free both to speak and to remain silent. At the same time, an *inability* to free associate can become a *desire* not to free associate for defensive purposes. This is the point at which interpretive approaches becomes appropriate.

Providing a safe space for patients to contemplate, to let their thoughts wander unimpeded, to be curious without interpretive, to choose whether to speak or not to speak, and to communicate by not communicating can be enormously valuable. It is important, too, to keep patients aware that they are in the consulting room for a reason—to reach a goal of their own choosing—and that at times they are their own worst enemies. Resistances and needs that thwart the therapeutic process should be addressed. A comprehensive approach that attends to underlying structural issues attends both to integrity needs and to the possibility that these may be turned to defensive purposes. It is also important to recognize that the way patients react to the notion of free association provides important information about the state of their psyches. Attention to these subtleties is congruent with the characterological approach, and its attention to, and evocation of, the patient's internalizations.

RECONSTRUCTION

Fonagy (1999) suggests that, "Therapies focusing on the recovery of memory pursue a false god" (p. 220). He goes on to suggest that "Psychic change is a function of a shift of emphasis between different mental models of object relationships. Change occurs in *implicit* memory leading to a change of the procedures the person uses in living with himself and with others" (p. 218, emphasis added). Further, "Truth in psychotherapy makes sense only in the context of psychic reality. Psychoanalysis is more than the creation of a narrative, it is the active construction of a new way of experiencing self with other" (p. 218). He is suggesting that change occurs through an understanding that develops through changes in the implicit fashion in which one lives one's life—one's habitual way of thinking, feeling, and behaving. He does not find that reconstruction of the past yields much in the way of benefit.

Every patient should be provided with the best treatment available, and helping a patient to develop a sense of continuity between the past to the present is optimal. Connections between past and present help patients to develop an understanding of how they came to be who they are. It solidifies the sense of self, the sense of identity. Gaps in memory and a lack of a sense of continuity creates a fragmented and incomplete feeling. Reconstruction of the past seems to me less useful than the *evocation* of the past within the present, including an understanding of how it relates to the transference. Similarly, helping the patient to understand how his or her mind works in the present yields good results and makes good sense, especially in the context of family dynamics. Treatment that relies on reconstruction of the *unremembered* past, however, occurs at an emotionally rather distant remove that limits its value and can be used defensively to get away from painful realities of the present, including the transference. There are many aspects of patients' past lives that require elucidation. Individuals subliminally know a great deal that become recognizable only when they, or the therapist, manage to verbalize them. Helping a patient to understand what in the past has led to particular present feelings and behaviors is of crucial importance.

Ms. J. struggled endlessly over her need to be perfect and was never satisfied with herself despite many successes. This struggle derived from a past wish to please a very difficult mother and from a present desire to please the internalized maternal imago and, in the transference, me. The patient was not able to know in any accessible way that her mother had had no interest in being pleased but had predominantly hated the patient. It was a cruel irony that this patient's wish to please her mother was doomed to fail; it was inherently impossible and not because of the patient's shortcomings. The only way to please this mother was to fail, and this resulted in a beating. There was no safe way for the patient to win approval from a mother who really hoped that she would fail. This dynamic became clear to me through careful observation and continued analysis of her transference and by my own countertransference, but though it infiltrated the patient's very being, it remained relatively unavailable to her because of the psychic pain it engendered and because of a family system of denial that disavowed the obvious.

A dynamic like this cannot be elucidated through the recapture of repressed memories. The patient had to *understand* the reality of her past in a way that made sense. All the events that led to this understanding were available to her; they had not been forgotten, but neither had they been put together in a way that was comprehensible. Once these experiences were put together in a comprehensible way, the patient began to see the import of this dynamic and to understand its impact on her life. This awareness was reached not through the acquisition of new memory, but through a deeper understanding of the *meaning* of events previously not comprehended. This is different from reconstruction of the unremembered past or of attempts to recapture repressed memories.

Patients obviously have memories and develop spontaneous recollections of the past; these should not be discounted, and they may provide important and vital information. Furthermore, it is hard to imagine transference interpretations without connections to the original template. Neglect of the past deprives the patient of crucial connections with the present and dilutes the importance of past childhood experiences and fantasies. It does not, however, seem to me particularly fruitful to engage in a concerted search to reconstruct memories of the very distant past, particularly of prehistoric and probably unreachable times or to risk an inauthentic treatment where guesswork becomes the norm. But as always this is not an absolute. There are times when reconstruction and attempts to recapture the past are vital. Trauma victims whose pasts have been obliterated must be helped to recapture aspects of themselves that have been lost through terrible experiences (to the extent that the patient can tolerate such recollection). Other patients who seem lost in the present and have no sense of continuity in their lives may need to find the past in order to develop a sense of meaning and connection. It is often useful to convey to patients some understanding of how the past informs the present, because it helps them to make sense of themselves, their thoughts, their feelings, and their relationships. Furthermore, patients often take comfort in understanding how their problems developed within a pathological family, as this diminishes the self-blame they feel over situations that were outside any possible control. These "lost" patients may need help to understand the subtle effects of their past upon their present psychology, because the difficulties in the family are often hidden and difficult to access consciously. Although they are fluent in the family "language," they often do not realize that they are speaking it; sometimes, too, they believe that they had learned a new, less pathological "language" in their own efforts to distance themselves from painful family dynamics.

To summarize, I think for all these reasons that it is most useful to concentrate on the past *within the present,* on the implicit characterological issues that define the individual and that impact upon the transference and on the patient's everyday life. Intellectualized reconstruction of a speculative, unremembered, or intellectualized past does not seem to me to be *as* useful, although establishing an understanding and an appreciation of past events can be extremely helpful, both in recapturing disavowed aspects of the self and in furthering a sense of understanding, continuity, and meaning. Intrapsychic conflicts are best elucidated within the everyday context with which they occur and within an emotionally alive atmosphere.

CONCLUDING THOUGHTS

In this chapter, I have suggested that the psychodynamic therapist makes choices throughout the treatment as to how to structure the therapeutic situation and relationship, and that these choices result in different attitudes toward the patient and the material the patient presents. They also affect what material comes up, as the patient responds to the therapist's preferred perspective. To the extent that inclusive, rather than either-or approaches are possible, these are greatly to be desired, as they facilitate access to the preconscious material that leads to the non-verbalized aspects of character.

IV

---◆---

The Art

of

Defense

---◆---

Defenses protect us from (that is, keep us from recognizing) certain painful realities and, like everything else, styles of defense are reflected in character. All of us develop characteristic ways of dealing with unpleasant thoughts and feelings that infuse our personalities and may be seen across all levels of personality functioning (conscious, preconscious, and unconscious). As I have been describing, attention to the "implicit" provides a convenient window into the psyche, and defensive strategies are not immune from this approach. Defenses, both as wishes and as needs to "not know," reflect family identifications as other psychic entities do, and they become internalized through self- and object representations. In this chapter, I concentrate on strategies of not knowing. I will consider first some aspects of the nature of "reality" and then some characteristic defenses, from the perspective of character structure. I will also discuss some defensive constellations that are less commonly addressed.

REALITY AND KNOWING

In all psychotherapies there are struggles around aspects of reality that patients believe must remain hidden. People alternate between the wish to know and understand and the desire to keep painful realities secret.

"Unknowns" are not always kept that way solely for fear of divulging forbidden feelings and desires; for instance, when preverbal traumas create wordless experiences for a child, these cannot be talked about directly in treatment—at least not initially. For this reason and others, defenses have many of the characteristics that I have been calling implicit. They are not usually verbalized as such; they must be deduced and interpreted by the therapist so that their meaning can be described and elaborated. Characterological issues, the implicit level of awareness, and the language of the family all fall into the category of phenomena that are not directly accessible to patient or therapist and that manifest themselves indirectly within the individual's defensive system

Aharon Appelfeld, noted Israeli author and Holocaust survivor, articulated some of these issues about what may and may not be known. He wrote upon visiting his homeland in the Ukraine, "I dreamed about nothing, as though I wished to flee this place" (Appelfeld, 1998, p. 51). He and his family had endured horrific violence, death, and deprivation after being driven from their home. In 1996, with much trepidation, he returned; he wanted, among other things, to recapture experience buried in response to physical and psychic pain. His statement sums up the experience of many people who deal with painful realities, whether they are material or psychic; all of us wish to flee our most painful experiences. Every individual struggles to come to grips with internal and external exigencies, and the ego's defensive apparatus helps us do this. Still, Appelfeld's description of his dream is striking. He does not say that he did not dream, but that he dreamt of *nothing*. To dream of nothing implies the negation of an occurrence. The destruction of a percept results in what Green (1997) refers to as a "negative hallucination." We shall see later in this chapter how massive psychic trauma can destroy the ability to remember and can create compensatory fantasies to replace horrific memories.

Appelfeld, recognizing the tricks that memory can play in wishfully altering reality, expressed the fear that "reality would come and slap me in the face" (1998, p. 48). This is the essence of the struggle for all of us, but reality *always* comes and slaps us in the face. The desire to know and understand is what impels us toward learning and curious engagement. The wish to "not know" is what keeps us locked in eternal psychological struggle. In psychoanalytic psychotherapy and psychoanalysis, patient and therapist confront this struggle in all the minutiae of treatment.

This struggle between knowing and not knowing finds expression in all psychological disorders. In this chapter, I concentrate on how individuals actually fashion the characterological solutions we have discussed—that is, their defenses against unpleasant or intolerable confrontations with reality—and the ways that these become embedded in personality structure. I will demonstrate the original adaptive aspect of these solutions, however pathological and maladaptive they eventually become, and why they therefore need to be treated with great respect. I will also focus on the ramifications of the desire to "not know" on patients' ability to function effectively and its manifestations in therapy and in the therapeutic relationship.

REALITY

Reality inflicts pain on all of us. The assessment of what is "real," however, is not a simple exercise. Therapists often operate from the premise that somewhere in the psyche, however repressed or denied, the patient "knows" reality even when it is neither accepted nor understood. But the question of what is "real" is not a simple one for the growing child. Certainly trauma, but often just the vagaries of ordinary growth and development, create confusions for children that may then become "institutionalized" or built in.

As an example, a young boy caught in the familiar Oedipal drama may feel terribly rejected by his mother's relationship with her spouse. The child cannot recognize the impossibility of the relationship that he longs for and consequently feels inadequate and unlovable. He may see his penis as small and inadequate and internalize an added sense of deficiency. These become *psychic realities* that are very resistant to alteration, and they may become manifest in the treatment where the young boy, grown up but still not recognizing the impossibility of his hopes, becomes convinced anew of his deficiency because the therapist does not love him. Patients hold on to their psychic realities with great intensity. It is the therapist's task to help the patient understand that psychic realities are developed in response to psychic forces and are not unalterable facts of life.

Adults can confuse psychic and external "reality" too. As I discussed in the previous chapter, disagreements over apparent "realities" may reflect transference/countertransference issues; this makes it hard to be doctrinaire about what is real, but it may also provide crucial information.

I saw Dr. R. for a reduced fee for a considerable period of time. Gradually, I became aware of my own dissatisfaction with the fee arrangement. I raised the issue of a fee increase with her, believing from her associations that she had more resources than she had acknowledged. She was upset with my request and insisted upon her relative poverty. I began to think about my request and wonder about its origins. I realized that I was frustrated with the treatment and that my request for more money reflected my wish that she give more to the analytic effort. More importantly, however, I realized that she was not really asking for much from me. I felt bored in the treatment and realized retrospectively that I was not being challenged. She had been taught to be satisfied with very little from her parents and transferred this poverty of desire to me and others.

Once I was aware of this dynamic, I conveyed it to the patient. I had told her previously that at times she seemed to me adrift and lost and that, as a result, I also sometimes felt uninterested. I now elaborated on this, telling her I felt that she was asking too little of me in the treatment; that she was making the therapy, paradoxically, both too easy and too hard for us: too easy because her distance created an indifference that discouraged me from trying to understand her, and too hard because it became an unpleasant, joyless experience for the both of us. This statement initially perplexed her, but as she became able to understand it there was a much-needed change in the treatment. This is not to say that she immediately began interacting with me in a more intense way. But it put us on the route to considering how little she had asked of herself and others in life and the reasons for this. She was able to tie it into the way she coped with the overwhelming stresses of her family life—removing herself and asking little of her already terribly depleted mother. My wish for more money was a clue not only to my own greed but also, via projective identification, to her greed, both denied and projected.

The "reality" of her financial condition was of little importance compared with the "reality" of her psychic state. It was the reality of the transference/countertransference paradigm, and the way it informed us as to her schizoid and deprived adaptational style, that needed to be addressed.

PSYCHIC VS. CONSENSUAL REALITY

Fonagy and Target (1996; Target and Fonagy, 1996) provide an important perspective on the interface between psychic and external reality. They suggest that in healthy children (and adults) a state of mind is established that enables movement between a subjective psychic equivalence mode (where perception and reality are congruent) and a pretend mode. The integration of these two modes of reality apperception moves the child toward a reflective mode of thought. They consider it essential that the therapist not hold to a rigid definition of reality as external. "If, on the other hand, the caregiver can frequently provide links between reality and fantasy in a way that retains an accurate, accepting reflection of the child's mental states, he affords the child a basis for organizing and comparing numerous experiences bridging the psychic equivalence and pretend modes. Gradually, the child becomes able to maintain a mentalistic stance himself, having internalised the process. . . . The child, using the parent's mind, comes to be able to *play with reality*" (Target and Fonagy 1996, p. 472). This attitude of playfulness, reminiscent of Winnicott, greatly enhances treatment with all patients because it helps organize and structure internal and external experience creatively.

We do have a sense of external "reality" though, and this sometimes needs to be addressed directly. Grossman (1993, 1996) and Renik (1992) suggest that the analyst must stand for and be an advocate for reality, particularly in so-called "perverse cases." By these they mean patients who purposefully and willfully distort or disavow aspects of reality, a phenomenon that I will discuss in more detail presently.

One patient felt frustrated with his progress in psychotherapy. He wished for a more intensive experience, and raised the question of more frequent visits. I agreed that these would be useful but, given the patient's financial situation, I wondered about the wisdom and practicality of increased sessions. The patient reluctantly acknowledged that in fact financial difficulties did make it impossible for him to afford more sessions. He then divulged, much more fully than ever before, how disorganized, chaotic, and out of control his affairs really were. The worsening of his financial condition, which he had been ignoring, was jeopardizing the treatment of his son who was seriously disturbed. This kind of disavowal of reality was not limited only to financial matters. There were other family needs that he did not attend to sufficiently either, including the desperately unhappy state of his marriage. This tendency infused his personality and was one of his characteristic ways of being and thinking in the world.

Views of "reality" evolve as patients improve and change in treatment. Gains in ego strength promote greater understanding of past and present events, and patients may reassess old events from new perspectives. Certainly, perceptions of the therapist or analyst change greatly over treatment, representing again an alteration in what was felt to be bedrock reality.

THE ADAPTIVE VALUE OF DEFENSES

Defenses protect against what feel to us to be unbearable realities, either external or psychic. These realities may include not only intense affects but also awareness of the situations that create these painful feelings. Defenses are not only pathological; they play an important role in saving individuals from hurt and helping them cope with overwhelming experiences.

> Dr. R. spoke about sexual and other desires, but she lacked passion and did not really experience pleasure of any kind. There were several reasons for this, but for now I will concentrate on her psychic reality of gender. She did not like being female, but she did not imagine herself to be male. She thought of herself as some sort of third sex—a psychic hermaphrodite. She wondered one day what treatment would be like if I were a woman. I chuckled and replied that that was not an option. She laughed, realizing that she entertained the belief that physical gender was not a fixed reality but could be chosen. She objected greatly to the reality of unalterable physical gender.
>
> She had been raised in a family with a domineering and violent father and a submissive and abused mother. She wanted to be in charge like her father, but this raised competitive fears. Her wish to dominate caused her to imagine fearful retaliation by her

father, both realistic (in the past) and psychic (in fantasy). She deprecated her mother for her weakness. She wanted to be close to both parents yet was afraid of her desires for sexual and emotional intimacy. Neither gender seemed attractive to her and her solution was to imagine a third one. This alteration of reality gave her a sense of safety under the press of gender and personal identity development.

"Mr. F." came up with a similar solution. This young man had three older sisters and a domineering and disapproving mother. He saw his father as distant and ineffectual. His sisters teased him unmercifully and, along with his mother, had enjoyed dressing him up in girls' clothes. He was in great psychic danger and developed a number of ways of coping. He felt unsafe in his masculine sense of self, yet he knew himself to be different from his sisters; therefore he too postulated a third sex for himself. This made him feel better. Even if he were castrated by his mother and sisters, he could maintain the illusion of intactness in his own individual kind of sexuality, thereby retaining status, satisfaction, and safety. He retreated to fantasy for solace in the face of the impingements he experienced within his family, and the fantasies he developed negated and denied the consensual external reality of two genders.

Both of these patients created solutions that assisted them in feeling safe and worthwhile under the press of family pathological structures that threatened their sense of self.

SAFETY AND PSYCHIC SURVIVAL

McDougall (1995) writes that psychic survival is the paramount need of everyone. From the adaptational perspective, defenses protect against threats to psychic survival.

For instance, I had a patient who abruptly decided to enter a seminary. He could give no cogent rationale for his new-found religious zeal, but discussion eventually revealed the emergence of homosexual desires that could be simultaneously (and secretly) satisfied and denied if he lived in close proximity to supposedly celibate men. This patient had struggled throughout his life with a barely acknowledged attraction to other men and feared that this would be so greatly frowned upon by his family that he had to hide it even from himself. This psychic safety came at a cost, however.. Before the emergence of his wish to enter the seminary, he had felt "safe" but had lived a very limited and unfulfilling life. With the recognition and analysis of this "solution" to the problem of his homosexual desires, we could look at the severity of his superego, his state of unfulfillment, and the characteristic defensive and compromise formation patterns that perpetuated both of them.

More extremely, victims of what Shengold (1989) calls *soul murder* must develop psychic mechanisms that maintain their sense of integrity, and these may look so pathological outside of their adaptational context that their original constructive function may not be appreciated. Shengold provides several definitions of soul murder: "It is a dramatic term for circumstances that eventuate in crime–the deliberate attempt to eradicate or compromise the separate identity of another person" (p. 2). "Too much and too little are qualities of experience. Too much too-muchness we call trauma. Too much not-enoughness inhibits maturation. Child abuse means that the child has felt too much to bear; child deprivation means that the child has been exposed to too little to meet his or her needs" (p. 1). Children in circumstances like this must develop techniques for staving off overwhelming affects and experiences if they are to save their newly emergent sense of identity and integrity. As they develop, these defenses may continue to keep psychic decompensation at bay, but at great cost. Long after the external danger has passed, energy remains invested in these defenses. Real external danger becomes internal danger, just as real and just as frightening.

One patient, a successful attorney, had been sexually abused by her stepfather. As is common in such cases, she had transient episodes of promiscuity in her adolescent years. Although this was not apparent to most observers, these gave her a feeling of triumph. When she was angry with her husband, she experienced him as potentially dangerous. She had internalized both the perpetrator and the victim roles; she could not accept her own abusing qualities and projected them onto her husband, thereby maintaining her own sense of innocence. This gave her a needed sense of safety, because she was more confident of her husband's non-violence than of her own. It also helped her feel less responsible for her own emotions. She was desperately afraid that she had done something to initiate her stepfather's advances, but at the same time she paradoxically wished that she had. That is, she was most afraid of being the powerless and fragile child that she had been when her stepfather attacked her. By secretly thinking of herself as the seductress, yet simultaneously denying the thought, she maintained a level of competence, control, and innocence that she had never really had.

Successful though she was in her given field, this woman was plagued with feelings of terror and anxiety. She had ways of thinking and behaving that helped her feel more in control and less vulnerable, but it was predicated on a hidden system that incorporated alternating senses of herself as victim and seductress. This system had developed out of her early family dynamics; it caused problems in her relationship with her husband, yet it helped her feel safe. It is worth pointing out that this system did not give rise to any discrete symptoms but manifested itself in pervasive personality characteristics.

A special case of the need to maintain safety and integrity is the need to maintain a consistent sense of self. The need for a coherent identity causes individuals to create interpersonal systems that reinforce the familiar. The patient described previously needed to maintain a consistent sense of innocence and could not accept the notion of her own aggression and sexuality. Her personality structure, her choices of mate and occupation, and her whole world view were constructed in a family language that required that aggression be hidden, that neither self nor others could be trusted, and that personal pressures could be taken out on others in the family (as her stepfather had taken his out on her) rather than contained. Accepting ideas distinct from her identifications meant relinquishing her sense of absolute innocence and owning conscious responsibility for her ways of experiencing the incest of her youth. It would result in wholesale changes in her sense of self.

THE NATURE OF DEFENSES

Brenner (1981) has made clear that underlying psychic processes can produce *any* defense or symptom, and that particular clinical manifestations are less important than the underlying dynamics. Ultimately, it is not symptoms that are useful to delineate in psychotherapy. It is the underlying psychic structure, defensive systems, quality of object relations, and dynamic issues (character structure) that guide the therapist to effective treatment. The *development* of symptoms, and the patterns of thought that gives rise to them, is important, as is the way the defense manifests itself *in action* (Grey, 1994; Busch, 1995). Especially instructive, from my point of view, is how defensive propensities become incorporated into character structure, independent of intrapsychic struggles, and become rigidified into ways of being and living.

But helping the patient understand the origins of whatever disorder required treatment includes attention to the unconscious fantasies that fuel thought, feeling, defense, and behavior. People's needs, wishes, and desires are the "motor" that drives behavior. Any approach that emphasizes the elucidation of character structure must keep an eye to identifying the affective forces that have formed the particular essence of the patient's personality. It must certainly include attention to underlying desires, to the responses (in defense and in action) to these desires, and to compensatory fantasies and inhibitory structures (superego). But it must not lose its recognition that the patient develops these psychic structures to fend off disappointment, to establish a sense of safety, and above all to ensure psychic survival.

DEFENSIVE PROCESSES

Negation

I understand defenses to be circumscribed responses to specific affects and thoughts. They arise in the context of a particular set of family dynamics, in that the child is a product of his or her family and tends to adopt family patterns of conflict and defense. They also reflect unique and creative responses to troubling psychological and situational experiences. As Freud (1925) points out in "Negation," the development of many defenses is an accomplishment. Rather than resorting to wholesale repression, a person with many defensive possibilities available can select and discriminate among the various aspects of some painful situation and respond to them with discrimination—this is a cognitive counterpoint to repression. Although their emotional impact may be hidden, thought about them is possible. This allows alternatives to be considered and decisions to be made.

All defenses, however, contain at least some quality of negation, as all defenses require a statement about what is and what is not. "It is not this, it is that." "I am not angry, I am loving." "I do not feel this way. I feel that way." Along with the affirmative there must always be a negative, and this negative is important. Consider the following example. (I am indebted to Karen Baker, M.S.W. for her kindness in sharing this case with me.)

The patient was a thirty-two-year-old man in long-term psychodynamic treatment. He was intelligent and well educated, and he worked in a prestigious law firm. He felt unable to form relationships, even with his therapist. Both of his parents, who were divorced, had died by the time he was in his teens. He remembers his mother as exceedingly depressed. His father had been more involved but was more interested in the young women he chased than in his young son. As the son moved into adulthood, he became socially isolated. His main sources of enjoyment were his work and his collection of ornate clocks.

The patient was compliant and cooperative, but the treatment seemed arid to the therapist. She often felt herself struggling to stay awake. He spoke about his fear of losing close relationships, as he had lost his mother and his father. If the therapist raised the possibility that he might have feelings of closeness toward her, he immediately spoke of his concerns about rejection. He could describe going to a mall and wondering why he never saw his therapist there, but he never spoke of positive wishes for attachment or of the excitement he might feel if he were in fact to see her unexpectedly. He always left out the wish, the desire. His focus was never on wanting to see his therapist but on not seeing her. He derided his father's promiscuity and defensively derided or ignored his own desires. Through the gentle interpretation of inhibited and denied wishes and desires, the patient began to become more energized, and the therapist no longer felt the sleepiness that she had previously.

As this example shows, negation is not always obvious if one focuses only on what the patient says; in working with defenses, it is often the *unspoken* part of the equation that is crucial. Like other "implicit" characterological phenomena, defenses depend for their identification on close attention to internalized self- and object representations, and these must be observed, as they cannot usually be verbalized.

This patient had had early shame experiences that left him desperately afraid of excitement. He was inhibited and defended against exhibitionistic wishes. His obsessive-compulsive qualities could be seen in his desire to collect instead of to experience. The therapist, a lively and engaging woman, felt as deadened as his parents had been. Her sleepiness in the countertransference led her to a sense of what was not being addressed within the treatment—the patient's denial of excitement.

This particular patient was all too aware of his explicit problems with loss and often pointed them out himself. But this was only one part of the picture. He did have significant separation and loss problems, but he was not likely to experience them unless he allowed himself to experience attachment, and his fear of excitement had led him to defend against the need to connect with others. His characteristic defense, the split between the affirmative and the negative, protected him from the perceived danger of excitement and defined the logic of the patient's disorder.

REPRESSION AND DENIAL

Freud's second theory of anxiety postulated that repression operates to keep anxiety-arousing material out of awareness. Repressed material cannot be known directly and is recognized only through its derivatives in a patient's associations, symptom formation (that is, the "return of the repressed"), dreams, transferences, enactments, and psychosomatic disorders—and, I would add, through attention to the implicit. Word associations are the link between the unconscious (symbolic and wordless) and preconscious (language-driven and accessible). It is sometimes possible to get a sense of the repressed at the beginning of treatment, during the assessment stage, but that does not necessarily mean it can be addressed instantly. A clinical vignette illustrates this.

A new patient described a work inhibition, which he felt was keeping him from attaining the level of success he deserved. He described his mother as very domineering and controlling and easily enraged at his strivings toward independence. He would hide from her under the tablecloth as a young child for fear of her criticism and her withering and shaming attitude. He described his father as a man who referred derisively to younger men as "young punks." In his profession he made sure that he deferred to older men, not wanting them to think of him as a "young punk." With me he was deferential; he insisted that he himself knew little about psychology, that I was clearly the expert, and that he had little interest in "poaching" on my territory.

Of course there is more to the story than this, but even this cursory perusal lays out the groundwork of his pathology. Oedipal issues are prominent. He is greatly afraid of being ashamed and will be reluctant to admit to perceived shortcomings out of a fear of embarrassment and humiliation. We might expect that beneath his meek exterior resides an extremely competitive young man, who will attempt to compete with and defeat the analyst.

If one were to relate this assessment to the patient, he would probably grasp it intellectually but not affectively. If he were asked directly about his competitive feelings toward his father and his desire to dethrone him, his response would likely be one of puzzlement and rejection. Only in the transference can dynamics like these be identified on a here-and-now basis that is useful to the patient. At the beginning of treatment, such central dynamic issues are unknown to the patient and probably more repressed than denied. But repression softens in many patients as treatment progresses, and defenses are used that allow more access to the unconscious. As treatment progresses, the intricacies of life and character are elucidated. Other issues that are defended against are identified, and material that had become more accessible to consciousness is dealt with via other defenses, including denial.

Denial

Attempts have been made to differentiate between denial and repression (Altschul, 1968); the most common view is that repression works against instinctual or id components, while denial operates against uncomfortable aspects of external reality. It can also be said that there is in the action of denial some discrimination: One aspect of a situation is accepted, while another is denied.

For example, a patient speaks about his wife's brother canceling dinner at the last minute. I ask him how he feels about it and he tells me that he himself had no feeling in particular about it, preferring anyway to spend the time alone. His wife, however, was annoyed. As he continues to speak, he mentions feelings of loneliness and sadness, along with a curious irritation. I draw his attention to his associations and displaced affect and wonder if he really does not have any feelings about the change of plans. Perhaps he does, he acknowledges. In this case, the situation is attended to, but feelings about it are denied and displaced.

A similar process is apparent in one patient's denial of guilt.

A man was involved in an extramarital affair. He said that he felt no guilt over it, and he had little moral compunction about his actions. He felt that his behavior was justified by his wife's outrageous treatment of him—what he felt to be her inattention. Notwithstanding, he was afraid of being found out. He claimed that it was his wife's rage that he feared, not any worries about the rightness of his actions. Still, he was putting himself in jeopardy in other areas of his life—he was not sleeping well and his associations were filled with ideas of punishment.

This man's defenses protect him from awareness of important aspects of himself—his guilt, his sadomasochistic dealings with his wife, and his need to feel blameless—and how they obscured the differences between genuine remorse and a fear of being caught. As he came to understand himself better, he was able to accept his own unacknowledged aggression and eventually to re-evaluate his whole way of thinking about himself and his wife.

Disavowal

Ms. S. visited an infertility specialist because she could not become pregnant. She did not tell the doctor, or acknowledge, that she and her husband did not have intercourse. She presented herself as if she had an infertility problem although, in actuality, her problem was a marital one.

In his "Fetishism" paper, Freud (1927) spoke of the splitting of the ego and the defenses of denial and disavowal. He uses these terms interchangeably but I believe that they can be differentiated accurately. Disavowal represents a relatively active and voluntary pushing out of consciousness. Denial represents less-conscious ego processes, similar in operation to repression.

Because these defenses operate at different levels of consciousness, they require different types of intervention. Disavowal is closer to consciousness than either denial or repression. Despite this, or perhaps because of it, patients who use disavowal as a defense against the acknowledgment of reality present particular therapeutic problems. Where denial, repression, or other such defenses are present, the patient has the conscious wish to get better and to understand, even if there are concomitant unconscious wishes to evade, deny, or repress. Those who disavow, however, have the conscious wish to get better by *not* understanding and by *not* accepting aspects of reality that are apparent to them and to the therapist. Consequently, the patient may willfully resist the introduction of truth and reality.

These basic defensive processes—negation, repression, denial, and disavowal—are used in varying ways in different characterological defensive styles. Now I would like to turn to some less commonly addressed defensive constellations and elaborate on how disavowal becomes operational with a frequency greater than commonly described. These clearly illustrate the way defensive styles can permeate the personality, as well as how they arise and the adaptive roles they play. They also illustrate how the analysis of defense can make a very important contribution to character analysis and psychic change.

FETISHISM

Fetishism is caused by a "rift in the ego" (Freud, 1938, p. 276). All defenses require a split but the split in fetishism is vertical rather than horizontal. In the horizontal split of repression, unwanted material is kept in the id (unconscious) by the unconscious ego. In fetishism and similar disorders, unwanted material is maintained in the ego (conscious and unconscious), representing a vertical split resulting in the simultaneous adoption of two contradictory percepts. For example, Ms. S. "knew" that she and I had a professional relationship and that it would remain just that, but she still maintained a fervent and *conscious* fantasy that we eventually would be united. In this important paper, Freud (1938) first illustrated how two contradictory percepts can be maintained simultaneously. He describes the horror of the little boy who has become aware of the penislessness of the female. Unable to tolerate such imagined evidence of castration, the boy denies the reality of the female genitalia and forms a substitute, a fetish, for reassurance. As the boy becomes a man, he "knows" that women do not have penises, hidden or otherwise, and he "knows" that they are not castrated. At the same time, however, he maintains his delusion of castrated phallic women and feels greatly endangered. Freud initially described this process in relation to fetishism, but he acknowledged that similar processes could be seen in other disorders as well.

A propensity toward disavowal and to the establishment of

fetishes may reflect more than a circumscribed fear of castration, however. All kinds of aspects of reality may be disavowed and disowned, and the tendency to do so becomes part of the character structure of the patient. It affects functioning in many venues, including, with a vengeance, the transference. In the previous example, the grown man has no awareness that his fetishistic behavior relates to repressed fantasies about castration (or, perhaps more accurately, about perceived defects). The "rift in the ego" however, allows contradictory percepts to exist without questioning, and this possibility may be exploited in other aspects of the patient's life. The woman who sought out infertility care knew that she and her husband were not having sex, yet she preferred to pretend that they were, wishfully altering reality to suit her preferred version. Disavowal runs the gamut from the more to less conscious, but it always contains a willful, purposeful pushing away of reality. In this it differs from repression, denial, and similar defenses and represents a characteristic way of dealing with uncomfortable realities.

Kaplan (1991) provides an interesting explanation of fetishes and related perversions. She speaks of the phallus not as a penis substitute but as a symbol of sexual potency for all men and women. The "defect" that a fetish is designed to replace is not related to the corporeal penis but to the sense of freedom and potency that is lost through parental and societal insistence on rigid sex roles. In other words, a boy may develop a fetish not solely out of castration anxiety. Boys who are ridiculed for not conforming to societal notions of masculinity may establish a fetish to hide their shame. A similar process occurs in women who feel that they cannot freely own behavior and attitudes that are judged to belong properly only to men. The development of a fetish is designed to reassure its inventor about disowned aspects of the self, either physical or psychological. It may relate to castration anxieties, but, equally, it may relate to any thought, feeling, attitude, or experience that must be disavowed. The consequences of this disavowal can be extremely detrimental to psychological functioning, and there may be an aggressive component to disavowal that creates havoc both for the individual and for those within his or her orbit.

Some patients who develop these disorders have had experiences where reality was constantly violated and where accurate perceptions were dismissed as false. Lying may be rampant but disavowed.

One patient, a carpenter, came to treatment complaining of anxiety and depression. He casually divulged as I took his history that his daughter was the product of an artificial insemination. When I asked him what he had told the child about this, he said that he and his wife had decided to keep it a secret. In fact he later described to me a situation where his daughter had questioned him about some of her inherited physical characteristics, and he had answered her as if he were her genetic father. When I pointed this contradiction out to him, he dismissed it as meaningless.

The child eventually had difficulty in school and was diagnosed as learning disordered; I hypothesized that she had been encouraged to have a "learning" disorder by her parents' nonverbal encouragement that she not learn the truth. Not only had they not told her of the circumstances of her birth, but what they had told her was not true. Reality was disavowed. My interpretations and observations were disavowed as well—listened to but essentially ignored and later almost forgotten. Sometime later I asked this man if he remembered our discussions about this matter, and he answered in the affirmative, saying that he thought he had some recollection. He had completely destroyed any meaning attached to it, and this was characteristic of his treatment. In some ways he manifested a negative therapeutic reaction, improving but insisting that he had not. He needed to see himself as all-suffering and masochistic, and any improvement in his functioning ran contrary to his preferred version of reality. When I pointed out this process to him, he would acknowledge its accuracy but disavow its import. It was only through continued interpretation of these issues on micro- and macroscopic levels that I was able to have substantial impact on him.

Renik (1992) and Reed (1997) suggest that the analyst and the analyst's interpretations may serve as fetishes for some patients. The patient does not use the treatment to obtain information, but as a substitute for perceived deficits. Treatment does not give rise to understanding, growth, and eventual separation but goes on interminably. The patient cannot make effective therapeutic use of the encounter, and interpretations are often ignored and disavowed—they have little relevance for the patient who is in therapy not to learn but to possess some quality that the therapist owns.

Ms. S. had a great desire to steal a painting on my wall. It wasn't an exceptional work but it was mine, and that endowed it with a power and meaning that she felt she lacked. She had little interest in a therapeutic relationship. She was determined that we would have sexual intercourse and that this would "cure" her of her deficiencies. She had what she called "dialogues" with me outside of the treatment hour, which felt intrusive to her and disrupted her attention at work. Once when she was describing these "dialogues" I asked her what I said. Abashed, she admitted that I had really said nothing. Just as in the treatment itself, she was not interested in what I said. Her "dialogues" were really monologues. They allowed her to feel more secure and capable in situations that made her anxious. But the belief that she was in treatment to learn or to change was a delusion. She did not use the therapeutic work to internalize a sense of me or of the analytic method. Rather, she wanted to possess me, to own me, like a fetish that would enable her to function. Clearly, this desire reflected fairly severe ego defects, and it was sufficiently driving that she threatened to leave treatment and would make appointments with other therapists when she felt she had to keep me in line.

The establishment of fetishes and/or the predominant use of disavowal alters reality in ways that the patient either experienced or imagined as a child.

Patients prone to disavowal, in my experience, are often very judgmental about the aggression that they see in others and portray themselves as innocent and blameless. Their separation, castration, and annihilation anxieties are such that they are terrified of being held responsible for any wrongdoing; this is all the more true as their archaic superegos lead them to expect overly severe punishment.

As I have mentioned, Ms. S. came to treatment for severe anxiety. She formed an immediate intense transference, erotized to the extreme. I never experienced the supposedly erotic transference as having much sexual intensity, however. To me it felt hostile and possessive. The patient began telephoning me after hours for "emergencies." Hang-up phone calls in the middle of the night caused me (and my wife) considerable discomfort and anger. These were designed to interrupt imagined sexual intercourse. Because I did not treat the patient as she wished—that is, I did not love her, desire her sexually, or treat her specially—she would try to retaliate. She often threatened to leave treatment and criticized me endlessly to her friends and family. If she felt hurt by something, she was consumed with fantasies of retribution toward me. But in spite of the hostility of these fantasies she saw herself as innocent and took comfort from this. She viewed me not as a person trying to help and understand her but as a disobedient object, and she wished to punish me accordingly. In the rest of her life too, those who crossed her paid for it, although she went about her revenge surreptitiously. When I confronted her about this, she would insist that she could not help herself. As a child, she had felt intensely competitive yet overwhelmed by her older brother. She became the supposedly "obedient" child and gained favor in the family in that role.

The liability of being the youngest and relatively helpless had become a defense for this patient. When she felt angry and vengeful, she became tearful and would insist upon her helplessness, thus reenacting her childhood experience, but this time using it to hide her hostility. Her revenge was exacted in hidden ways. She could speak one moment about how furious she was and in the next disavow any hostile intent. The reality of her hostile actions was not repressed or denied—it was disavowed. She clung to the fantasy that I would provide her with all that she lacked in the world—a penis, a baby, status, prestige, greater intelligence, and financial success. She was enormously competitive with me. This prevented her from using our work therapeutically, as she was more interested in proving me wrong than she was in gaining understanding. Early in treatment she divulged that she always carried a "lucky charm." This was a concrete fetish without which she felt panic. Throughout the treatment she attempted to ward off uncomfortable thoughts, feelings, and fantasies by willfully withholding them from me. She would "forget" about them or would say that she had a fantasy but would not elaborate. Her wish was for me to try to seduce the fantasy out of her, resulting in sexual pleasure for her. My interpretation of this wish helped eliminate its occurrence. Nevertheless, she was not using the treatment for understanding; she was using it for sexual pleasure and was disavowing its psychotherapeutic purpose.

This patient had been raised in a family where reality was constantly disavowed and disowned. Her family, she was told, "did not believe" in jealousy—not that it was not acceptable, but that it did not exist.

This was the kind of distortion of reality through which her family saw the world, and it put enormous pressure on her to disown jealousy and other "negative" feelings. Not surprisingly, many members of her family suffered from anxiety disorders; normal and expected feelings were perceived as dangerous when they insisted on arising despite the insistence that they "did not exist."

Proper understanding of a patient includes the recognition of the wishes and desires that underlie defensive fears. If this is lacking, a collusion develops that stunts growth. Allowing this patient to externalize her disowned aggressive and sexual aspects and remain "innocent" and "blameless" would have led to a gratifying but unproductive treatment. I had to address her need to feel innocent and her avoidance of any responsibility for the way she ran her own life. Yet it is not always easy to avoid this when a patient's internal psychic structures repeat sadomasochistic relationships and the therapist becomes embroiled within that dynamic by being reluctant to confront the defended against hostility.

Anality

Shengold (1985) and Chasseguet-Smirgel (1974, 1978) have made important contributions to the understanding of a particular mode of defense: anality. The anal defensive style *obliterates* reality by ignoring differences between self and other, between generations, between genders—in short, by *obliterating awareness of* any aspect of reality that the individual finds troublesome, as the alimentary canal reduces separate "realities," or discrete bits of food, into an undistinguishable mass of unwanted and soon-to-be-discarded feces.

Shengold (1985) calls this defensive stance anal narcissism. A fantasy world is fabricated in which differences between genders are eliminated, generational prerogatives and characteristics are subverted, and dirty becomes clean and vice versa. Shengold feels that "All basic psychological dangers (which include narcissistic injury—envy of breast as well as of penis) can bring on the threat of regression toward nothingness: toward non-discrimination, anonymity, need-fulfillment rather than love, loss of identity and individuality, loss of the ability to care about others, and finally, dehumanization. If any developmental level gets too charged with 'archaic affect' (cannibalism and murder), an 'anal,' 'sphincteric' regressive defence that revives narcissism can be initiated" (p. 56).

In other words, the individual caught in anal preoccupations and fantasies becomes "King Shit," master of the kingdom and slave to no one—perfect, the creator of the fecal world (Shengold, 1985). This "perfection" can be projected onto others, as can the "shit," resulting in a characteristic alternation between idealization and devaluation. Sadomasochism rules and pre-genital sexuality is highly valued, as it allows denial of the painful realities of a child's sexual, intellectual, and personal vulnerabilities and inadequacies.

Chasseguet-Smirgel (1978) describes the anal fantasy as "the fantasy of having reduced the object to excrement, of having, in breaking down the barriers which separated mother from son, daughter from father, brother from sister, the erogenous zones from each other, and the body molecules among themselves, *destroyed reality and thereby having created a new one, that of the anal universe where all differences are abolished*" (pp. 31–32).

Chasseguet-Smirgel believes that because fecal material is "renewable," anal patients do not value time or take its passage seriously. Treatment may go on interminably, as time is never lost; it can always be regained. Relationships are of little value because they are never as valuable as the sacred feces, always present and immeasurably wonderful. When relationships *are* established, a high premium is placed on the patient's feeling in control. The regression or fixation in anality can promote the development of perversions. Because generational differences can be altered or changed at will, pedophilia is acceptable. Reality is determined by the individual's proclivities at the moment. The notion of another's subjectivity is irrelevant because the anal narcissist is only concerned with his or her version, which is wholly self-referential.

Ms. S., whom I've been describing previously, has some characteristics that could be described as fitting the definition of anal narcissism. She denied my own reality to a very irritating extent sometimes and, at least to my mind, violated the chief precept of psychoanalytic work—the search for truth. She wanted to obliterate and destroy my interpretations, as she experienced them as diminishing her. She was so terrified of being inadequate that she always felt that she should know in advance anything I conveyed to her. She treated interpretations not as helpful information but as assaults on her competence or as intrusions that made her feel like "shit." Consequently, she fought me in her efforts to establish that she was right and I was wrong. She had fantasies of intercourse with me but only anal intercourse—she fabricated a vol-untary act of "sexuality," which was really aggression. If I were inside her anally, I would be under her control, subject to her whims and desires. In her fantasies, she could castrate me, turn me into feces, or get rid of me violently. Her view of interpersonal interactions was "rape or be raped."

How should we understand the need to obliterate meaning through regressive anal defenses? Patients who are prone to these kinds of solutions have been subject themselves to obliterations of meaning, particularly as children. Ms. S.'s mother not only disapproved of jealousy, she told her daughter that she "didn't believe in it." What can a child do when she feels an emotion that is not supposed to exist?

Obliterations of meaning like these cause serious disjunctions in the development of a child's capacity to place thoughts and feelings in perspective. The child has to come up with solutions that allow her to feel safe and secure in the "real world" without violating the strictures of her family. Anal defenses, like the others we have discussed, are attempts to cope with overwhelming affects. Children forming identifications within their families develop self- and object representations that mimic, for good or ill, the unverbalized personality characteristics of the parent. Family defenses become individual ones and are used when necessary to adapt and adjust. When they are resorted to often enough, these attempts at solutions become rigidified aspects of the personality.

As I have tried to demonstrate, assessment of the patient's level of development is always essential, but it is especially important in those prone to anal defenses. If the therapist does not understand anal thinking and internalizations, interpretations and interventions will not be useful. And because the patient is likely to treat them "like shit" anyway, countertransference sadism is a danger for the therapist who neglects the processes of the anal defensive style. It is easy to become embroiled in sadomasochistic interactions when one's hard work is treated with disrespect, but it is useful to remember that such hostile defensive maneuvers represent to the patient the last best hope of safety and sometimes even of sanity. Furthermore, the countertransference can inform the therapist of the nature of the transference. That is, by experiencing the patient's desire to demean, the therapist can understand the patient's past experiences of being denigrated and present transferential fears of more of the same.

THE EMPTY CIRCLE

As I indicated in the first chapter, I believe that trauma, both catastrophic and cumulative, has profound influence on the nature and development of psychic functioning. Catastrophic trauma compromises the ego's ability to process painful situations and affects, in ways that resemble and ways that differ from the destruction of meaning characteristic of those with the anal narcissism. Laub (1998) has given the name "the empty circle" to the psychic breakdown and ego disintegration that massive trauma can cause. "The empty circle...is a term that symbolizes the absence of representation, the rupture of the self, the erasure of memory, and the accompanying sense of void that are the core legacy of massive psychic trauma" (Laub, 1998, p. 507). Laub (1998) has also applied this concept to the children of survivors, who must contend with the emptiness and destructiveness passed on by parents incapable of psychically ordering the constellation traumas that have befallen them.

In trauma, a psychic split (similar to the "vertical split" described previously) occurs such that the victim simultaneously experiences the horror of the trauma and withdraws into an objectless and non-representational state. Memory may be permanently impaired and retrieval of painful events impossible or extremely dangerous. The trauma victim who has suffered *psychic breakdown* may respond with terror, panic, and a sense of blankness when confronted with further trauma or its symbolic equivalents.

Aharon Appelfeld witnessed the slaughter of his mother and grandmother at the hands of Nazi murderers, which experience can certainly be called a massive trauma. When he returned to the scene of the villainy, the villagers reacted to him with the same repression, denial, and disavowal characteristic of his own attempts to come to grips with psychic pain. Psychic pain requires a response, whether one is perpetrator or victim.

Appelfeld's dream, which I described previously ("I dreamed about nothing . . ."), suggests the psychic breakdown of which Laub speaks. To dream of nothing implies the destruction of something. He is not saying that he did not dream. He is dreaming of negation. Laub's viewpoint suggests that the effects of the trauma that Appelfeld endured keep him from using the dream to rework and integrate the experience of returning to the scene of the trauma. Appelfeld returned as an adult years removed from the trauma, however, and has used his writing adaptively to come to grips with the trauma in his life. Many trauma victims do not have resources that they can use so productively, however, and consequently end up with unmanageable psychic pain, with the possibility of suicide ever present.

Laub and Auerhahn (1993) suggest that survivors of massive trauma achieve different levels of knowing in their incorporation of their experiences. They list eight such "forms of knowing," ranging from "not knowing" to "a consciously deeper and more integrated 'level of knowing'" (p. 290). "During massive trauma, fiction, fantasy, and demonic art can become historical fact; this blurring of boundaries between reality and fantasy conjures up affect so violent that it exceeds the ego's capacity for regulation. To protect ourselves from affect, we must, at times, avoid knowledge. We defend against intense feelings of rage, cynicism, shame and fear by not knowing them consciously" (p. 287). Furthermore, they suggest that in evaluating trauma victims for treatment it is essential to evaluate the level of traumatic memory in order to know where the therapeutic intervention should focus.

Traditional treatment emphasizing defense and resistance analysis may not be useful for trauma victims. To the extent that psychic structure has been destroyed, the ability to symbolize—to represent by language—is also damaged, and the patient's capacity to recapture or verbalize experience is diminished. Those who can still use metaphor or transference may be able to come to grips with their traumatic experiences in a traditional psychotherapy, but those who cannot may require a different orientation that accommodates the trauma, perhaps by relinquishing attempts at reconstruction. Ongoing assessment of trauma victims' ability to symbolize and verbalize experiences is necessary to make sure that retraumatization does not occur.

People who have suffered intense and massive trauma have not destroyed meaning in their lives. External forces have destroyed meaning. This distinction must be continued within the treatment. Although it may appear that trauma patients disavow or destroy meaning willfully and for gratifying purposes, they are not necessarily trying to reduce treatment to the fecal level. They themselves have been reduced to that level by the perpetrators of their abuse. Consequently, interpretations that emphasize such patients' use of their symptoms as a compromise formation may be experienced as intrusive and attacking and may very well be inaccurate.

Patients with trauma backgrounds may not be willfully withholding and resisting. They are trying to maintain a sense of safety under the press of psychic forces that feel overwhelming and destructive. Respect for the patient and for his or her adaptive efforts requires that the therapist tread lightly with trauma victims. The effects on the psyche of massive trauma are great and tend to result in diminished ego functioning. For many trauma victims, conflict-free spheres are few and far between, and almost any stimulus can trigger intense emotional reactions. This is another way of saying that early trauma infuses the personality.

TRAUMA, KNOWING AND NOT KNOWING

Many therapists never treat patients who have lived through such large-scale catastrophes as the Holocaust, but almost everyone sees trauma victims of other sorts from time to time. So it behooves us to be aware of the effects of trauma on character—particularly on characteristic ways of knowing and not knowing—and how these effects differ from other defensive styles.

Some patients are able to transcend their traumatic experiences and form more elaborate defensive apparatuses that provide some gratification. Ms. S. was not a victim of severe trauma but she did suffer early parental loss, and we have seen how she used her early liabilities and inadequacies to hide her aggression. People who have been abused in other ways may similarly incorporate both victim and perpetrator roles and then try to defend against awareness of their abusive selves. This defensive need may restrict their thinking and their ability to discriminate in other areas of their lives.

Ms. T. called me to request an appointment. She had recently been suspended from her job at a government agency. She presented herself as extraordinarily frightened and distraught. She talked non-stop, in a tangential and confusing manner. She seemed very suspicious and imagined great conspiracies among prominent government officials. She insisted that she had been wrongly accused; this belief, I later discovered, was correct, and she eventually hired an attorney and won a large monetary settlement from the state.

Guilt over childhood issues made her very fearful of being accused of wrongdoing. There was some suspicion of sexual molestation by family members, as well as considerable physical abuse by her siblings. When she came to my office, she expressed a fear of the oddly dressed people who tend to gather around university towns.

She also talked incessantly about the "liberals" who were ruining the country. I told her that although I could appreciate her concerns and it was clear that she had been treated unfairly by the state, it was not in fact oddly dressed strangers or liberals who had done her the most harm. It was familiar family members of a political persuasion similar to her own. She could not grasp this and continued to rail against her perceived enemies. Here was a woman who had truly been wronged by the state, but who had incorporated this traumatic event into her belief system in such a way that it aided her denial of her underlying psychic distress and the experiences related to her early abuse by family members.

It is interesting too that although Ms. T. was exquisitely sensitive to the abuse she herself had suffered, she was quite neglectful of her children and her husband. Her relationship with me, though not abusive, reflected this characteristically rather cold-hearted approach to others. She felt no connection to me despite my intense work on her behalf. She did not recognize my emotional investment in trying to help her. She focused mainly on her own needs and pain, as the other members of her family of origin had focused mainly on theirs. Her basic character structure was never altered in treatment, which she terminated once the settlement had been reached and she felt exonerated. This woman had been traumatized as a child and had used denial, disavowal, displacement, and splitting as defenses. She did not wish to know beyond what she already knew and, I suspect, felt incapable of tolerating the truth.

TREATMENT CONSIDERATIONS

Helping patients deal effectively with what they know and do not know (or do not want to know) means keeping track of several variables. To list the defenses used by an individual says little about that person or about the direction that therapy should take. As always, thorough assessment is necessary, and assessment with regard to defensive style includes attention to the usual considerations: the level of ego functioning and the ego's brittleness or flexibility; the nature of the problem (neurotic, borderline, narcissistic, psychotic, traumatic: i.e., what is being defended against); the quality of the patient's internalized object relations and capacity to establish a therapeutic alliance; the ability to withstand the rigors of interpretive treatment; and the desire to be introspective and ascertain the truth.

Like other psychological characteristics, a patient's defensive apparatus does not operate in isolation from the rest of the personality. In my view, as I have attempted to make clear, neurosis is character neurosis: defenses are interwoven into an individual's personality structure and do not operate only in response to conflictual issues. The terror of knowing, or the need to "not know," spans all disorders and diagnostic categories, and the particular approach taken to the problem depends on constitutional variables, family upbringing and identifications, and circumstances of fate.

People will go to great lengths to feel safe. Many years ago I worked in a maximum-security prison. The prisoners knew that the parole board wanted an acknowledgment of guilt, a statement of remorse, and an assurance that the prisoner had learned from his incarceration. Yet prisoners commonly went to their parole hearings denying involvement in the crime, in spite of their knowledge that this would not be looked upon favorably by the board. It is possible that these men were acting out of repressed guilt, but I think that less likely than primitive fears. I hypothesized that early annihilation and castration anxiety prevented them from acknowledging their guilt—that they unconsciously feared worse retribution than continued incarceration. In fact, many of these prisoners had become so practiced at trying to convince others of their innocence that they had convinced themselves. Their internal need to deny culpability was so great that they could not use experience in any kind of self-reflective way; this deficit was unwittingly conveyed to the parole board. This self-delusional process may have been helpful to society in continuing to keep possibly dangerous men incarcerated, but it also speaks to the lengths that people will go to maintain a sense of psychic safety.

Helping patients understand how they think and how they try *not* to think can lead to profound changes. This is not say that such a process orientation does not run into strong resistance. People are taught to "not know" and to "not think"—that is, not to see reality as it is—and it may feel very unsafe to them to do otherwise. All patients come to treatment looking to feel better. They also want their versions of reality confirmed. It is the therapist's task to help patients to understand that they *can* feel better, but that this may require giving up a preferred version of reality. To understand the impact of desires not to know upon one's personality and one's life is illuminating; it leads to increased ego strength and a greater ability to know oneself and one's world. But a process like this must occur in an atmosphere that allows patients to be safely held and contained. Ignoring people's aggressive and sadistic qualities does not help them feel safe; on the contrary, it leaves them feeling alone, bewildered, and out of control. All of us are best served by attention to what is real, to the extent that we can tolerate it. To strive for understanding within the context of the patient's character structure is helpful in that it makes clear what is "real" in the patient and also the approaches that may best enable this reality to be tolerated.

V

◆

SYMPTOM,
DEFENSE,
AND CHARACTER

◆

All people struggle with the uncomfortable realities of pain and help-lessness. It follows, therefore, that people develop strategies for coping with these unhappy eventualities. These strategies–which ultimately manifest themselves in symptom, defense, and character–have important adaptive functions, and in this chapter, I will explore this aspect of their development.

A maturing child confronts internal and external pressures that make constant demands on the psyche. Out of these pressures and ex-periences, a personality structure develops that reflects that child's solu-tions to the complex problems that life presents. Enduring personality patterns or character structure as a whole (what I call the implicit as-pects of personality) embody everyday forms of functioning and con-tain, in encoded form, adaptations to the problems of life. Symptoms reflect relatively circumscribed attempts to adjust to internal and exter-nal demands while still achieving as much as possible the desired satis-factions. Defenses, as the last chapter has illustrated, develop to protect the psyche from painful realities and are held in constant readiness against a sudden need for protection.

From the classical perspective, symptoms develop when a per-son, kept by internal prohibitions from direct satisfaction of instinctual demands, fashions a behavior that affords both indirect satisfaction and the requisite punishment for it. Symptoms do not address only the classic instinctual needs; they may reflect attempts to cope with other kinds as well. Attachment and relationship, independence and autonomy, and safety and security are only some of the many needs that push for satisfaction in developing individuals. Like symptoms, defenses and larger character organizations are responses to a wide variety of needs.

Symptoms and defenses develop in response to danger and then become incorporated into character structure. As Baudry (1989) says, "In general, a behavior that appears maladaptive to an outside observer will often turn out to be the best available solution for the person under the given circumstances. Much of analytic work deals in part with the reconstruction of the setting in which certain characterologic choices were made" (p. 684). The formation of a particular person's compromises and adaptations are manifestations of the creativity of the developing child. One of the marvels of being a therapist is the opportunity to witness the cleverness—however desperate—with which people manage, when they must, to cope.

> One of Dr. R.'s techniques in tense interpersonal situations was to survey the situation silently and then, with varying degree of consciousness, maneuver herself into the position that she saw as most likely to meet her needs. Generally, she was able to escape scrutiny and criticism by appearing guileless while she pursued her goals, and she described these scenarios as if they played out as they did by serendipity, rather than by design. On occasion, I pointed out her cleverness, and she enjoyed these comments. They worried her at first, however, as they challenged her "incompetent" persona and left her feeling, as she put it, "found out." I don't usually relish patients feeling "found out," because this is an experience very closely related to shame. But Dr. R.'s disavowal of her competence increased her sense of alienation from herself, and she was relieved to relinquish her burdensome façade. Owning her competence helped to reduce her sense of desperation.
>
> In her family, her father's rule had been absolute, and rebellion was met with physical abuse. There was some suggestion that her father had been too seductive with her. Her beaten-down mother had degenerated into a distant and forgetful shell of a woman. Neither parent offered a satisfactory safe or reliable model for identification. Fantasies of attachment to her mother were just that, fantasies; her mother offered little opportunity for real attachment or

connection. (As the patient got older, she found herself strongly interested in older women, often taking an apprentice-like role with them.) Her father was frightening in his brutality. He gave her little opportunity to work out Oedipal issues in safety, and these were denied; her ambition and sense of entitlement became invisible along with them. As the analysis progressed, it became clear that she had a considerable desire for success and that she had in fact managed to run her life more effectively than she let on. Acknowledging this felt dangerous to her, though, and her successes caused her anxiety. They meant the loss of her identification with her depressed mother and represented a competitive rivalry with her frightening and abusive father. The incorporation of these issues into her personality style gave rise to her presenting symptoms, defenses, and character. The symptoms were her depression and listlessness; the defense was her insistence on her own incompetence; the character style is as I have described it previously.

CHARACTER FORMATION

Freud (1926) elaborated the formation of character pathology in "Inhibitions, Symptoms and Anxiety." He described how "The ego now proceeds to behave as though it recognized that the symptom had come to stay and that the only thing to do was to accept the situation in good part and draw as much advantage from it as possible. It makes an adaptation to the symptom—to this piece of the internal world which is alien to it—just as it normally does to the real external world" (p. 99). The ego then develops an apparatus for incorporating emerging symptoms within already existing personality constellations. The symptom then becomes elaborated into character structure.

Ms. S. came into treatment with debilitating anxiety and a profound sense of inadequacy. The anxiety had developed out of a childhood fear of being "caught" in her hostile fantasies. It was maintained into adulthood for the same reason. Having been overmatched as a child by her siblings, she developed a conviction of incompetence that she eventually used to her advantage in adulthood. That is, she savagely retaliated when real or imagined wrongs were done her, but always in a way that was hidden from view. When confronted, she feigned innocence. The anxiety was both symptom and defense (ego function); it obscured her rage, and the incompetence was her characteristic opening gambit in presenting herself to others.

Hartmann (1952) states that "Defensive ego functions can lose their defensive nature in time and become valuable and integral ego assets serving a far wider function than the original defensive one" (p. 248). He says too that character formation helps people integrate the effects of trauma. The development of character transforms feelings of helplessness and vulnerability into adaptive responses. This comes at a cost, as character by its nature is choiceless; it exists beyond volition and has a compulsive quality. Adaptively, however, character formation creates a sense of independence from forces that seem beyond the individual's control, as alien sources of stress are integrated within the personality and used adaptively.

For example, we can see that Dr. R.'s normal ambition and competitiveness felt very risky to her given her family circumstances, and she adapted to the stress by pursuing them secretly, behind a façade of incompetence. Her symptoms—depression and listlessness—were not discrete entities, nor did they operate in isolation from this persona. Although she obtained some secondary gain (see following) from her personality structure, a more compelling motivation was her wish to achieve the normal and expected gratifications of success in an internal atmosphere of fear and self-punitiveness—the only safe and acceptable way she could imagine to exercise her desires. This is not to say that instinctual gratification is not a prime motivating force, but the search for it is *embedded* within a personality structure, which takes on a life of its own.

Symptoms also help patients maintain a stable sense of self and gain some satisfaction in life even while coping with overwhelming situations. Freud suggests that the ego draws "as much advantage from the symptom as possible." This advantage—which has become known as "secondary gain"—is usually thought of pejoratively; it connotes manipulations by the patient in the service of ill-gotten gains. This can certainly happen, but patients do not use their symptoms only to obtain instinctual gratifications, and even when they do the gratifications they seek may be legitimate and appropriate.

It is not always easy to distinguish among wish, fear, and defense. People with histories of early abuse, for example, are afraid above all of being helpless in situations that re-create the past. They may defensively establish lives in which wishes for sexual and aggressive gratification appear to be primary. However much satisfaction the gratification of these wishes may afford, however, the wishes are not primary. They are responses to the original trauma and represent in their essence an attempt to maintain a sense of safety and integrity.

For instance, a young child who has been abused may develop a sadomasochistic personality style that provides some gratification. Although sexual gratification is a compelling need and may seem like the primary need in such cases, people who have been abused are also trying to figure out how to feel special, or even worthwhile, after having been damaged. The primary motivation of the sadomasochistic behavior is to deal with the horrible feelings engendered by the abuse. This is accomplished by transforming the abuse from physical or emotional trauma to sexual triumph.

As I indicated in chapter III, needs do not exist in isolation; they generalize into a personality that includes characteristic internalized relationships and ways of thinking and behaving. Conflictual issues, too, become embedded within the personality structure, and that is the therapeutic context in which they must be elucidated, identified, and in-terpreted. Clinicians must attend to the affective needs that underlie conflict and the resultant compromise formations that motivate characteristic ways of behaving and thinking. As Fenichel has pointed out, psychoanalysis must recognize "That not only unusual and suddenly erupting mental states but also ordinary modes of behavior, the usual manner of loving, hating and acting in various situations can be comprehended genetically as dependent on unconscious conditions; and that ordinary volition is determined just as are disorders of the will" (1945, p. 463).

Another illustration of this perspective, again using the experience of abused children as an example: Abuse itself compromises ego function, so traumatized children must process more trauma with fewer resources. They may develop elaborate fantasies to defend against the recognition that they were hated by their presumably loving parents, a shocking reality and a bewildering and confusing one to a child. The desire not to know the reality of the parents' hatred may be generalized to other kinds of learning situations—such as school. Similarly, truth in treatment may be feared as the representation of the dreaded truth of parental hatred.

I saw a paranoid patient for a number of years whose stated response to any impeding vacation of mine was pleasure—he knew it would be good for me to get away. He wanted me to be well rested, so as to be in top shape to help him. This man was similarly helpful and considerate within his network of friends and colleagues, his whole personality structure having become infused with the need to deny hostility. He considered himself a caring and compassionate person, and he was. But he was not only that, although any inquiry as to other motives was met with polite disinterest. It was only late in treatment that he began to understand that he might be defending against angry feelings, let alone to acknowledge the possibility of hostility as a primary motivating force.

A psychotic mother had abused this man physically and emotionally. In his need not to accept the reality of his mother's abuse he established a style of thinking that obscured his understanding of people's motives (including his own). This cognitive style rigidified into a personality structure that hid his own intense rage as well as his mother's, because he used his confusion about reading himself to obscure his hostility.

Of course, his concern about my well-being during vacations was a reaction formation. The concern was there, but it was there partly out of his subliminal awareness of his rage and his concern about it getting out of hand. His paranoia represented his need to disown the fearsome and murderous rage that linked him with his similarly constituted mother.

CHARACTER FORMATION AND NEED SATISFACTION

Character structure is an elaboration of the adaptations that allow a child to maintain a stable sense of self in the face of developmental and environmental pressures. A child as he grows internalizes self-object representations that develop into a sense of who he is—his sense of identity, of "me-ness." As Sandler and Sandler (1978) point out, internalization occurs not only of the self- and object representations, but also of the representation of the relationship between the two. All of these representations, particularly the last, become part and parcel of the individual. This is crucial for an understanding of the subtleties of personality functioning and can be seen in the following example.

A law student railed constantly against my inadequacies. I was too analytic and too emotional, too superficial and too intellectual. I could rarely please him, and on the occasions that I did, he barely acknowledged my contribution. He had seen other therapists and found them useless. I did better than the others, he thought, but was still essentially worthless.

This man had suffered a traumatic separation as a child when his mother became seriously depressed. His attacks against me represented attacks against his mother for her inadequacies and also attacks against himself for his own inadequacy at getting his mother to love him. He attacked me outwardly, but he was inwardly attacking himself. Similarly, his lukewarm praise was a repetition of his own experience of his mother's relative disinterest, and his reluctance to accept my help repeated his experience of not having been helped by his mother when he needed her. He had become the essence of this early traumatic relationship, playing out the internalized relationships between early self- and object representations. I pointed out to him the link between his present state of depression and his internalized self-object representation; this allowed him to make some sense of his self-loathing and helped move him toward a depressive position whereby he could begin to feel the tragic and profound loss of his mother.

Sandler (1981) suggests that people look for specific "wished-for interpersonal interactions" and to that end evoke certain responses from others. The wished-for interaction is one that is felt to be familiar and to convey a sense of "safety, affirmation and well-being." He goes on to say that "[. . . Character] traits are not only the expression of instinctual wishes, the product of defenses against such wishes, or combinations of the two, but are also ways of evoking responses from our significant object, or rather their present day representatives" (p. 707 parentheses added). He points out the wish-fulfillment aspect of character traits, which explains in part why they persist even when they appear to be damaging to the person, and suggests that character traits endure because of the aforementioned sense of safety that they afford. "The aim of all ego functioning is to reduce conscious or unconscious representational discrepancy and through this to attain or maintain a basic feeling state of well being" (Joffe and Sandler 1987, p. 229).

I conceptualize this same process in terms of internalization of *structure*. That is, people internalize in their totality representations of their families' modus operandi. Each family unit has unique group dynamics, myths, and ways of thinking, relating, and functioning. In the individual's identification with the culture of the family, these intricate ways of being structure his individual personality and relational "language," and provide a sense of familiarity and comfort. These internalizations, or structures, define the essence of a person—but they may also lead to rigidity of character and do not yield easily to change.

Ms. S.'s psychic organization had a strong narcissistic and sadomasochistic quality. In our early years, I heard a lot from her about the "unfairness" of life—that was how she described disappointment. Similarly, she often called others (especially me) "mean" when they failed to meet her needs or desires. Her retribution for such "mistreatment" was to be extremely mean and unfair to others herself. Because I would not love her as she desired, she criticized me publicly, trying to damage my reputation.

This was how she had operated all her life. Alternative ways of processing hurt and anger felt alien and confusing to her. In her family, someone who was hurt returned it, in spades and with relish. This was one aspect of Ms. S.'s family language; another was a devaluation of independent thought. The combination made Ms. S.'s vengeful retaliation for disappointment quite resistant to change.

I find this metaphor of "family languages" useful in clinical work, especially with couples. Spouses are often not "bilingual," and an introduction to the concept and intricacies of the partner's language can be quite illuminating.

CHARACTER AND THE UNCONSCIOUS

One fair criticism of the characterological approach is that it neglects unconscious material. I counter this charge with my own belief that much of the work of psychoanalytic treatment occurs, or should occur, in the preconscious. Heavy emphasis by the clinician on the past or on unconscious processes seems to me to point to an uncomfortable transference/countertransference issue that seeks relief in distance from the immediacy of the moment.

This is not a rejection of the unconscious, however, as I also think, somewhat paradoxically, that a concentration on implicit issues, on the preconscious, and on character structure is an excellent mode of access to the unconscious, that most difficult of venues. What is the "unconscious," though? Is it repressed material from the past? Current feelings and thoughts that are defensively kept from awareness? Experiences that have not yet been formulated and can only achieve clarity and "consciousness" once they have been formulated? One risk of the quest for a repressed past is that it may become an intellectualized exercise. But the patient's implicit functioning (family language and internalized self- and object representations) provides a natural link between past and present— and also among conscious, preconscious, and unconscious, between the transference/countertransference and past relationships, and between the immediate and the experience-distant.

Psychological preoccupations and conflicts pervade all levels of consciousness and all aspects of personality. The ones that can be most meaningfully addressed exist in what I have been calling the "implicit" aspect of the preconscious. The "implicit," residing as it does in the preconscious, is relatively accessible to the patient, and so are the recognition of the characteristic family language and culture; allusions to these are easily understood and appreciated by patients. Attention to these primarily characterological phenomena provide a facilitative *context* in which unconscious material can emerge. We are all aware that as psychotherapies progress, access to the unconscious increases and the material deepens; dreams are not the *only* "royal road to the unconscious." Forays into the hidden are most profitable when the contextual variables are right. Present-day life experiences of the patient, accessible transference/countertransference issues, and attention to the "implicit" provide a context from which the unconscious may readily emerge.

SYMPTOM

Psychoanalysis since its earliest days has focused on the question of symptom etiology. The current trend in psychoanalytic theory and practice is a broadening of the focus away from concrete or specific symptoms and toward more encompassing and more elusive concepts such as self, authenticity, and character. My adaptational perspective is in keeping with this trend, and I will turn it now upon a consideration of symptom formation. Symptoms are signposts to underlying issues that require attention. The specific symptom picture is less important in the context of a focus on these preconscious and characterological signposts.

All children in their development are confronted with pressures that require response. Symptoms are attempts to cope with the demands of conflicts and other stresses upon the ego. A symptom may represent a compromise formation, such that gratification and punishment are achieved surreptitiously and together. Alternatively, it may reflect an attempt to contain overwhelming affects as comfortably as possible. We all do our best to keep pain to a minimum and to obtain what satis-faction we can as we try to survive in a world of perceived danger. We try to use creatively, and to our (perceived) advantage, the circumstances presented to us, just as we try to make the best out of the situations we encounter and to avoid dysphoric affects. This is the context in which instinctual gratification has its say. It is a powerful say and it exerts a very strong influence, but it is not the only need pressing for satisfaction.

The obese patient that I described in chapter I presented for treatment complaining of depression and anxiety. She had a number of physical problems related to her eating habits, including high blood pressure, gastrointestinal problems (worsened by the high-fat diet she favored), diabetes, and a strong family history of cardiovascular disease. Rage was a constant psychological problem, and she had frequent conflicts with co-workers and other acquaintances. She had been fired from her previous job in a real estate company for physically threatening a co-worker. We established a good relationship and were able to begin to look at what was going on.

   Although she often spoke of herself as a "follower," she was actually very rebellious. Whenever the importance of losing weight (for health reasons) came up, she would stop after the appointment for some unhealthy treat. She was constantly in trouble with her boss for not following through on assignments. She made an imposing figure, noticed by all. She kept a marvelous number of doctor appointments, and I wondered how she tolerated all the pricks and prods that they entailed with such equanimity. I suggested to her that she must get some satisfaction out of all of this, so resistant to intervention was it—and it began to appear that her symptoms did indeed solve several problems for her, while, of course, accomplishing their task of making her miserable. As a child, she had been afraid of her physically abusive mother, and her large size afforded her protection. Her family held fundamentalist religious beliefs, and although sexual and angry feelings were disapproved of, gluttonous ones were allowed. Her sexual and aggressive needs were subsumed under her eating behavior. A turning point in treatment occurred when she was able to identify that she wished to eat when she felt sexually aroused.

Part of my work was to convey to her that the needs she was attempting to satisfy were *not* pathological; they were natural and normal human needs that had been subverted. We could also see that her rage responses represented identifications with her enraged parents as well as anger toward them. Her family was intrusive and boundaryless, and saw her attempts at separation and individuation as betrayals that would leave her depressed mother empty and lifeless. Her family did not value delayed gratification, so the patient was never able to learn how to regulate her affects, or to differentiate them.

Throughout the treatment, we looked at the adaptive functions of her obesity—what it did for her and how difficult it was to give up the gratifications it provided for other needs that felt less within her control. She began to understand that she was essentially distrustful of others and that she felt that only the bliss of overeating was a reliable comfort, as one could not depend on others.

In this patient's very difficult family, obesity had been one of her few possible routes to satisfaction. She was able to fashion for herself a modicum of contentment and control while at the same time maintaining a conscious belief in her fecklessness. The variety of medical procedures that she underwent provided her both with attention—masochistically derived and sexually exciting—and with punishment for her hidden sexual and assertive needs. She denied the seriousness of her disorders as her family had taught her to deny the reality of its own maladaptiveness.

The needs and anxieties that produced a symptom such as this woman's obesity are many and varied. A complete analysis requires the careful elucidation of each, *along with recognition of the value of the symptom to the patient.* In this particular treatment, we had to address issues relating to the patient's aggressive and sexual needs, relationships, self-esteem, identity, affect regulation and differentiation, and feminine identity. Attention to transference manifestations as well as to their counterparts in her everyday life assisted in illumination. This broad focus, including attention to characterologically based internal representations, eventually enabled her to lead a life of greater satisfaction and accomplishment.

SYMPTOMS AND INTERNALIZATIONS

Psychological problems may arise in response to many different kinds of forces. Victims of Shengold's "soul murders," for instance (trauma, overstimulation, and neglect), create symptoms that represent internalization of the traumas; internalization of external traumas, which includes representations of self and object, creates an internal world in which the traumas are re-created. These become compelling dramas that are acted out in the patient's relationships. Such activities are not instinctually based. They are compelling, and compelled, re-creations or repetitions of pathological relationships.

As Sandler (1981) points out, the patient internalizes *both* self and object *and* the relationship between the two, in the context of a "wished for interaction." These internalizations may begin to be used adaptively as the child develops, but they may occur without initial volition. That is, traumatic events have an imprinting potential such that the trauma may become part of the individual's psyche without any intentionality. The symptoms in their existence reevoke the language of the family.

An essential part of treatment for many patients, therefore, is the identification of their qualities and characteristics *without* any attribution of motive or desire. A description of a patient's characteristic modes of thinking, feeling, and relating can be of crucial importance, as these form the background of that person's psychic functioning and provide the specific context out of which conflicts and other needs develop. Sandler (1960) refers to this as a "background of safety."

This notion of "background" is not unlike Winnicott's concept of the "environment mother." Infants require both an "object mother" and an "environment mother." "The object mother has to be found to survive the instinct-driven episodes, which have *now acquired* the full force of fantasies of oral sadism and other results of fusion. Also, the environment mother has a special function, which is to continue to be herself, to be empathic towards her infant, to be there to receive the spontaneous gesture and to be pleased" (1963, p. 76; emphasis added). This distinction applies to the therapist's functions as well; one, the "environment therapist," is not interpretive, but appreciative and observing. The other, the "object therapist," is transferential, engaged, and able to "survive" the projections of the patient.

Kumin's (1996) work on what he calls "pre-object relatedness" provides an important perspective on this notion of the *background* of the patient's psychic functioning. He holds that infants establish very early relationships with their significant caregivers and that these precede the child's ability to experience the object as an object. It should be noted that he is not supporting the notion of a symbiotic union. He is suggesting that there is a quality of relatedness that recognizes the individuality of the other but that predates symbolic thought. "Pre-object relatedness denotes a modality of experience that develops prior to the baby's conscious, reflective awareness of itself and others as being real, permanent, independently motivated individuals. Pre-object relatedness is characterized by the preverbal exchange of emotional shape and regulatory function between mother and infant and persists as a background capacity in all interpersonal communication throughout life" (p. 4).

This foundation determines the shape and quality of the personality and so imbues a person's life, yet it is ephemeral within the treatment. It is the elucidation, identification, and elaboration of these unverbalized qualities that provide the most lasting and meaningful changes in psychotherapy. When such unthought realities can be understood, the patient may be able to become "unstuck" from incomprehensible and confusing situations.

Kumin provides further explanations for projective identification and other situations of nonverbal interpersonal affective interchange. He believes that individuals comprehend each other's communications through a variety of modalities. For example, an infant who sucks upon a textured pacifier will spend more time looking at it than at a smooth one. Learning is transferred from one mode (sucking) to another (seeing). Hearing (one mode) a particular feeling tone may create a pictorial representation (another mode) that then creates a verbal interpretation (still another modality). Therapists, too, "read" a patient's affects and form mental representations of them that can then be redelivered to the patient. These "intermodal exchanges" often operate preconsciously, yet they often provide the "meat" of interpersonal interaction, and they may operate without question or awareness. In that sense they are syntonic; they feel to the patient like his or her very essence and are not even identifiable for discussion. Yet they are vital for treatment, because it is this "implicit" aspect that defines character and that contains embedded conflicts and dynamic issues. The "implicit" is often not attended to in treatment and the crucial nature of internalized representations are not brought to the surface and consequently not worked through.

SYMPTOM AND DEFENSE

People are very creative in their struggles to maintain equilibrium and satisfaction in the face of internal and external exigencies; attention to this creativity allows us to see how symptom and defense interact and interweave. Ms. S. provides a good example here. As previously described, she was able to turn what was a disadvantage, her inadequacy relative to her older siblings, into an advantage where she hid her hostility behind a persona of incompetence. As a symptom, she was besieged by anxiety and feelings of inadequacy. As a defense, she could maintain the illusion of innocence and purity, denying her sexual and aggressive strivings.

This—the transformation of a disadvantage into a hidden victory—is not an uncommon occurrence. This patient's treatment was quite successful, as attention to this process enabled us to examine and understand the feelings of entitlement that underlay her helplessness, and she eventually was able to take much more control in her life. It is important not to forget that the solutions that patients achieve to maintain self-esteem under pressure represent an achievement. At times, they may be used manipulatively or in other ways that engender countertransferential reactions, but they are an achievement nonetheless, and the patient rarely benefits from being "caught" or "found out" in such *sub rosa* uses. When emphasis is placed solely on a search for hidden gratification, however, this may be a counterproductive result.

SYNTONICITY

It has sometimes been suggested that character is ego-syntonic while "symptoms" are ego-alien or -dystonic (Fenichel, 1945). Because I suppose that symptoms are produced by processes that infuse the personality, this is a distinction that does not entirely hold. Syntonicity can exist consciously or unconsciously; most symptoms and characterological problems that are identified by the patient as dystonic may be dystonic consciously, but have some degree of unconscious syntonicity. The symptom came into existence to solve an internal psychic problem, and the patient has an emotional investment in maintaining its existence.

Obviously, syntonicity exists in degrees. Some patients feel uncomfortable with their situations and have strong conscious wishes to change. Others express discomfort but want the environment to change rather than themselves; this perspective becomes quite clear once the surface is scratched. Some patients have symptoms that are uncomfortable, but they lack the wherewithal to consider anything but superficial "whys," or they find alternative ideas so threatening that they can't make the analytic space to explore their psyches. The tenacity with which a patient clings to a characteristic way of functioning is diagnostically and prognostically significant. People who are open to possibilities and able to engage in the play of the analytic encounter tend to possess more ego strength and to have a much higher probability of success.

Some patients keep areas of their psyches or lives "off limits" and sequestered from discussion. This is a character structure that is especially difficult to treat. At times the therapist may feel a great deal of pressure to keep away from these "forbidden" topics, yet the pressure may be so subtle that it is consciously recognized only when the case is supervised or when the patient tries a different therapist. Other individuals operate from hidden basic premises which, even once they are identified, are maintained with a rigorous and vigorous tenacity. Some patients with a strong sense of entitlement fit into one or another of these categories. They feel that life has shortchanged them and are forever angry at the unfairness of it. Most people with these characteristics would be aghast to hear themselves described so. Nonetheless they truly *do* feel entitled, and considerable effort must be expended before they can understand the ramifications of this stance in other areas of their lives.

Or, consider the example of one patient of mine, who superficially deplored a psychological symptom, but in reality clung to it with vigor. This woman and her husband had substantial assets and a large income, but their financial arrangements were such that they lived from paycheck to paycheck. Some months when she was "short" she had trouble paying me. It was very hard for her to appreciate that she and her husband had constructed their situation—that it was not "real" in the sense of their actually being short of money. It was even harder to help her see that her "trouble" paying me reflected a wish *not* to pay me. The stinginess that she and her husband exhibited in their financial dealings was characteristic of their psychic organization and of their relationships. They were ungenerous with each other to the degree that it was hard for them to fulfill even their *own* needs. They gained masochistic gratification from their self-denial, and she (and perhaps he) got sadistic pleasure from creating discomfort for me. These personality characteristics were syntonic and were, in fact, viewed by them as admirable—an example of responsible frugality. The patient had no conscious appreciation of the expanded context of these behaviors.

Patients may acknowledge intellectually the validity of an interpretation, and yet have no actual intent of making any changes. Some affects and fantasies become embedded in belief systems in ways that feel unalterable, leaving the patient able to see no alternatives and reluctant even to explore what their behavior might mean. Anderson (1999), speaking of the pressure toward enactment, describes Bion's conception of how patients' desire to alter psychic reality—"both internal reality (one's needs) and external reality (nurture needed)"—"stems from the omnipotent demand that the pleasure principle need never be relinquished, that adaptation to the reality of an increasingly complex world, internal as well as external, need never be acknowledged" (Anderson, 1999, p. 511). The patient pays lip service to the therapist's interventions and interpretations, but seeks a closed, solipsistic world of his or her own making. These are omnipotent defenses, and to analyze and understand them requires diligence and attention to detail. Transference interpretations are particularly helpful in identifying and elucidating these issues, because the material is so readily available. Furthermore, the patient's need to control and dominate may contribute to the development of an enactment. The therapist often feels pressured to not address those aspects of reality that the patient wishes to disown. This countertransference affect can be used as an effective signpost to such maladaptive but syntonic belief systems.

REPETITION COMPULSION

Freud (1914) suggests that patients repeat instead of remembering. "We have learnt that the patient repeats instead of remembering, and repeats under the conditions of resistance" (p. 151). In "Beyond the Pleasure Principle," he suggests that the repetition compulsion helps the patient master early trauma, but that it reflects also the influence of the death instinct. "Enough is left unexplained to justify the hypothesis of a compulsion to repeat—something that seems more primitive, more elementary, more instinctual than the pleasure principle which it over-rides" (p. 23).

The existence of an inborn death instinct may be questionable, but given the level of rage and destructiveness that we see both within and without the consulting room, it is not difficult to imagine that aggression and its vicissitudes are inherent. People's tendency to repeat maladaptive and self-destructive patterns can be breathtaking in its tenacity. Over and over, we see patients rush headlong into relationships or activities that are clearly ill advised and appear to be yet another rendition of some recurring disaster in their lives. Much of treatment is spent deconstructing such repetitions so that the patient can understand the compelling reasons for their existence.

Sandler (1974) explains this compulsivity in his concept of the "unconscious peremptory urge." Patients are driven, he suggests, in a way that feels involuntary, to find ways to meet their desires. Freud's view of the repetition compulsion as a manifestation of a death instinct provides one *explanatory* perspective, and if the repetition compulsion is an instinctual by-product, it is irreducible and stands on its own. However, to me it makes more sense to see the repetition compulsion as a *descriptor* of a complex of psychic maneuvers, especially as the nature and raison d'être of repetition compulsions have not yet been well elucidated. What produces such a strong need to keep reproducing and re-creating seemingly traumatic situations? In a sense, all compulsions are repetitive, and the compulsive propensity has not really been sufficiently explained.

It is important to point out here that "compulsion" refers to the *drive* to repeat, not to the general repetitiveness that is seen in all psychopathological conditions. People maintain consistency and structure in their lives, and this includes consistency in their psychological difficulties. However, there are some people who are irresistibly drawn—compelled—to activities that, to the outside observer, and sometimes even to the individual, seem to be doomed to failure. Although a repetition compulsion is typically self-destructive, it is not the outcome that defines it; it is rather the need to set up, repeatedly, situations of a compulsive, driven quality such that the patient does not consider the nature of the activity.

Patients with refractory compulsions like these are typically people with relatively serious psychological disorders. Here is another instance in which the therapist's language influences treatment. The compellingness of the repetition desire can be viewed from a whole spectrum of positions, from a judgmental one that envisions a person seeking undeserved gratification or retribution, to a more sympathetic viewpoint taking into account the patient's representational and security needs, and everything in between. The therapist's perspective will directly influence how the patient comes to view the compulsive behavior and also how the pair work with it in treatment.

Shabad (1993) suggests that the repetition compulsion exists when individuals have not been able to transcend and integrate "traumatic themes" that are passed on from one generation to the next. "The chronicity of the traumatic theme derives from the unmourned and therefore, repeated aspects of the parent's history that have become entrenched in the parent's character and are continually enacted on the child; the helplessness engendered by the traumatic theme derives from the child's continued incapacity to change the parent into a wished for figure" (p. 65). From this point of view, the individual is continually trying to undo disappointments and disillusionments—to make the parent whole—and is thus condemned to search endlessly for an impossibility. An approach that emphasizes an acceptance of the reality of loss, disappointment, and impotence, and that encourages mourning over lost possibilities, is seen as desirable.

At times, this desire to alter reality can be seen in the development of perverse solutions that may themselves take on a compulsive quality (Lepisto, personal communication, 1999). As I discussed in chapter IV, reality itself can be the enemy that points out the pain of the loss of the patient's infantile omnipotence (Akhtar, 1997; Anderson, 1999). When that happens, the patient must deny the reality of the impossibility of the desired relationship in order to maintain the illusion of symbiotic bliss. The ability to think and consider becomes antithetical to the goal of omnipotence. This situation needs to be identified and worked through over and over and over again.

Novick and Novick (1996) indicate that pathological omnipotence protects masochistic patients from overwhelming fears of chaos and psychic disorganization, and that these fears contribute to the persistence of masochistic symptoms. This also helps to explain the "stickiness" of patients embroiled in repetition compulsions. The belief in the possibility of a desired relationship may represent an omnipotent solution defending against regressive fears of helplessness and extreme passivity. The terror engendered by such fears is considerable and is compelling. The need to repeat represents a belief that is like a house of cards. Any suggestion that it may be maladaptive evokes a fear of psychic disorganization and is mightily resisted. Novick and Novick suggest that special attention should be given to these omnipotent needs lest termination occur prematurely.

TRAUMA AND THE COMPULSION TO REPEAT

As I have said before, victims of trauma develop intrapsychic features for dealing with extraordinarily painful experiences, and they internalize the roles in the trauma of victim and perpetrator both. A sense of shame, humiliation, powerlessness, helplessness, and hopelessness infuses the personality structure, causes great grief, and gives a lifelong cast to the personality. This may become manifest in a compulsion to repeat unsatisfying and sometimes damaging interpersonal patterns. Why does trauma create this compelling need to fling headlong into self-defeating activities?

Trauma, according to Krystal (1978), needs to be understood in terms of its effect on affective development. "Although the aftereffects of trauma are many, there is a syndrome of affective disturbances which reflects *direct* sequelae of trauma and is related to the nature of the traumatic state. In these individuals we see a lifelong disturbance of affectivity" (p. 90). These lifelong disturbances are manifest in the repetition compulsion, which develops out of attempts to cope with trauma and its overwhelming affects, whether the trauma was catastrophic or "ordinary." Although not all of those with the compulsion to repeat are victims of trauma, I would venture to say that those with serious, repetitive self-destructive behaviors have endured serious assaults to their egos and their ability to cope with the everyday demands of life has been severely compromised.

Greenacre (1967) provides a definition of trauma that includes less intense experiences than the obvious catastrophic ones. "In my own work I have not limited my conception of trauma to sexual (genital) traumatic events, or circumscribed episodes, but have included *traumatic conditions, i.e., any conditions which seem definitely unfavorable, noxious, or drastically injurious to the development of the young individual*" (p. 128). Similarly, Khan (1963) points to "cumulative trauma": ongoing impingements on the developing child that present pressures beyond the capability of the emerging ego to handle. He speaks of the failure of the mother as a "protective shield" (Freud, 1914). Shengold (1989) aptly describes ongoing "soul murders" that have cumulative traumatic effect.

Experiences like these create lifelong, enduring personality characteristics that pervade all relationships and activities, and people who have lived through them feel that they *must* engage in these ongoing activities–in that way they are experienced as syntonic, although they may be superficially acknowledged to be maladaptive.

These different writers all point to the conclusion that repetition compulsions represent, especially in traumatized patients, a sense of the inevitable. As aspects of character structure, they transcend simple motivational etiologies and exist, in part, to maintain a sense of self and to provide a sense of stability. They feel essential to the patient, and a thorough explication requires attention to internalized self- and object representations based upon past traumatic events. The following section expands upon these notions.

REPETITION COMPULSION AS STRUCTURE BUILDING AND MASTERY

Every significant psychic event has an impact on the structure of the mind; trauma is no different. Brenneis (1997) cogently describes how traumatic experience becomes melded into the patient's psyche in a way that allows the patient to make the experience his or her own, and to *represent* it in a palatable and familiar way. Brenneis describes how trauma creates a representational need that co-exists with individual and preexisting aggressive, libidinal, and narcissistic needs. Brenneis's work is significant, because it identifies a need that may very well fuel the maintenance of the repetition compulsion: the need to represent, organize, and structuralize experience meaningfully.

Cohen (1980) suggests that "Repetition compulsion (replica production) aims at the actualization of an unconscious trauma so that it can be retrospectively mastered." In repetition compulsion, "The primary affect being defended against is intense unpleasure associated with traumatic experiences of loss of control, over-stimulation, or perhaps primal depression" (p. 426). He suggests that repetition compulsion may not be driven by the pleasure principle, but rather that it operates out of a drive to master unsymbolized experience, which has as its hallmark diffuse affects and a strong somatic component. He suggests that as the patient improves through treatment, a new level of organization (wish-fulfillment) comes to the fore. Trauma creates poorly organized intrapsychic structures and these are manifest in the repetition compulsion. "Such experiences, because they were overwhelming and disorganizing to the child's capacity to perceive, represent, and form memory traces, are not only unrecallable in the ordinary sense that repressed memories are. Rather, they are unavailable for recall because *they do not employ adequate mental representations,* even in the unconscious" (p. 423). The patient, unable to structure the traumatic experience, has no choice but to act it out repetitively. Cohen emphasizes that because repetition compulsion represents a defect in memory organization, the goal of treatment is not the recapture of memory but the *formation of* memory.

These writers support my belief that trauma creates internalizations of the traumatic event. Distorted self- and object representations become structuralized, as do fantasies about the nature of the trauma and of the relationships among the participants. These renditions of the trauma help define the person's character and result in a perspective tainted by the experience.

Traumatic experiences, whether they are catastrophic or cumulative, thwart ego development, and once internalized they become heartaches, so to speak, that require soothing and resolution. This need drives patients to seek out relationships that match the original trauma, in order to rework it into a better resolution and perhaps even to capture lost memory. The patient is convinced that one solution only will suffice; that it is essential. A disconsolate infant wants *only* the mother, and although substitutes may provide the needed physical nourishment, they do not provide the emotional connection that the baby yearns for. It is this yearning that becomes manifest within the repetition compulsion. How is this different than ordinary life experiences? Trauma patients have typically used fantasies of the omnipotent, unsullied mother as a way of carrying them through the deprivations and terror of the traumatic experience. They have not been able to gain sustenance from the more ordinary experiences of life that those less traumatized can take solace in.

This need for representation resembles the feelings that drive artists and other creative individuals. The drive to express oneself–to represent one's feelings, thoughts, and essence–is universal and often irresistible. It becomes pathological when it serves needs that are more negative and self-destructive than creative and life-enhancing. The drive that fuels the repetition compulsion is the drive to structure experience– to make sense of experiences that make little sense. The "culture" of the trauma, whether catastrophic or cumulative, creates the only language that the patient understands and compels the re-creation of situations where that same language and culture may be experienced. Although many aspects of the repetition are premotivational, adaptively the patient tries to obtain satisfaction within the trauma by expressing both sexual and aggressive needs; elaboration of the trauma occurs in fantasy, such that the patient develops identification with the perpetrator and designs modes to create affective satisfaction within relationships that are inevitably, repeating the trauma as they do, maladaptive. People who experience early trauma are drawn to repeat because they cannot do otherwise. As one patient put it, in speaking of her irresistible need to repeat maladaptive relationships, "It's like home, you get a taste for it in childhood."

A thirty-year-old secretary entered treatment because of difficulty in an affair with her boss. She was unmarried, he was married, and he was putting great pressure on her to discontinue the relationship. She was plagued by pervasive and debilitating anxiety. She had a history of overstimulating and oversexualized early experiences; her mother had had a variety of relationships with men, sometimes including sex for money. The patient had memories of seeing and hearing encounters between her mother and her lovers which she experienced as bewildering yet enticing. She did not know her father.

    As the evaluation proceeded, I discovered that in spite of her relative youth she had been married three times already, each time to a man with whom she had first had an affair. As with her other husbands, she had decided that this present man, her boss, was the love of her life, and she was despondent over the possibility that she might not be with him forever. She hid many of her real feelings from her lover, hoping that if she were "perfect" he would leave his wife for her. Nevertheless, she managed to be quite demanding and often complained of not being sexually satisfied. Not surprisingly, the transference was imbued with erotic desire, although I never experienced her desire as having much sexual heat, similar to that which I experienced with Ms. S.'s. Her desire for me, as for her boss, was more acquisitive than erotic. We were objects that she felt unable to live without. As the transference intensified, she would follow me in her car, demand extra sessions, and insist that I see her for no charge, on her own schedule. She was demanding with me as she was with her lover, insisting on phone calls rather than requesting them and responding very negatively to vacation breaks or to my decisions not to respond to some of her questions.

    The traumatic experiences of this woman's childhood had imprinted upon her a particular way of understanding relationships: as exploitative and narcissistic. The desire to repeat, via identification, her mother's behavior, reflected a desire to reestablish a relationship with her mother that felt familiar and provided a modicum of soothing. Because much of the trauma had been prerepresentational in nature and without memory that could be retrieved, the patient lived out the experiences instead of using them for structure building. Her own narcissistic and sadomasochistic character caused her to view relationships through those lenses and to gain satisfaction from manipulating others.

As a child, she had desired to be included in her mother's sexual relationships, and her desire for married men reflected this compelling need. Her insistence that these men were her salvation derived from unresolved mourning over the reality of her father's absence. It also reflected her sense of herself as a little girl who always felt inadequate in comparison with her fully developed, physically mature mother. Possession of a married man would prove her the equal of her mother. All of these complicated and involved issues needed to be identified, explicated, and worked through repeatedly. Her suffering was such that she felt an intense need to maintain her illusions, and she believed that these desired relationships would salve her pain. Successful treatment required microscopic attention to each of these identified issues, using the transference to assist in making these issues manifest.

Work with repetition compulsions is complicated still further by the fact that people embroiled in them tend to evoke strong countertransference reactions in their therapists. It is very frustrating to work with a patient for a long time, to put an enormous amount of thought and effort into helping the patient to become more reflective, and then to find the patient continuing to act impulsively and compulsively. Certainly with the patient just mentioned it was hard for me not to become angry and condemning. I had to recognize my feelings, and without denying them, refrain from using them as an opportunity to exercise my own sadism. Besides being hurtful to her, it would have actually served to perpetuate the dynamic, because of her desperate need to get a "rise" out of me.

When I became aware that a patient of long standing had begun turning sideways as she walked through the door into the consulting room, I noted it and waited for an opportune moment to address this behavior. When I brought it to her attention, she responded that she, too, had noticed it and had thought to herself that she wished I would give her more room. She had no other thoughts about it and I dropped it for the moment. I was struck by her comment, and upon reflection I realized that she was correct; uncharacteristically, I had been standing in the doorway in such a way that she did not have sufficient room to pass. I said nothing about my awareness of my own contribution at this time. She was quite often silent, but soon after I raised my observation of her turning away she became even quieter than usual. When I remarked upon her silence, she became quite distressed, saying that she felt she could do nothing right. "I can't even free associate properly."

It finally became clear to me what should have been obvious before. I was pressuring this woman to comply with my notions of what a "good" patient should be. I *was* pressuring her, both literally and figuratively. I realized that my crowding her in the doorway, and my insistence on "free" association, represented an enactment. I had often felt frustrated that this patient talked so often about cutting down her sessions and "resisted" a sense of closeness with me. She was a person who favored obsessional defenses and tended to keep emotionally distant from many in her life. Out of my own need for closeness and to feel important to this patient, I had unconsciously created a situation (blocking her way) that I could then use to point out to her—her need to distance herself. I also realized that I had brought it up at a time when I was irritated with her because she had once more been thinking of reducing her sessions.

This whole incident informed me greatly about the impingement issues with which she was contending and reminded me of some of my own issues about needing to be appreciated and sufficiently attended to. I also speculated that her need to distance herself represented a defense against a desire to impinge upon *me*, to become merged with *me*. My awareness of these constellations allowed me to back away from the patient, both literally and figuratively. This resulted in her feeling more relaxed and more "free" to associate or to not. She still turned sideways through the door, although not to the same extent, but that was based on her insecurities and not on my own. As I backed away to give her more space, she became more reflective and transference issues came to the fore of their own accord.

ENACTMENTS

Like many psychoanalytic concepts, enactment has no precise consensual definition. To my mind, it is not synonymous with acting out or acting in, because neither of these concepts necessarily postulate an interactive dimension, while enactment does. "Enactments are symbolic interactions between analyst and patient which have unconscious meaning for both" (Chused, 1991, p. 615). In fact, the evolution of the term *enactment* is based upon the awareness that the therapist or analyst is doing something different from the usual when a patient brings emotionally charged material to the session. In nonenacted mode, the therapist will listen to the material, may even have an emotional reaction, but does not find him- or herself responding behaviorally to the material in a way that is uncomfortable.

According to Sandler (1976), enactment refers to a particular kind of "free-floating role responsiveness" (p. 45). "My contention is that in the analyst's overt reactions to the patient as well as in his thoughts and feelings what can be called his 'role-responsiveness' shows itself, not only in his feelings but also in his attitudes and behaviour, as a crucial element in his 'useful' countertransference" (p. 45). Sandler's position is that patients may very well evoke in their therapists a certain role-responsiveness that matches up with early wished-for interactions. The countertransference is "useful" because it informs the therapist and the patient of issues and conflicts that could not be articulated in any other way. He further states, "What I have been concerned with in this paper is the special case of the analyst regarding some aspect of his own behaviour as deriving entirely from within himself when it could more usefully be seen as a *compromise* between his own tendencies or propensities and the role-relationship which the patient is unconsciously seeking to establish" (p. 47). He lays the bulk of the responsibility for the enactment upon the patient but certainly does not view its existence as problematic or as an indication of harmful countertransference; on the contrary, it is "useful."

Not surprisingly, different theories see enactments differently—some as inevitable but potentially useful and others as part and parcel of the intersubjective process and not deserving of any particular label. I will offer a brief review of the literature to establish a context for my discussion.

Jacobs (1986) is generally credited with having given structure and meaning to the term. He tactfully suggests that the typical history of those in the therapy professions includes the role of being an empathic listener within the family. This responsiveness to the needs of others often serves the therapist well but can sometimes predispose toward becoming embroiled in "enactments which, subtly, can alter and distort his perceptions and understanding" (p. 297). Like Sandler, Jacobs does not view the existence of enactment as necessarily problematic. It is only detrimental if it is not picked up and worked through. "It may happen, too, that there is formed between patient and therapist a defensive collusion that has as its unconscious purpose the exploitation of the transference so as to avoid the emergence of other anxiety-laden material" (p. 304). Enactments may reflect these collusive elements from both participants' unresolved childhood anxieties or may reflect more generalized countertransference reactions that relate to the patient's need to evoke certain reactions from others.

Most clinicians do not feel that enactments are necessarily problems. Chused (1991) suggests that enactments are to be avoided, if possible, but acknowledges that their existence informs the treatment and can be exceedingly helpful. She suggests that the patient pressures the analyst toward a countertransference response, which may or may not have referents in the analyst's own pathology. "*Enactments occur when an attempt to actualize a transference fantasy elicits a countertransference reaction*" (p. 629). For Chused, enactments exist because patients do not always have the capability to verbalize their conflicts and thus must rely upon the only mode available—action. The role responsiveness of the analyst creates a countertransference response.

Intersubjectivists (among them Freedman and Natterson, 1999) suggest that enactments are inevitable and that those who think otherwise deny the intersubjective realm and privilege the therapist. They believe that enactments are co-constructed by the analytic pair and that this perspective provides an immediacy and meaningfulness that is lost in perspectives that maintain the separateness of the participants. They do not view enactments as unique within the analytic process. Rather, "We would state that enactments are continuous in analysis and are *essentially just another way of describing the analytic process*" (p. 226). Maroda (1998) suggests that although patients may strive to evoke a role responsiveness in the therapist, it is incumbent upon the therapist to maintain proper boundaries despite this provocation. "The experience of being in control is an essential aspect of adequately defending or coping. When patients repeat the past, they do so at their own behest, and a measure of control makes the experience manageable. But when analysts re-enact their pasts with their patients, they remove control from the patient, which leads to confusion and anxiety at best and, at worst, to trauma, despair, and self-destruction" (p. 525).

Kumin (1996) suggests that people with traumatic backgrounds search out others in their environment with whom they can actualize them. The enactment is designed not only to repeat the trauma but also to help the patient internalize the therapist's ability to deal with emotional upheaval. "The patient, in a small way, reenacts the developmental successes of the analyst and gradually internalizes the therapist's more mature and adaptive response to the patient's enacted trauma" (p. 181). The enactment is viewed as an inevitable construction reflecting the failures and successes of both participants' histories.

It is important to note that the term *enactment* differs from *re-enactment*. These experiences are new ones; they have roots in the participants' pasts, but are not veridical expressions of past experiences. An enactment is a present-day creation that provides information and meaning to aspects of patient, analyst, and their relationship that were previously unavailable. The *pressure* to enact is ubiquitous. The *potential* to enact occurs when the clinician feels this pressure in an uncomfortable way, even if no real change occurs in his or her overt behavior. It is this feeling that should function as a signal to the clinician that an underlying issue has been activated and needs to be addressed.

Let us go back to the example that I provided at the beginning of this section. I have been seeing this patient for a long time. She and I have gone through a lot together, with regard to both transference/countertransference issues and to this woman's very intense struggles to stay alive. I feel, and I think she would agree, that I have been very helpful to her. Could someone else possibly be more helpful? Certainly. But the relationship she and I constructed is different from the one she would have formed with any other analyst. This imagined clinician might have been more helpful in some ways and less helpful in others. Yet we are, in a sense, stuck with each other, just as family members are. We both try to do our best, and we pick up the pieces when we don't do as well as we should.

I think it would have been better if I had felt less insecurity about my place in her affections; she would have been spared an impingement that caused her pain. On the other hand, we were not very aware of the importance of this issue in her life, and our construction of it, with the help of the enactment, resulted in great clarity and a deepening of the material and of the transference. We hope that I am up to the task of keeping my countertransference to a minimum and that when it emerges we can identify the meaning that we each derive from it and its impact on the treatment. The treatment is about the patient, however, and my view (my own way of looking at patients, that is my language, my worldview) is that our time should be devoted primarily to an understanding of her inner life, not mine.

In an earlier work (Hooberman and Hooberman, 1998), I suggested that it is helpful to consider whose pathology was making the overriding contribution. It is the patient's drama or the analyst's drama that is being played out? There are some patients who evoke similar responses in almost everyone they meet. It is not surprising when this happens in treatment. On the other hand, analysts, human and imperfect as they are, have issues that impose certain pressures upon the treatment regardless of the patient's individual pathology.

Then, of course, there exists the "primordial soup" in which patient and analyst struggle to find ways to talk about feelings, fantasies, ways of being in the world, and issues about essence and meaning that transcend verbal explication. Those with traumatic backgrounds often have no way to explicate that which exists beyond verbal meaning. People for whom symbolization is not available, as identified in the work of Kumin (1996), may have no avenue of communication available to them except action, and their therapists may have no other path toward helping them except to become intricately involved in their drama. For some patients, an analyst who insists on remaining emotionally uninvolved is not helpful, and an emotional storm may even be created out of the feeling of terror evoked by the sense of being alone. My previous example was relatively mild in intensity, yet it was crucial in that it called to our attention both my impingement and the patient's issues in this area.

Patients who have endured far greater traumas and deprivations than this one may evoke countertransference responses that are in some sense independent of the analyst's pathology; notwithstanding, these responses may still derive their shape from that particular analyst's pathology. This paradox can allow the therapist and patient to find a space—the "analytic third" (Ogden, 1996a)—within which these issues can exist and where careful delineation and analysis can occur. This is the place where a determination can be made as to the origin(s) of the enactment. Subjectivity is inevitable. Whatever the specific origin of the pressure to enact, it occurs within the subjective relationship of the participants and must be addressed and understood within that realm.

CONCLUDING THOUGHTS

The development of personality structure represents both failure and success. It is a failure in the sense that the individual feels forced to develop neurotic (in the best case) choices in order to solve intrapsychic and interpersonal problems. It is a success in the sense that these choices are often creative underpinnings for future problem solving. Access to healthy compromise formations, sublimations, and other defensive possibilities helps us cope with the wide range of pressures that we all endure. Symptoms and character development develop out of the tension among the needs for psychic survival, for need satisfaction, for ego development, for a sense of safety and security, and for reasonable levels of self-esteem. The internalization of family dynamics, and the "language" of the family in which they are expressed, create psychic structures that support identity. They are consequently stabilizing but also highly resistant to alteration. These identificatory processes must be respected if the patient is to feel safe enough to explore their utility, and they must be attended to if the therapeutic process is to deepen in the direction of more satisfying and comprehensive change.

VI

◆

ANARCHY,
PERVERSITY, AND
SADOMASOCHISM

◆

In this chapter, I continue my look at the effects of trauma on personality development—this time by focusing on the development of particular personality constellations that reflect attempts to gain satisfaction and superiority in situations and relationships that evoke memories of encounters that were defeating and demoralizing.

Over years of practice, I have become more and more convinced that the ongoing assaults on individuals that have come to be called "cumulative" trauma have pernicious effects indeed. Patients under such assaults must protect and defend themselves, and often they do this by fashioning responses to them that lessen their hurt by (apparently) turning defeats into victories. The need to alter reality in this fashion may generalize within the patient's character structure; because these assaults also create severe disruptions in self-esteem regulation, narcissistic disorders are often the result. The anarchic, perverse, and sadomasochistic defenses that I will discuss in this chapter are found most clearly in the narcissistic disorders, and so I will use examples from those to illustrate my argument. Many patients have suffered serious narcissistic blows that may cumulatively become traumatic, and thus may have some of these characteristics embedded within their character structure.

The young child is vulnerable to narcissistic injury as both ego and self-development are still incomplete. Children treated too often as narcissistic extensions of another person may learn from this experience to externalize their own internal conflicts onto others to maintain a sense of safety and competence—this is what they have seen done to them. Victims of trauma have suffered in addition repeated violations of the commonly accepted rules and standards of human behavior; they tend to have a hard time establishing boundaries that protect their own integrity and recognizing the integrity needs of others. Unable to regulate affects effectively themselves, traumatized individuals must depend on other people and on external events to maintain psychic equilibrium and necessary levels of emotional gratification. Given their experience of boundary-violating relationships, this dependence may not recognize or respect the individuality of these others.

People who eventually develop anarchic, perverse, and sadomasochistic personality configurations have typically been the victims of anarchic, perverse, and sadomasochistic behaviors by significant caregivers. Harshly treated, they have not internalized a gentle self-concept, and the painful realities of life have been overwhelming and *too* painful. They must be disavowed or somehow transformed.

Profound violations of the ordinary rules and order of society may result in what I call the "anarchic" disorders; these represent the need to create a world where the realities that reinforce feelings of disparagement and self-disgust are denied. By *anarchic* defenses, I mean the wish to obliterate reality and meaning and imagine a world where rules and standards are non-existent and painful realities can be transformed by the use of fantasy and disavowal. I have discussed some of the general aspects of this defensive posture in chapter IV. Similarly, *perverse* defenses may create a sense of meaning and comfort out of childhood occurrences of pain and rejection. They attempt to turn pain into pleasure and the unpleasant realities of life into gratifying fantasy. Finally, *sadomasochistic* disorders result when early childhood relationships are experienced primarily at the two poles of domination and submission. Pleasure and competence appear possible only when the individual either is in pain or inflicting pain on another.

Although these three personality configurations may intermingle, I will discuss them separately, hoping to illuminate each more clearly. These constellations manifest themselves within the treatment relationship, of course, and contribute to very strong countertransference reactions and enactments.

THE ANARCHIC DEFENSES

Our patients, like everyone else, must cope with the unpleasant realities of life and of psyche. The psychoanalytic relationship is at times very painful to the participants and, more often, to the patient, who is in the more vulnerable position. Protests against the therapeutic enterprise often match protests against past traumas and hurts, and an entire anarchic history may be unconsciously created within the psychotherapeutic relationship. By anarchic history I mean experiences in the patient's past life in which boundaries of integrity were breached. Sexual, physical, and emotional abuse; overintrusiveness; and nonconsensual perverse behavior are all examples of anarchic experience. They are shocking and disorganizing to young children, and puzzling and bewildering as well, because they betray the order of society as it is generally represented to children. Generational, gender, and relational rules are ignored and broken, with predictably profound and serious consequences. Psychodynamic therapists sometimes concentrate on the aspects of the Oedipal conflict that are problematic and possible precursors of psychological disorders. At the same time, however, the attainment of the Oedipal position is an accomplishment—it defines appropriate generational boundaries for the child in an ultimately reassuring way. In their extreme manifestations, the anarchic disorders seek to dismantle Oedipal triangular relatedness, resulting in a loss of internal structure.

Anarchic manifestations are very easily seen in the all-too-common criminal activity that pervades society. Many people in less obvious ways try to deny and alter the unpleasant realities of life, however, by ignoring or disregarding commonly accepted obligations. As always, what occurs outside the consulting room finds its way inside, and throughout the remainder of this section I will examine further ramifications of this desire to alter and deny unpleasant realities.

ANARCHY AS A SOLUTION

Anarchic predilections represent attempts to maintain a sense of competence and self-esteem under the pressure of attacking and belittling internal representations. People who desire to create a world without rules and order have had their own personal and societal boundaries violated; the resulting humiliation and shame is overwhelmingly painful, and the sufferer will go to great lengths to avoid situations that evoke such despair.

The flight toward anarchy negates gender, generational, and other fixed realities that have been identified as the source of the pain. Past helplessness in the face of overwhelming stimulation leads to fantasies of a world in which the small stature and genitalia of childhood will no longer seem deficient. In this anarchic world, juvenile sexuality is valued, not scorned—the child rules the roost and, in fantasy, is no longer the victim of stronger predators. Identification with the aggressors of childhood is characteristic of the anarchic defenses. These people re-create with others their humiliating experiences, and the reversal of victim and victimizer soothes their desperate sense of inadequacy. Turning actual past (and internalized present) passivity into an advantage instead of a disadvantage allows them to retain some shreds of self-esteem in the aftermath of pervasive feelings of smallness and incompetence. The externalization onto others of a pervasive sense of badness also feels cleansing and mitigates self-destructive feelings. The fundamental metaphor of the anarchic world is the anal one.

ANAL NARCISSISM

I pointed out in chapter IV that Chasseguet-Smirgel (1974, 1978, 1984) and Shengold (1985, 1992) think perversions are both fixations of, and regressions to, the anal level. As expected, people with anal personality organizations have issues around dominance and control, and both these theorists suggest that anal regression and fixation tend to reduce relationships to a fecal level.

From my perspective, this has several consequences. It promotes a sense of grandiosity—an artifact of the belief that one can magically transform oneself and one's relationships into that any form one wants. Gender and generational differences are obliterated such that Oedipal dynamics become irrelevant. The child, in fantasy, is no longer denied access to the desired parent by the realities of generational constraints, immaturity, and the incest taboo. One is no longer constrained by gender; one can be whatever one can desire or create. The adequacy of immature genitalia becomes a non-issue since pregenitality is idealized.

In "On Transformations of Instinct as Exemplified in Anal Erotism," Freud (1917b) characterizes the intensity of desire and control of the anal period. "There are people whose anal erotism remains vigorous and unmodified up to the age preceding puberty (ten to twelve years); we learn from them that during the pregenital phase they had already developed in phantasy and in perverse play an organization analogous to the genital one, in which penis and vagina were represented by the faecal stick and the rectum. In other people–obsessional neurotics– we can observe the result of a regressive debasement of the genital organization. This is expressed in the fact that every phantasy originally conceived on the genital level is transposed to the anal level–the penis being replaced by the faecal mass and the vagina by the rectum" (p. 131). The child, dealing with the narcissistic injuries of immature genitalia and the reality of gender constraints, fantasizes a limitless world where generational differences recede and where one is not limited by gender or any other unpalatable aspect of reality. This anal world is solipsistic; boundaries exist there only when condoned by its creator, who is no longer bound by the need for relationships. Possessor of fantasized penis and vagina both, an individual at this level of organization is self-satisfying.

This "anal narcissism" and "anal defensiveness," as Shengold calls them, protect the individual from hurt and danger. People go to great lengths to maintain their illusions of dominance, control, omnipotence, and self-sufficiency. Kinston (1980) suggests that to maintain a stable internalized self-representation, "the individual will tolerate considerable injury to his conscious idea of himself when it preserves his (unconscious) self-representation" (p. 383). In other words, for optimal success in treatment, a patient who wishfully regresses to an anal world in which he or she is creator and ruler, must be confronted with the reality of a rather mundane and ordinary (in the sense of being not quite as special as is desired) existence.

THE HOLOCAUST AND THE
OBLITERATION OF MEANING

The desire to reduce and diminish others can clearly be seen in the horrors of the Holocaust. It is not just the murderousness of this catastrophe; it is the excrementalizing process, by which human beings were reduced to the level of fecal material and treated as such, that makes it so horrific. Language and social contracts lost all meaning; personal integrity and control were obliterated; humans were devalued in a maelstrom of destruction and hatred–these are mind-boggling, absolutely disordering experiences, and beyond the ability of most people to contain rationally.

The victims of the Holocaust once lived in a world, which they believed to be governed by rules of law, language, and social order, where triangular Oedipal relationships consistently maintained generational, gender, and relational structures. The Nazi regime was a Sadian world, organized at the anal level, that idealized the pregenital and devalued human development and intelligence. It turned the world of reason topsy-turvy in an unimaginable way and obliterated secondary processing and rationality.

Bluhm (1999), in a fascinating article originally published in 1948, describes the anality of the Nazi regime. In a description of the survival mechanisms of concentration camp internees, she speaks of the *"anarchic power of accident"* (p. 98). "If a person happened to lie next to the door through which a group of drunken SS-men entered, he may have been tramped or kicked to death, while his neighbor suffered no harm. If a prisoner met a guard who asked him to walk closer to the wire and he did it, he may have been shot; if he refused to do it, he may have been shot as well. . . . This anarchic power of accident, of the unexpected, of terror, not only ruled over the inmate's life and death in a physical sense, but was perhaps the strongest force in the mental dynamic of concentration camp life" (p. 98).

Bluhm goes on to describe how the traumatizing effect of such atrocities overwhelmed the prisoners' egos' usual psychic survival techniques. Sublimation, symbolization, and dream formation were greatly impaired, further diminishing their ego resources for accommodating the trauma. Victims of severe trauma, particularly early trauma, have difficulty using symbols to comprehend their experience.

In chapters IV and V I described many of the deleterious effects that trauma often has on character structure. As traumatized patients are often incapable of metaphor, the usual symbolic psychoanalytic language is beyond their capability. A colleague of mine had a patient who was thought to have multiple personalities. She had been horrifically traumatized as a child—so traumatized that she could not use ego defenses to symbolize or metaphorize her experiences at all. Consequently, they continued to exist in archaic form within her mind, continually traumatizing. She coped by developing alternative personalities that dealt with the trauma and the resulting affects—the ultimate "it's not me" experience. The task of the treatment was, in part, to help her become able to use language to help create alternative ways of coping, understanding, symbolizing, and transforming her experiences into more tolerable forms. (I am indebted to Michele Rivette, M.S.W., for this example).

Patients like this with backgrounds of severe trauma often report dreams that they claim to be veridical renditions of the day's events, with no apparent distortion or symbolization. However veridical the dreams *feel*, there is evidence that they are not absolute truths but are influenced by the patient's preexisting psychic structure and preoccupations. The patient doesn't have the symbolic capacity, however, to experience or deal with them except as veridical. From the patient's perspective, it is as if these dreams and the corresponding experiences are not processed at all; they become incorporated photographically. The patient's ego cannot process experience; the ability to derive meaning from experience has been destroyed, leaving life flat and sterile.

ANARCHIC DEFENSES AND THE COUNTERTRANSFERENCE

The countertransference as described in this work can present both danger and opportunity to the therapist. Patients are not the only ones who sometimes distort the therapeutic enterprise to other ends. Occasional extreme examples of this arise, as for instance when a therapist encourages a sexual encounter. But much more often it happens subtly, to create a particular feeling in the therapist that may be contrary to the best interest of the patient.

A therapist most often becomes aware of personal needs intruding on the treatment when disquiet and urgent feelings make themselves felt. Reactions to these feelings may vary, but it seems to me that the need to rationalize, or to persuade oneself that one is acting in the patient's best interest, is a tipoff that something may be amiss. Clinicians are not immune from the desire to create their own anal worlds.

Anarchic patients can be extremely provocative, and they elicit strong countertransference reactions. It is hard not to respond to their dominating and excrementalizing with anger, distaste, or retaliation, and we sometimes fail to manage it. When the therapist, because of countertransference pressures, becomes susceptible to the pull toward the anal world, enactments may result, and the therapeutic pair may be distracted from thoughtful consideration to mud-slinging accusations.

These people, with their extremely fragile sense of competence, are defending against intense experiences of terror (Anderson 1999). They externalize these feelings and the receiving therapist may well begin to feel sufficiently terrorized by the patient that reflective thinking is temporarily lost. As the patient fears annihilation and has been terror-ized into complying with others' unreasonable demands, the therapist feels similar pressures—not to bring up painful interpretations and agree to covert frame and boundary agreements. When they become manifest in enactments, these pressures can provide information about the patient's internal structure that is unavailable in words.

PERVERSITY

Effective treatment provides patients with new experiences. When the desire for new *affective* experiences transcends the desire for change, how-ever, a perverse treatment may arise—one where the patient desires to bend and maneuver the treatment such that pleasurable experiences, not cure, become the priority. The treatment becomes a venue not for learning but for reinforcing the patient's belief in a desired altered reality. Perverse treatments often masquerade as effective ones, because the patient may be very affectively involved and appear to be working hard and introspectively. Yet the patient may be changing little and, on closer scrutiny, is seen to be using the therapy to bolster rigid yet well-disguised beliefs.

Freud (1905a) suggested that, "neuroses are, so to say, the nega-tive of perversions" (p. 165). "The motive forces leading to the formation of hysterical symptoms draw their strength not only from repressed *normal* sexuality but also from unconscious perverse activities" (p. 51). For Freud, in this instance, perversion is a failure in sublimation or in symptom formation. The perversion becomes manifest without un-dergoing the structuralizing and symbolizing activities of the ego, and is thus quite a direct representation of the unconscious. In later writings, Freud (1927) suggested that neurotic people defend against uncomfort-able wishes while the pervert tries to disavow uncomfortable reality by vertical splitting.

More recent writers have also concluded that perversity exists within us all, albeit in varying degrees of strengths and compulsion. Coen (1998) suggests that perverse defenses exist to maintain self-esteem against the onslaught of painfully impinging internal and external realities. Neurotic defenses may be designed to the same ends, but perverse and neurotic patients have different psychic organizations and one of the most important of these is a difference in the capacity to accept reality.

Perverse Solutions

As I've said, I view symptoms as attempts at problem solving. Perverse activities and personality orientation also represent attempts to solve vexing or overwhelmed psychic problems. As Freud (1919) described in "A Child Is Being Beaten," people try to make the best of a bad situation, and when necessary they imagine circumstances where a painful interaction can be interpreted as a mark of specialness. People who resort to perverse thoughts and practices are trying to create meaning and comfort out of pain and rejection. They are looking for a sense of wholeness, and they imagine that the achievement of their particular fantasies will provide this. Perelberg (1999) suggests that some very disturbed patients are prone to violent behavior because of their fragile sense of identity. In healthier patients, however, it is "only the feelings of security engendered by attachments to objects of both sexes that prevent the individual from feeling overwhelmed by the pressure of the phantasies and desires of the pre-genital sphere, because they may then be anchored in a set of secure object relationships" (p. 39).

Perversity as a defensive or characterological constellation does not require the existence of frank sexual perversion. Perversity may exist in a hidden form, without overt behavioral manifestations, and the therapist must pay careful attention to the details of the subtle but very powerful influences of the patient's desire to alter reality to conform to perceived needs. The mark of perversity is the hidden pleasure that the individual attains through the presumably therapeutic encounter.

Many patients look for gratification within the therapeutic relationship. They look for love and for the satisfaction of many other needs unmet in their lives so far. Most patients have observing egos, however, that maintain some distance even upon the turmoil of the treatment, and they understand deep down that the true point of the enterprise is to promote their own capacity to help themselves. A perverse patient desires the relationship as an end, not as the means to the end. A neurotic patient may feel tremendously competitive with the therapist and may *to some extent* thwart the treatment to express that need. A perverse patient will thwart the treatment *in the extreme* to maintain the pleasure of being able to do it—that is, to dominate. There are many motivational underpinnings that can fuel perversity, but it can be identified in the transference by the ongoing desire to exchange therapeutic benefit for pleasurable gratification. Treatment is not seen as a venue for change and growth but for stasis and satisfaction. Pleasure seeking is the object, not insight and development.

Transitional Objects and Perversity

The transitional space is the place where therapist and patient meet, where transference/countertransference struggles intersect, where patient and therapist can play with the real and the not-real, and where the work of therapy occurs. As Bollas (1987) suggests, the concept of "transitional" implies movement. Winnicott (1953) said about the transitional space that there is in each human being "a part that we cannot ignore, an inter-mediate area of *experiencing,* to which inner reality and external life both contribute. It is an area which is not challenged, because no claim is made on its behalf except that it shall exist as a resting-place for the indi-vidual engaged in the perpetual human task of keeping inner and outer reality separate yet inter-related" (p. 230).

The transitional space is experiential but with a movement to-ward growth. Perverse patients are not interested in the experience of growth, however, but in an experience of pleasure that validates their right to be alive. They have typically been treated as part-objects by their parents—as narcissistic extensions, not whole individuals in their own right. Existing as they did only in the context of their parents' needs, they feel annihilation anxiety when not satisfying the needs of another. This is the shape of the internalized relationships that they reenact. Inner deadness is what perverse patients defend against, even to the extent of risking their physical well-being. The normal activities of life (feeding, excretory functions, relationships) become overly sexualized and gratify-ing because they represent life-affirming and enlivening situations. The search for sensation, connection, and aliveness propels the perverse indi-vidual toward activities that in some tragic cases eventuate in death. As an example, think of those who engage in extremely risky behavior for the "thrill."

Winnicott suggests that the mother must provide the illusion of omnipotence and control and also gradual disillusionment. The infant must have the unquestioned belief that he or she has created the breast—that it can be destroyed at will and then be re-created without enmity. But the gradual internalization of a sense of competence and well-being is only achieved when the child's omnipotence is disillusioned in such a way that realistic limitations can be realized and the child can be soothed despite his or her failures.

A person with a perverse personality organization does not have this experience. This child never attains the illusion of omnipotence and remains dependent on external sources for gratification and soothing. The original object remains just that, an object—it never becomes a separate subject with its own independent life. The patient cannot soothe him- or herself and must search always for the missing or lost object, yet must discard it after use because it is empty and useless once the need for it has disappeared. It has no regenerative capacity. A healthy infant creates and destroys and then re-creates the object. A patient with a perverse personality organization has never created anything but feels like a passive recipient of fortune and dependent on serendipity.

Consequently, such people need to establish worlds of their own of control and omnipotence, where satisfaction and pleasure can be achieved. Because anal organization is the fixation point for such control, mature genitality is not possible and pregenitality is idealized. Other people are not seen as whole objects but as part-objects to be manipulated and controlled. People with anal personality configurations have little concern for the well-being of others and are ruthless in their relationships. This manifests itself in the transference; the therapist is not viewed as a flesh and blood individual with needs but as one who should satisfy the needs of the patient no matter what the satisfaction would cost either one of them. Requests for accommodation become demands, and the demands may be insatiable. As I have said, angry responses by the clinician to these demands are not uncommon. I find it helpful to remind myself that at the moments of greatest urgency, the patient is expressing most clearly the sense of emptiness and despair.

Khan (1979) suggests that inadequate "holding" in the Winnicottian sense means that transitional objects get used in the service of perverse sexual relationships. "In perversions, the object occupies an intermediary position: it is not-self and yet subjective; registered and accepted as separate and yet treated as subjectively created; it is needed as an actual existent not-self being and yet coerced into complying with the exigent subjective need to invent it" (p. 21). Individuals prone to perverse relationships recognize the separateness of others to some degree, but more fundamentally believe others to have been created by them, in their own image. This is a paradoxical self and not-self concept akin to that of a transitional object. But although subjects are viewed as separate, they are still imagined to be subject to ultimate control and manipulation. The other exists to satisfy the individual's needs and is seen as having been created expressly for that purpose.

Khan further suggests that the pervert employs the "technique of intimacy" to gain satisfaction. The patient makes every relationship and every encounter one of great emotional intensity and imposes a sense of heightened sensuality upon relationships even where it does not belong. The lack of ego integration encourages a lack of whole object relationships, and the agglomerated internalized part-object relationships result in what Khan refers to as a "collage" (as opposed to an integrated) ego structure.

Ms. S. saw relationships through the lens of her own needs. The transference was perverse; she saw me as a created object to be manipulated and used for her own needs. She had experienced considerable early abandonment by her mother and did not trust others, but she attempted to deny her separation fears with omnipotent fantasies of control and possession. She did not trust that I would consistently be there for her and, instead of viewing me as independent, she viewed me as hers to control. She eroticized our relationship to possess me. I was annoyed by her supposedly sexual fantasies, which were in fact hostile and objectifying. I felt pressure not to pursue my therapeutic goals because she got so angry when I interpreted her frustration with the reality of our relationship. Vertical splitting and disavowal were two important defensive mechanisms for her; she used them to brush away such reality considerations, and greatly prolonged the treatment by her reluctance to work in therapy to resolve her problems (instead of to gratify her many fantasies).

The satisfaction of a gratified fantasy may be intense, but it has little staying power. This evanescence demands continual repetition and concomitant despair. One aspect of Ms. S.'s transference was especially illuminating. As I have mentioned previously, before I truly understood her personality structure, I found myself being seduced into an enactment. She would mention that she had had a fantasy or a dream and then not tell me about it, prompting me to ask. This teasing represented the first layer of motivation in the formation of the fantasy and gave her a sexual satisfaction that she desired.

Continued interpretation of her need to pervert the treatment resulted in a strengthened ego and a reduction of her demands. My refusal to allow these continued hidden gratifications allowed her to identify her grandiose fantasies and then to mourn the loss of her grandiose controlling self, resulting in more enduring satisfactions in her relationships both in the transference and outside it.

Perversity and Part-Objects

People with perverse personality organizations have particular ways of conceptualizing relationships, and these can be seen in the transference. Internalized self- and object representations are composed of part-objects and other people are viewed correspondingly. Ms. S. had a fantasy that I possessed a "healing penis," which she thought would cure all her defects. She used this concept of the "healing penis" as a fetish. Because she did not see me as separate, my penis was hers, and its possession would fill her empty spaces, both metaphoric and real. Her inability to acknowledge me as a separate individual with a therapeutic task was an indication of her part-object orientation and also of her need to impose an eroticized relationship over the therapeutic one. Before our sessions she spent long periods in the office restroom, preparing herself for the sexual encounters she so desperately desired.

Early in the treatment, she told me stories and incidents without giving me information that was essential for understanding them. This left me confused but, by her reckoning, I already knew whatever she did (so much did she experience me as an extension of herself).

The urgency of the need to fill their emptiness can propel these desperate people into exploitative relationships. Stalkers appear to possess perverse personality structures. They attribute to their victims an intimate relationship where none exists. They eroticize feelings of separation, longing, and loss. Rather than experiencing directly their own sense of emptiness, they fantasize an erotic relationship with the object of their desire, imagining that it will salve their internal despair and prove their worthiness. Ms. S. had experienced the significant disappointments of her life as narcissistic injuries. The resulting sense of inadequacy caused her to idealize me and imagine that a sexual relationship with me would elevate her to the level of adequacy that she desired. This kind of idealizing is very destructive to the individual who does it, because the externalizing on which it depends depletes the person of a sense of his or her own good qualities.

Vertical Splitting

As I have said, people prone to perverse relationships tend to use vertical splitting to deal with uncomfortable aspects of reality. They are able to hold contradictory perceptions in their minds despite evidence that proves one or another inaccurate. An example of this is Ms. S., who consulted an infertility specialist even though she very well knew that she was not pregnant because she and her husband did not have intercourse. This inclination can make treatment difficult, as the patient may seek a confirmation of cherished beliefs more than an expanded conception of "truth" or "reality." Britton (1995) makes an important point supporting his contention that it is very hard for people with narcissistic and perverse disorders to let go of their pathological solutions. He indicates that some patients concretize their fantasies into beliefs and that these fixed beliefs count, as far as the patient is concerned, as "knowledge," despite considerable conscious evidence of their inaccuracy. The presentation of alternatives by the therapist is often superficially accepted but rejected in practice, as the patient truly "knows" what is real or not real.

This perspective gives an added dimension to the refractoriness of certain disorders and of the repetition compulsion. Grossman (1996) suggests that "The defining characteristic of the perverse way of thinking is that potentially distressing perceptions, although noted, can be treated as if they did not matter" (p. 512). Further, "The pathology is in the license that he grants himself to *keep his treasured beliefs untested*" (p. 512).

The patient's behavior in therapy may challenge or even stymie the therapist's ability to think, out of the need to disavow important aspects of reality. The patient may talk in such a way that it is very difficult to ascertain meaning, for example, or so flatly and affectlessly that the therapist can't maintain interest. Some patients talk about extraneous matters with little association, and others create such chaos that thought and consideration become very difficult for both parties. The clinician must be alert to these strategies and reflect back what the patient seems to be experiencing to bring the disavowals back into the therapeutic purview.

Perversity and Hostility

Perversions arise when narcissistic disorders become infused with unmodulated hostility and unintegrated eroticism. Stoller (1975) suggests that every perversion has a hostile component. In well-organized individuals, sex and aggression are fused; they co-exist and they modulate each other. In perversions they are unlinked and one operates at the bidding of the other. Relationships, for example, may not be seen as a source of satisfaction of attachment and affectional needs. They are infused with aggression and seen as conquests or competitive challenges. Aggressive situations are pervaded with raw hostility without the softening influence of attachment and affectional desires. Similarly, a person without appropriate degrees of aggression cannot function properly in a sexual relationship where assertiveness is an essential component.

To promote modulation in therapy, it is often helpful to indicate the linkages that have been denied between sexual and aggressive needs. For instance, a patient anxiously embroiled in a conquest, whether romantic or in business, may feel more comfortable if once made aware of the hidden attachment needs that the hostile actions disguise. Correspondingly, the exploitativeness exemplified by narcissistic and perverse patients can generate countertransferential reactions, and these reactions may be easier to handle if the *therapist* is aware of the hidden libidinal and affiliation needs.

On the other hand, some patients seem to think that they possess no aggression. Typically passive-aggressive and passive-dependent in presentation, these individuals have convinced themselves of their essential purity of motive. Consciously, at least, they have obliterated any aggression and therefore lack the ability to maneuver effectively in the world. Identification and interpretation of underlying hidden aggression creates the necessary links that enable appropriate assertion. "In other words the defusion of the instincts has gradually to change to fusion in any successful analysis" (Rosenfeld, 1971, p. 171). Countertransference responses of irritation may be engendered by the patient's denied and externalized hostility.

Rosenfeld feels that a patient whose psychic structure is strongly influenced by aggressive needs can develop a perverse psychic organization if this aggression becomes eroticized.

Mr. G. was a young professional who came to treatment suffering from profound depression and suicidal ideation. He initially established what appeared to be a good therapeutic alliance. He improved in treatment, regaining his equilibrium, and returned to his career. This level of adjustment did not last and he was soon in my office again. This time, however, he was obstreperous and resistant. He quit his professional position, refused to work at all, and gradually became more and more reclusive. I referred him for a medication evaluation but he refused to take any medication. He stopped coming to appointments, although I maintained contact with his parents, hoping to help them modify their enmeshed relationship with their son.

The parents had a very disturbed relationship, the father having been something of a tyrant while the son was growing up. My patient was very close to his mother—too close, in fact, which caused his father to resent him even more. By refusing to leave their house, he replaced his father, exercised considerable tyranny by means of his "mental illness," and got great pleasure from this revenge. His mother felt trapped by his demands, as his suicidal threats frightened her; however, they also enabled her to act out her unhealthy symbiotic need for her son. The father, older and now somewhat enfeebled, felt impotent and helpless. The son desired no treatment. He had managed to fashion a compromise that at once fed his destructiveness and hid his fear of not being able to function adequately in the world. Furthermore, he was now able to take his father's place with his mother—an Oedipal victory.

"The whole self becomes temporarily identified with the destructive self, which aims to triumph over life and creativity represented by the parents and the analyst by destroying the dependent libidinal self experienced as the child" (Rosenfeld, p. 173). Mr. G. felt forever condemned by his hostility and the damage he created and could see no way out of the cycle he had desired and created, particularly because his parents were reinforcing his drama.

Perversity in the Transference

People with perverse personality disorders often create perverse transference relationships and with them perverse transference/countertransference struggles emerge. They greatly fear whole object relationships, as these raise the possibility of emptiness, pain, separation, dependency, and unmanageable envy. As such, the therapist is often treated as a "part-object," who is designed to provide pleasure and satisfaction to the patient. Part-objects are formed by excessive deprivation and harshness with the patient's early life. Having internalized the horror of their treatment, the present day patient transmits that sense of terror to the therapist; in effect, subtly threatening the therapist to maintain a part-object tie and provide gratification rather than insight. Therefore great pressure is placed on the therapist to engage in activities, subtle and overt, that undermine the treatment just as the patient's early relationships were subverted from growth producing to that which provided inappropriate parental pleasure. One common manifestation of this is the attempted creation of an exciting and presumably sexually stimulating relationship.

Perversity develops in response to early traumatic experiences; indeed, Stoller (1975) has suggested that perversions represent a triumph over past indignities. To people with a perverse personality organization, every relationship–including the therapeutic one–is a possible humiliation and degradation. Consequently, every relationship offers the temptation to humiliate and degrade preemptively as a defense. Only two positions are imaginable: victim or victimizer. The possibility that two people might be working toward a mutually beneficial goal is alien to the patient with a perverse personality organization.

The perverse relationship also defends against the terrors of abandonment and emotional disconnection. Carnigan (1999) states, "Perverse transference enactments were often surreptitious, and picked up initially or mainly through countertransference feelings of malaise, a sense of being deceived, provoked, manipulated into playing a role, or a measure of induced excitement" (p. 925). Ogden (1996b) suggests that people with this personality constellation are trying to animate a relationship that they fear is dead and empty.

I think it is essential that the therapist help the patient become aware of these externalizations. Perverse dynamics are acted out and not verbalized so it is the therapist who must give voice to them, and the therapist's countertransference responses provide crucial data from which to inform the patient.

For instance, a patient told me about a sexual encounter in such detail that it was clear that she was trying to arouse me. My discomfort made me aware that this kind of eroticization was distracting us from the essentially empty nature of the relationship she was describing, in which she was being exploited. Her attempt to exploit me and our relationship for anti-therapeutic purposes helped keep her from the awareness of the emptiness of her relationship with the other man and of her envy of the full and meaningful relationship that she imagined I enjoyed with my wife. In her fantasies she could turn a defeat into a triumph by inducing in me envy of her romantic relationship. As I helped her understand the motivation for her involvement with this man, along with her need to try to arouse me, she became able to understand and appreciate the disavowed emptiness, the fear of deadness, and the malignant envy. This, in turn, allowed her to return her externalized idealization of me to its rightful owner and make a more realistic appraisal of herself and her abilities. Mourning the lost grandiose self enabled her to move on with her life and find partners that are more loving, genuine, and giving.

SADOMASOCHISM

Sadomasochism is a pathological solution to a feeling of endangerment. It is both a type of behavior and a state of mind. Some people have been hurtfully impinged upon by their parents and treated in demeaning and dismissive ways. This has been their way of life; sadomasochism is their language and they know no other. It is the clinician's task to introduce alternative ways of thinking, behaving, and understanding to a patient who is very fearful of many things. I will be concentrating in this section not specifically on sadomasochistic sexual behavior but on sadomasochistic psychic solutions.

Stolorow (1975) suggests, "The inference to be drawn, then, is that masochistic activities, as one of their multiple functions, may serve as abortive efforts to restore, repair, buttress and sustain a self-representation that had been damaged and rendered precarious by injurious experiences during the pre-Oedipal era, when the self-representation is most vulnerable" (p. 442). The patient, fearing dissolution of identity and the dread of emptiness, moves toward painful relationships as a way of feeling vital, alive, and real. The sense of identity is so fragile in these individuals that real intimacy results in a fear of loss of self. Consequently, painful relationships—and physical pain—solidify the sense of separateness. Pain establishes the boundary between self and other, creating the temporary illusion of self-sufficiency and competence.

Internalized Sadomasochism

People raised in sadomasochistic environments become modern renditions of their early family relationships. Beaten and demeaned as children, they reenact this experience with their own children and in other relationships. This includes the relationship of psychotherapy, which becomes a venue for struggles over domination and submission. The need to maintain an identification with early family imagoes is particularly intense when real security within the family is not possible; the object relationship is maintained through the painful tie (Grossman 1991).

Sadomasochistic behaviors and personality attributes serve many masters. Like all psychic structures, they have adaptive and problem-solving purposes. Work with sadomasochistic patients requires constant attention to underlying motivation so that the dynamics of the sadomasochistic processes at any given moment can be elucidated. The connection between hostility and pleasure is usually firmly established and well entrenched, and it creates particularly tenacious defenses. As in the related constellations I have been describing, the transference/countertransference pressures toward enactment can provide crucial information in situations where verbalization is limited or unavailable.

Sadomasochism may develop out of a number of different family constellations, but in all of them the family has not established a secure stimulus barrier that protects the child from traumatic impingements, either catastrophic or cumulative.

In some families, for example, there is an imposition of premature eroticism. No firm generational boundaries exist, and everyday activities are tinged with sadomasochistic eroticism. Typically, the parents have not appropriately combined sexuality and aggression. Each is used in the service of the other, confusing the child as pleasure becomes associated with pain and vice versa. A traumatized child may eroticize the experience to create some pleasure out of an unbearably *un*pleasant situation.

In some cases genuine pleasure and satisfaction are actively discouraged. The normal bodily experiences that serve as the background and foundation for later more sophisticated pleasurable experiences may be absent, condemned, or contaminated by aggression; the child must create satisfaction out of nonhedonistic pursuits. "Masochism is the active pursuit of psychic or physical pain, suffering, or humiliation in the service of adaptation, defense, and instinctual gratification at oral, anal, and phallic levels" (Novick and Novick, 1996, p. 46).

Primal scene fantasies are another prime source of sadomasochistic development. It has been established that children imagine parental intercourse to be sadistic (Novick and Novick, 1996) and cannibalistic. In healthy families the genuine affection between the parents softens such fearsome fantasies until the child becomes able to incorporate a notion of intercourse in which hostility and sadism are seen in context; the sexual act is comprehended as not solely aggressive but infused as well with eroticism and pleasure. In less healthy families, however, the ambient level of hostility reinforces the notion of brutal sex. As a model for interaction, the primal scene creates fear of sexuality and interpersonal involvement in general. Children may avoid relationships, inhibit aggression out of fear, or become highly aggressive and sadistic as a counterphobic defense against terrifying fantasies. As adults men may depend on an exaggerated view of imagined sexual prowess (sometimes to the point of sexual violence), believing that this protects them from danger; contrarily, they may become impotent, fearing their own violence and/or that of the devouring vagina. Women may respond to the same dynamic with reaction formation, by becoming pseudosexually seductive—an attempt to bolster them in the face of their terror—or they may become sexually inhibited or even on occasion fashion themselves as predator.

Even hurt and violated children use their relationships for ego-structuring purposes. But under those circumstances object ties become known and maintained through pain and rejection; that is, pain is a source of satisfaction (Novick and Novick, 1996). The patient in the transference doesn't believe that the analyst desires a healthy resolution of problems but that the analyst, like everyone else in the patient's psychic experience and apparatus, wishes to inflict pain and suffering. For this reason too the patient resists success, believing that it undermines the desperately clung-to therapeutic relationship as the patient envisions it—that is, based upon failure and punishment. The patient craves for the therapist to disapprove, to beat, to denigrate.

I had a patient who sometimes got angry with me over a missed session or a difference in perspective. Rather than working collaboratively toward an understanding and resolution of the conflict, she wanted me to fight with her. The satisfaction that she had achieved as a child by provoking her parents into physically attacking her was the only satisfaction that she knew, and the only alternative she could imagine was to be left empty and alone in the context of her mother's affectless and preoccupied state and her father's disinterest in children. She got some attention from, and was enlivened by, the fights that she provoked.

Sadomasochism and Pleasure

Because the usual sources of pleasure are lacking, the child in this kind of family lacks the kind of hedonic self that can be based in affirming ways on satisfaction (Krystal, 1978). Families that value self-denial and abstinence over pleasurable activities discourage healthy eroticism. The therapist must proceed gingerly in such cases because the encouragement of behaviors that are affirming and pleasurable may be perceived as encouraging the violation of moral standards. Patients may comfort themselves with the heroism of their self-denial and view any suggestion that they become "ordinary" in their desires with derision. The moral superiority of suffering brings great satisfaction to the sadomasochist, who whenever possible turns defeat into victory. A situation that is fraught with unhappiness and violence and ruled by stultifying or destructive parents becomes an opportunity for imagined heroic denial of self and of needs. Thus, the sadomasochist transforms physical abuse and psychic hurt into pleasurable successes and derides those who cannot do likewise. "Pain is the affect which triggers the defense of omnipotence, pain is the magical means by which all wishes are gratified, and pain justifies the omnipotent hostility and revenge contained in the masochistic fantasy" (Novick and Novick, 1996, p.64).

Sadomasochism-engendering parents are often so profoundly depleted in themselves that their children fear to ask much from them. "Consequently, the self is regarded as ruthless, omnipotently destructive, and as having robbed and depleted the parent of vitality. A parasitic view of human interaction develops; experiences of pleasurable mutuality are alien" (Markson, 1993, p. 932).

Patients with these negative, lifeless dynamics are often mistakenly thought depressed. Certainly, they do present with a downcast and defeated demeanor and without a doubt their words suggest a depressive disorder. Less than an awareness of deep sadness or loss, however, these disaffected patients tend to feel empty and lost themselves. They are not suffering from an affective disorder; rather, they suffer from not being able to *not* suffer. Suffering is valued. It feels wrong not to suffer. Their "depression" is not motivated by guilt; on the contrary, guilt is what happens when they are *not* depressed. In treatment this process needs to be identified, because a negative therapeutic reaction will quickly become established and time and energy will be deflected into a misguided effort to alleviate the patient's discontent. Awareness that the discontent is *valued* directs patient and therapist to consider the need to suffer and its antecedents.

Sadomasochism and Countertransference

Because of the exploitative nature of sadomasochistic processes those with a primary sadomasochistic bent can evoke strong countertransferential reactions. They inevitably feel hurt within the therapeutic relationship, and they strike out against the therapist in ways both large and small. It is not always easy to tolerate these provocations without wishing to retaliate.

Furthermore, therapists often feel impatient with the tenacity of these disorders. Treatment can last for years and years (Novick and Novick, 1996)—not always an advantage to a therapist who is constantly being assaulted by the patient for his endless misdeeds. Yet treatment is often the patient's last chance to fashion some real satisfaction out of life, and it is essential that the therapist maintain realistic hope in the face of the patient's destructiveness and hopelessness.

Mr. M., described in chapter II, was a thirty-five-year-old auto executive who presented with depression and psychosomatic complaints. He had been put on antidepressants by his family physician, so I referred him to a psychiatrist for continued care. He insisted that he was receiving no help from the medication, and the psychiatrist tried him on eight different ones despite my suggestion that the patient's need to suffer would not allow him to perceive any benefit from medication however "successful" it might be in the abstract. Eventually the doctor gave up, and the patient devoted his energy to the psychotherapy. He progressed, felt less anxious and depressed, and no longer woke up in a panic. His relationship with his family improved, and he was able to adjust to some downturns in his career. Nevertheless, he continued to complain that he had made no progress in treatment. I would gently point out the contrary position and wonder why he had such difficulty in recognizing his improvement.

He complained similarly to his family about his depression until they were sick of hearing about it, which allowed him to express his outrage over various other hurts without seeming to do so.

Over a considerable period of time, we came to the conclusion that to admit to success in treatment would mean that I was a success, which he did not want to acknowledge. Envy of my abilities and potency increased his sense of inadequacy. In a crucial way, he really did not want to feel better. He maintained a secret (even to himself) pleasure over such maneuvers as the thwarting of my therapeutic zeal and the constant scolding of his family.

He had been raised in a joyless household where his mother pressured him to be a "good boy"—that is, duty-bound and without pleasure. He had issues about his adequacy as a male, and the hidden victory of thwarting me (even though it thwarted him as well) increased his sense of competence. He portrayed himself as incompetent in relation to others but without conviction. Similarly, he spoke about what an "evil" person he was but without any apparent affect and with no consequent changes in his behavior.

Progress in treatment was slow, but he did progress despite himself. Constant attention to the identification of hidden satisfactions like the two I have described created a greater sense of adequacy. He began, for instance, to take pride in his ability to fight back against his (perceived as) domineering wife. Eventually, he was able to recognize how he had diminished his own sense of competence by secretly idealizing me. All of these gains resulted in increased ego strength, which enabled him to feel less secretive and reclusive. He began to understand that he could express competitive and angry feelings toward me directly without being endangered.

Mrs. B., a computer programmer, exemplified a number of these hidden sadomasochistic qualities. One was that she was, as she put it, a "quid pro quo" kind of person. Any hurt that she experienced required a response in kind. If I hurt her, as I naturally often did, she paid me back surreptitiously. This same dynamic appeared in her relationship with her husband, a "quid pro quo" kind of person himself, who then retaliated himself, escalating terrible arguments in which ferocious accusations flew back and forth. Her interest in showing me what a fine person she was kept her from expressing these vengeful feelings overtly; nevertheless, I was often treated to silent withdrawals and distancing. She felt particularly frustrated with me for not automatically knowing what she was thinking or feeling. She resented having to tell me, expecting me to be as omnipotent as she felt herself to be.

Mrs. B.'s mother had seemed joyless to her as a child; she also had a sadistic and hurtful bent. When the patient transgressed the mother responded hatefully, with withdrawal accompanied by nasty and sarcastic comments. The patient developed a false compliant self, hiding her vengeful and other lively qualities from herself and others. She recounted one story of having been scolded for wanting to go shopping with her friends instead of attending a family function, and then taking a cooking pan and hitting herself over the head repeatedly. She gained victory by being more punitive than her mother.

Overt masochistic behavior like this still offered her some relief, and this led to a paucity of relationships because she was afraid of her aggression. She developed an aura of self-sufficiency that was really a way of eliminating any hostile envy toward others.

This patient responded well to elucidation of her secret hostility, which eventually empowered her to assert herself in more reasonable ways. Understanding her vengeful and sadistic fantasies freed her from having to act upon them and allowed her a wider range of ways to express herself. Additionally, helping her understand the degree of hurt and devastation that she experienced in our relationship enabled her to direct her anger toward me directly instead of displacing it elsewhere, as upon her husband. Awareness of the acuity of her sense of narcissistic injury helped her mourn the loss of the idealized mother and of the omnipotent self, healing past wounds and allowing her to establish more gratifying relationships in the present.

TREATMENT CONSIDERATIONS

My focus in this chapter is not frankly perverse or sadomasochistic sexual behavior. I want to show instead that these disorders in their less overt forms are much more widespread than is commonly recognized. Many

patients have underlying narcissistic issues that are never addressed because they are not perceived. Once they *are* identified, however, it becomes possible to focus on helping the patient understand the narcissistic
injuries and the resulting rageful responses and making sense out of their
present-day renditions in the transference and in the patient's life. Unlike
other serious disorders of developmental deficit, people with narcissistic
personality organizations often do have sufficient stability of personality
that they can tolerate interpretations of hidden motives. They need to
understand the whole complex of personality characteristics that become
involved in sadomasochistic and perverse solutions. To look at the adaptive power of these behaviors is a nonpejorative stance that rings true
and is palatable to the patient.

Patients with anarchic, perverse, and sadomasochistic propensities all struggle with a damaged sense of potency. They tend to use vertical splits (see chapter IV) to maintain belief systems that have taken on
the power of fact or knowledge (Britton, 1995). These beliefs are not
always directly available to the patient or to the analyst for scrutiny because they operate pre- or unconsciously. But working in the implicit
arena of character, as I have said, requires careful attention to the countertransference, and this is exactly the kind of attention that can provide
crucial information as to these belief systems. The pressure on the analyst to conform to the patient's dynamic system can be intense and is
a clear signal that an enactment is being activated. Irritation with the
patient and the desire to say or do hurtful things are all ind'cations
of a sadomasochistic enactment. These patients need to deny certain
aspects of reality in an urgent way that is hard for them to articulate,
yet the subtleties of these disavowals must be addressed if the split-off
parts are to be re-owned and integrated. This can happen only if the
therapist stays exquisitely sensitive to the hurts engendered within the
relationship and repeatedly makes the connection between them and
the grandiose and omnipotent solutions offered by anarchy, perversity,
and sadomasochism.

VII

◆

AMBIVALENCE

◆

The capacity for ambivalence is a major accomplishment, reflecting as it does a whole as opposed to part-object engagement in relationships, and the ability of an integrated personality to contain contradictory affects. On its face this may seem paradoxical, as the possession of two opposing feelings appears to show a *lack* of integration. Yet all relationships contain elements of conflicting emotions (Freud, 1917b), and an individual who cannot contain them all is doomed to relationships that do not do justice to the complexity of human interaction. Healthy ambivalence is the ability to maintain apparently contradictory affects in a relatively nondefensive way. This differs from those prone toward anarchic and perverse defenses because these pathological characteristics are designed to alter reality wishfully, not to accept conflicting emotions inherent in human interactions.

As it is popularly used, the term *ambivalence* suggests mixed feelings and often connotes indecision. Yet ambivalence does not in fact reflect indecision, but rather the simultaneous existence of two or more contradictory feelings. The attainment of ambivalence is what allows us to consider opposing viewpoints and wishes, and then make a responsible decision with the potential to maximize satisfaction. The dialectical stance that is often the most creative alternative to conflict can be attained only when a number of different points of view can be simultaneously identified and addressed.

Perhaps a brief review of the pertinent literature will help set the landscape. Abraham commented that "Freud has made the very significant observation that the serious conflict of ambivalent feelings from which the melancholiac suffers is absent in the normal person" (1924, p. 435). I disagree with this, believing as I do that conflicts over ambivalent feelings exist in everyone, normal or "melancholiac." *Problems* exist, however, not because contradictory feelings are present, not when conflictual feelings are present but when a *conflict* is experienced *over* their *existence*. As Holder (1975) says, "It is of some clinical importance to distinguish between those individuals who are capable of tolerating the coexistence of ambivalent feelings without being neurotically conflicted about them and those individuals who do experience conflict over their ambivalent feelings and are capable only of finding pathological solutions to it. . . . It might be a useful diagnostic pointer to assess not only a child's frustration tolerance but also his *ambivalence tolerance*" (p. 209). Parker comments similarly, "Ambivalence itself is emphatically not the problem; the issue is how a mother manages the guilt and anxiety that ambivalence provokes. Hence I will speak of manageable and unmanageable ambivalence" (Parker, 1995, p. 6). Any realm of human endeavor is subject to ambivalence.

Freud (1917a) introduced the concept of ambivalence in relation to the development of melancholia. Abraham (1924) describes Freud's discovery well. "He showed that the patient, after having lost his love-object, regains it once more by a process of introjection (so that, for instance, the self-reproaches of a melancholiac are really directed towards his lost object)" (p. 419). The patient doesn't suffer because of mixed feelings per se, but because of discomfort over *hostile* feelings. Freud speaks of ambivalence throughout his writings, and it gains special prominence in his description of the formation and resolution of the Oedipal conflict.

Abraham (1924) goes on to describe the oral and anal phases, each of which consists of two stages. The primary oral stage is preambivalent. "Within the first—the oral—period, the child exchanges its preambivalent libidinal attitude, which is free from conflict, for one which is ambivalent and preponderantly hostile toward its object" (p. 453). This first stage represents a desire to incorporate the object, and because there is still little differentiation between self and object, the object is not subject to destruction; hence there is no ambivalence. The second stage of the oral phase represents a desire to bite, and thus the desire to incorporate is accompanied by ideas of consumption and destruction. This is an ambivalent attitude. Similarly, says Abraham, two stages exist in the anal phase: The first is the desire to contain and control; the second the desire to expel and destroy. He is postulating an inherent ambivalent state for all infants, that is, by consequence not pathological.

These processes may *become* pathological under a variety of conditions, some constitutional or biological, relating to physical ailments, and others perhaps relating to extended disappointments. As I have said, it is not the fact of ambivalence itself that is problematic; it is when hostility predominates in a relationship that there may be difficulty in accepting contradictory feelings. Parents' ambivalence does not necessarily damage their children; it is a normal occurrence. Children do, however, suffer in relationships when parental hostility, and then through internalization, their own hostility, overwhelms other more affectionate feelings. Parents who can tolerate mixed feelings can help their children accept, and accommodate reasonably to, their own hostility.

INTEGRATION OF "GOOD" AND "BAD"

As therapists trying to help patients accept their conflicted and imperfect selves, we must be attuned to how contradictory affective states co-exist. All of us must come to grips with qualities within ourselves that we find uncomfortable and less than desirable, as well as the ones that we tolerate, accept, or even admire. How this accommodation occurs in individual people is based on the flexibility and fluidity of their psychological functioning, The therapist needs to be attuned to the specific way any given patient deals with competing or contradictory affects.

Melanie Klein, who first described splitting as a mental process, provides a valuable perspective on ambivalence. She places great emphasis on the inborn aggressive instinct, but she also elucidates how the internal sense of "badness" may be altered through experience. Through an accumulation of benign experiences, the infant gradually builds up a positive sense of self and becomes able to integrate contradictory feelings of goodness and badness (with regard to both self and object). Klein (1940) states, "Not until early anxieties have been sufficiently relieved owing to experiences which increase love and trust, is it possible to establish the all-important process of bringing together more closely the various aspects of objects (external, internal, 'good' and 'bad,' love and hated), and thus for hatred to become actually *mitigated by love*–which means a decrease in ambivalence" (p. 349, emphasis added). "When in the course of normal development a balance between love and hate is attained, and the various aspects of objects are more unified, then also a certain equilibrium between these contrasting and yet closely related methods is reached, and their intensity is diminished" (p. 350).

Winnicott (1963) also speaks of the importance of the fusion of love and aggression. "This is the achievement of emotional development in which the baby experiences erotic and aggressive drives toward the same object at the same time. On the erotic side there is both satisfaction-seeking and object-seeking, and on the aggressive side, there is a complex of anger employing muscle erotism, and of hate, which involves the retention of a very good object-imago for comparison. . . . Ambivalence has been reached" (pp. 74–75). The mother needs to tolerate her own ambivalence, allowing without retaliating the infant to use her "ruthlessly." Tolerance of ambivalence is internalized through identification with the tolerant mother and enables the child to develop a certainty of self and a certainty of how Erikson (1963) described basic trust. It allows the baby to incorporate a sense of concern and regard for the mother even in the presence of hostile feelings, and by generalization, for self and for others.

SPLITTING

Splitting or the lack of ambivalence tolerance can have deleterious results, and in the following I would like to describe these in more detail. Accumulated aggressive feelings must be mitigated by loving feelings in order for these contradictory experiences to be integrated. In treatment, first patients must be able to give full vent to their rage and their loving feelings without initial interpretation in order for this mitigation process to occur. Interpretation, essential as it is in treatment, should be used to provide explanations of material that is not understood, but only after the patient has experienced the full extent of the feelings that have been defended against. Too early interpretation prevents the full expression of affect, reinforcing defensiveness. Furthermore, therapists' own discomfort with intense affects may make them reluctant to address their patient's strong transferential feelings, and countertransference reluctance to tolerate the patient's raw rage also may drive it underground, creating severe distress for the patient and sometimes resulting in an unresolved negative transference and consequent early termination.

At times, patients may deny or suppress critical or angry feelings out of a need to protect their internal and external (i.e., the therapist) objects from destruction by their rage. One of the ways this can be accomplished is for the patient to maintain "ownership" of the critical feelings and project the more positive ones onto the therapist. Idealization results, as the patient has projected all worthy attributes onto the therapist, increasing the therapist's perceived worth, and now feels left with a preponderance of "bad" aspects. This process may lead to an iatrogenic increase in depression. It may be difficult to perceive because of the pleasure that the therapist obtains from the idealization and leaves the therapist feeling better while the patient feels worse.

When percepts are split into "good" and "bad" components, however, and an idealization-disparagement paradigm results, eventually the internalized "bad" feelings become intolerable to the patient and are projected onto the therapist. I have certainly experienced situations–very perplexing and disturbing ones–where I am suddenly seen as the source of all of the patient's unhappiness in life. The patient's rage and disillusionment are profound, which fuels still more depression and despair as the feelings are re-introjected. This process can sometimes be avoided if the therapist is constantly on the alert for the overidealization that obscures negatively tinged transference affects.

Erotic transference feelings can be both gratifying and uncomfortable. Some patients who manifest intense erotized feelings toward their therapists are, in truth, working through unmodulated but disguised rageful feelings. This may confuse the therapeutic pair into searching for hidden libidinal sources instead of the true obscured anger. Countertransference feelings of discomfort and therapist irritation can be good indicators of the underlying affect. When the patient is creating distress for both, it is likely that hostile feelings–even disguised as sexual ones–are exerting considerable influence.

A patient may also project a sense of badness onto the environment, and as a result may feel persecuted. The psychic roots of this feeling may be quite subtle, and the therapist may come to believe wholeheartedly in the patient's stories of being poorly treated. Sometimes the therapist is accused of being condemnatory and persecutory–and may well be feeling that way in the countertransference, along with considerable internal pressure not to bring up areas of the patient's behavior that may rouse his or her ire. Such projective identifications provide information about the persecutory nature of the patient's internal objects.

Patients who excoriate their spouses while disavowing any responsibility for the problems in the marriage are usually operating out of an unintegrated unambivalent state that prevents any constructive examination of their own sense of badness, which is instead externalized. If the externalization process remains unanalyzed, the vested interest in maintaining innocence at all costs remains untouched, with the result that real-life problems are not likely to be resolved. It is a vicious perpetual cycle, as the need to feel perfect must be protected with more and more vigor as "bad" experiences pile up.

THE EROTICIZED TRANSFERENCE
AS PART-OBJECT RELATEDNESS

Some patients idealize their therapists and develop an intense, eroticized transference. Those who do so are doing so in order to maintain the part-object relationship to which they have become accustomed. As children, patients prone toward eroticization have themselves been treated more as possessions than as separate individuals. Any abuse that occurred within these families became eroticized as a defense. Consequently, in treatment, positive and affectionate feelings do not seem that way; they feel hostile and acquisitive. Any hostility is not expressed directly but comes across through intense sexual feelings that feel more hostile and sado-masochistic than erotic.

Within these eroticized transferences, therapist and patient, at least in the patient's mind, are allied against the world, in a semblance of the early fantasized all-gratifying mother-infant bond. Unfortunate spouses are unfavorably compared with the therapist, and marriages have been known to fail when this dynamic is left unanalyzed. Such an apparently "unambivalent" relationship discourages the development of a realistic sense of self, as it supports the belief that self-esteem can only be based upon this kind of illusory, symbiotic relationship (Chasseguet-Smirgel, 1988). Real aspects of the professional relationship are ignored and disavowed. Negative feelings toward the therapist are projected outwardly, sometimes with such vehemence that one is reminded of projectile vomiting. Patients may become involved in terrible displaced altercations as denied hostility toward the therapist is projected onto others in order to maintain an "all-good" relationship. If this process goes unchallenged, however, the hostility eventually comes home to roost, resulting in tre-

mendous disillusionment in the therapist and a virtual certainty of atten-
dant rage and depression.

Although it is usual within the Kleinian schema to think of the
persecutory aspect of "bad" internalized objects, it is important to remember that "good" internal objects can be equally tyrannical. The young
child is not able to modulate aggression (this is true of some patients as
well), and thus must keep internal bad and good objects separated, lest
the good become contaminated. "As I have mentioned before, the ego
endeavours to keep the good apart from the bad, and the real from the
phantastic object. The result is a conception of extremely bad and *extremely perfect* objects, that is to say, its loved objects are in many ways
intensely moral and exacting. At the same time, as the infant cannot fully
keep his good and bad objects apart in his mind, some of the cruelty of
the bad objects and of the id becomes attached to the good objects and
this then again increases the severity of their demands" (Klein, 1935,
p. 268). The intense self-punitiveness seen in some patients does not
reflect only hidden guilty feelings over bad behavior or thoughts, but
may represent instead a structural problem such that no "badness" at
all can be tolerated for fear of this contamination. The patient feels
the intolerable pressure to live up to unrealistic expectations of perpetual
"goodness."

This lack of integration must be addressed prior to fruitful analysis of the *content* of feelings and behavior. An acting-out dynamic often
will be seen where patients use self-destructive behavior paradoxically—
they confirm their "badness" in order to protect their hidden, split off
"goodness." People need to be able to understand and tolerate imperfec-
tion. Internalization of the more benign aspects of the therapist, of a more
realistic notion of what constitutes "goodness," is essential. Helping the
patient to deidealize the therapist moves the patient toward a
reinternalization of the disowned "good" self and results in a lessening of
despair and of acting out behavior.

AMBIVALENCE AND HOSTILITY

"Thus the shadow of the object fell upon the ego, and the latter could
henceforth be judged by a special agency, as though it were an object,
the forsaken object. In this way an object-loss was transformed into an
ego-loss and the conflict between the ego and the loved person into a

cleavage between the critical activity of the ego and the ego as altered by identification" (Freud, 1917a, p. 249).

The loss Freud describes can refer to any aspect of a relationship, not only the relationship as a whole or the actual physical loss of the person. This wonderfully evocative passage gives full weight to the problem of accepting ambivalent feelings in the context of uncomfortable or unacceptable aggression. It appears to the child that under adverse circumstances the love and affection expected from the parent is lost. The loss of the beloved parent imago does not destroy the identification with the once-beloved parent, but that parent is now resented for the perceived abandonment. This loss of the object (loving parental imago) results in internalization of the child's hostility toward the parent which transforms a sense of loss into negative self structure ("object loss . . . transformed into an ego loss"). The anger and disappointment are internalized and can be reified into an internal self-hating representational structure.

As we know, we all must contend with less than perfect parents who, in a variety of tolerable ways, abandon and disappoint us. For some, however, the abandonment and disappointment have lasting deleterious effects. As an example, consider the patient I described in chapter V who suffered an early loss through his mother's intense depression and who later developed an intense negative transference. The absence of his mother created a severe depression, but the patient developed as well a sense of self-loathing, based in part upon an internalization of anger toward his mother that had become part of his ego structure. An object loss (his mother's ability to be a warm, nurturing presence) became an ego loss (self-loathing). This type of process may give rise to a variety of disorders, depending on the degree and nature of the trauma. Again, it is not ambivalence that creates the problem, but ambivalence contaminated by too much hostility.

Consider another example.

Ms. D. was a very bright young woman and a perpetual underachiever. She worked on a factory floor assembling auto components and was bored and listless, finding little to engage her interest in her job. As we discussed her situation and her family, it became apparent that she could not maintain, in her mind, the possibility that she could remain connected with her perpetually depressed and dissatisfied mother while pursuing more intriguing career options. As a child, she had been discouraged from independent thought and action, and had been encouraged to take care of her mother. Consciously she experienced herself as incompetent and capable only of menial tasks. She had never considered college or a move away from her family. As we talked, it became apparent that she was afraid of her conflicted feelings toward her family and denied them by convincing herself of her ineptitude. Becoming aware of her anger was liberating for her and enabled her to begin to look at options for herself. The pull toward the family was intense, and much more work on loyalty issues, competitive conflicts, and identity concerns was required before she could deal with it; even the simple awareness of her defended-against anger enabled her to begin to think differently about herself and about her life.

This young woman had had an ineffectual father. The absence of a strong paternal influence deprived her of a model for maintaining perspectives that differed from those of her mother. It also weakened the triangular Oedipal conflict that might have moved her beyond a two-person symbiotic perspective and helped her learn to tolerate independent thought and a separate identity. Her inability to maintain a viewpoint of her own prevented my patient from considering other options in life. Her one-dimensional perspective was a wholesale incorporation of her mother's view of things. What her mother felt about her we don't know, but we speculated that she herself could not tolerate her own ambivalence toward her daughter. Perhaps she could not manage the loving and hating feelings in a healthy way that would allow her to withstand separation without acting upon her wishes to control and dominate.

All parents have contradictory feelings toward their children. Even before a child is born, the parents develop fantasies about the child and their lives together. These are inevitably doomed to disappoint. The parents must be able to tolerate the disappointment of the failed fantasy in order to permit the development of a healthy relationship such that the child feels free to pursue healthy ambitions. A parent whose disappointment is too great resents the child and the child's independence, and acts out this resentment in destructive ways. When children feel that their life is owned by their parents, they often go on to unsatisfying and futile lives. Their failure to please the parent is perpetual and without possible solution. They forever search for parent substitutes or for imagined situations that they believe can satisfy the internalized imagoes. As rooted in childhood, these are, of course, doomed to fail. Their lives become dominated by this wish to please; their lives become devoted to their parents without the necessary separation and individuation that leads toward healthy and productive lives.

The patient described in chapter III, Ms. J., believed that if she were only to become perfect she would please her mother. She failed to realize that her mother had never been particularly interested in whether her daughter was perfect or not. Aggression, unmitigated by sufficient love, held sway in her. This mother seemed more interested in hurting the child than in the meeting of (seemingly impossible) goals. The patient was caught in a terrible bind—she always failed, in that she never pleased her mother; yet she succeeded by failing, because her mother seemed to enjoy her pain. This unhappy dilemma gave rise to suicidal feelings and self-destructiveness.

This patient's growing recognition of her mother's essential hostility toward her eventually alleviated her intolerable despair. Mrs. J.'s recognition that it was impossible to please her mother enabled her to recognize the negation of her own self-love and helped her to a more realistic perception of herself that contained positive self-attributions as well as negative ones. Her mother's lack of healthy ambivalence had prevented the patient from feeling that way—that is, ambivalent—toward herself. She could not tolerate any imperfections, as they activated a sense of self-hate. As her therapist, I often felt a pressure not to point to any "culpability" because of the patient's intense self-loathing. As she internalized a more realistic self-appraisal, I felt that I could introduce conflict-derived interpretations and that these could be heard and tolerated.

Another patient had never as a child been taken to the doctor or dentist. Her mother's belief in a symbiotic omnipotence that could provide for all of her daughter's needs eventuated in the daughter's contracting the polio virus. Although she recovered, she developed "post polio syndrome" as an adult. A major accomplishment of the treatment was that the patient ultimately learned to care for herself. This represented a resolution of her own underlying omnipotent fantasies, which also served to maintain a tie with the very early symbiotic mother. Although (consciously) mercilessly critical of her mother, her poor caretaking of herself indicated an unconscious identification with the early omnipotent mother-child dyad that effectively obliterated the ambivalent feelings necessary for healthy growth and development.

AMBIVALENCE, ATTACHMENT, AND SEPARATION

Separation issues also have great potential for conflicts over ambivalence. Children and parents have to negotiate attachment and separation. Parents who use their children as narcissistic extensions lack the security to let their children live their own lives. The need to hold too tightly is tantamount to a hostile attachment, as it denies the child the right to independence and autonomy.

Of course, these issues are extremely complex, and parents achieve the necessary compromise between attachment and separation with varying degrees of success. As Winnicott points out, parents need not be perfect, only "good enough." Good enough in this regard means being aware of their own ambivalent needs both to hold and to let go, and neither letting go too soon nor holding on too long. This dynamic is germane to the treatment process; one therapist's need to be needed may create an interminable, stultifying treatment, while another's fear of closeness may result in an arid one that ends, perhaps, prematurely. In the former situation, the therapist's own insecure attachment is being actualized in the treatment. In the latter, the therapist's hidden sense of depletion creates an abhorrence of closeness, as a defense against the intense desire for closeness, because closeness can represent a fear of being drained by the patient's needs and can also awaken painful feelings of loss, neglect, and abandonment. All countertransference issues are subtle as are these and are rarely available to the therapist for self-analysis.

The developmental deficits of neglect and trauma prevent the development of an integrated sense of self and other, and the heavy burden of too much internalized aggression narrows the viewpoint of those who bear it.

A young salesman sought treatment for unremitting depression and a general sense of ennui. He had had a perfectionistic father who was prone to violent outbursts; his view was always correct, he insisted, and could never be questioned. The patient grew, not surprisingly, into a version of his father. His view too (which he focused on religion) must be always correct. He tolerated no opposition and insisted that any viewpoint other than his own was "liberal" and "wishy-washy." He could not see that his belief system was essentially the same as his father's. His inability to integrate his own imperfections caused him to project them onto the world in a black-and-white fashion. He was judgmental in relationships, and before he made some gains in treatment he had suffered from psychosomatic problems that seemed to demonstrate how unable he was to use thoughts to deal with conflicts. For him, ambivalence represented weakness, in contrast with his idealized image of strong (that is, absolutist) belief.

As I mentioned in chapter IV, Freud (1925) suggested that negation helps people discriminate among various aspects of perception and that this in turn facilitates the development of judgment. Reciprocally, too much aggression interferes with the establishment of careful consideration, both because so much of the individual's energy is taken up by defense against it and because alternatives are not allowed to enter into thought. Aggression does not lend itself to fluidity of thought and flexibility. One who is angry or enraged is limited in ability to use thought in careful consideration of possible alternatives. A child who is taught to not consider alternatives is at a real disadvantage when confronted by the mysteries of life. Children identify with their parents' ways of apprehending the world, and parents who cannot tolerate ambivalence in themselves do not tolerate it well in their children, either. This intolerance is internalized and becomes an integral aspect of the child's way of functioning, but at the cost of a stunted ability to comprehend the complexities of the world, of thoughts, and of emotions. Unhealthy ambivalence results when a person cannot make up his or her mind about someone (or something) *because of unresolved conflict*. This leads to a paralysis of action and thought, and a flatness and staleness of experience. Healthy ambivalence does not reflect indecision, but the ability to consider options and possibilities and develop dialectical solutions. This is a very useful capacity in navigating the rigors of life.

ALEXITHYMIA AND FRAGMENTATION

In thinking about ambivalent symptomatology, it is important to differentiate between obsessive-compulsive disorders and more schizoid and fragmented states.

It is widely believed among psychodynamic psychotherapists that obsessive-compulsive patients defend against awareness of anal-sadistic desires and that their characteristic indecision obscures preoccupations with potentially aggressive, unmodulated, or "messy" actions. There are other people with similar symptoms, however, whose apparent indecision reflects an inability to organize thoughts and feelings cohesively. These emotionally distant people find it hard to feel whole and to see others as individuals in their own right. Their indecision comes from having no firm sense of self and little connection with internal desire states and may lead to trouble in such seeming trivialities as ordering in restaurants or picking out clothes.

Some of these people suffer from what has been called *alexithymia*. Krystal (1988) has said about this condition that "The inability for self-reflective self-awareness (which enables one to identify one's "feeling" as being an appropriate response to one's self-evaluation) is typical of alexithymia. . . . Many alexithymics learn to use the common expressions denoting affective response when they think they should experience them or in situations in which they have observed others reacting emotionally. Therefore, they frequently behave like the color-blind who has learned to cover up his deficiency in perception by using a variety of clues from which to infer what he can not discern. However, they are missing a quality in their self-perception that would enliven their self-view and give it conviction and vigor" (p. 244).

Krystal describes alexithymia as a response to severe or catastrophic trauma, but it is my feeling that many people who can be described as alexithymic have histories of cumulative trauma (Khan, 1963) in their relationships with their mothers—specifically the sorts that destroy internal vitality through overwhelming externally derived stimulation. Affects become associated with pain and are avoided at all costs. The normal and natural desire for pleasure and pleasure-seeking activities shrivels out of the fear of being hurt and overwhelmed.

This kind of situation can result when parents do not establish a stimulus barrier sufficient to protect the child from harmful impingements. Parents of these children may themselves be detached, schizoid, and unattuned, resulting in "benign" neglect. Moreover, parents who cannot modulate their own aggression can neither protect the child from it nor detoxify the child's own aggression. As we have seen, overwhelming aggression impedes the development of healthy ambivalence; self- and object representation become disturbed and distorted, and cognition suffers. The capacities to maintain subjectivity and to symbolize are also affected, resulting in an increased dependency on operative thinking. "This characteristic 'operative thinking' involves a preoccupation with 'things' at the expense of object relations. The combination of impairment in the capacity for fantasy and abstract thinking, and the lack of affective clues, deprives the patient of the ability to emphasize and to be emotionally involved with significant others. This development results in a particularly 'dead' and dull transference relationship as well" (Krystal, 1988, p. 266). To one degree or another, alexithymia connotes a life lived without joy, without passion, and without even much pleasure.

When asked for preferences or for descriptions of affects, these patients may appear to be indecisive, but their problem is not indecision; it is the inability to ascertain their needs and desires. They do not experience fear of punishment should they make the "wrong" choice as some patients might. They do not understand the language of affects. One such patient of mine described his view of the world as if looking through a black-and-white prism. Another patient tried to initiate fights with me because, as she put it, "I am just trying to feel something." My work in prison settings and with seriously disturbed patients has shown me some examples of individuals who have been known to seriously hurt or kill others or themselves in order to attain some sense of being alive and meaningful.

Treatment often consists, initially at least, of helping the patient identify and own affective states. People like these are not easy to treat. They tend to re-create in the transference their fragmented internal state. Associations, and indeed the relationship itself, lacking affective referents, may seem to the therapist to be without meaning or substance. Yet learning to differentiate affects is vital for these people, who live bewildering lives without the emotional compass most of us take for granted. If this underlying personality constellation is not identified, treatment can take on an inauthentic tone that mimics the disconnectness of the patient's early life. The treatment becomes an "as-if" experience, lacking depth and meaning.

Alexithymic patients are not necessarily trying to communicate content; they are often trying to develop a way of attaching without feeling overwhelmed. Although their presentation and their self-experience often lack affective resonance, some of their defended-against affects do become manifest in the treatment, although not always in ways that are easy to conceptualize. I had one patient whose sessions, devoid of obvious emotion, felt assaultive to me. His lack of emotional connectedness felt battering, as if I were being attacked. Certainly he had no conscious awareness of any hostile intent, at least in the beginning. It was only much later, after his tremendous denied and suppressed anger had been identified, that he was able to vent his anger more directly, much to my relief.

Therapists must survive these "attacks" and manage to keep themselves "alive" while trying to find the genuine affect that underlies the layers of abstraction or fragmentation that defense or deficit has imposed. The moments when the patient can appreciate a sense of aliveness are welcomed by both participants, however brief and sporadic they are.

AMBIVALENCE AND BORDERLINE DISORDERS

Borderline patients with their propensity for splitting internal (and consequently external) objects have a lot of trouble maintaining contradictory feelings simultaneously, and therefore do not have an easy time with the accomplishment of healthy ambivalence. It is disconcerting to work with patients who can so thoroughly under the stress of splitting "forget" a long history of a warm and helpful therapeutic relationship. As in the related disorders I have addressed in this chapter, gradual experiences that facilitate integration of good and bad internal objects result in an increasing ability to deal with contradictory feelings.

TREATMENT IMPLICATIONS

In his seminal paper, "Hate in the Countertransference" (1949), Winnicott points out that a patient can know his analyst only from the perspective of his own characteristic way of thinking. "In the matter of motive: the *obsessional* will tend to be thinking of the analyst as doing his work in a futile obsessional way" (p. 195). He suggests that some patients experience a "coincident love-hate state" whereby contradictory emotions co-exist in a way such that they are not easily separated, or described independently. He points out that "[The child] does not yet appreciate the fact that what he destroys when excited is the same as that which he values in quiet intervals between excitements. His excited love includes an imaginative attack on the mother's body. *Here is aggression as a part of love*" (1950, p. 206, emphasis added). Contradictory emotions exist, but not in a coherent or stable state. Consequently, the individual has no confidence that love will continue to exist predictably. "Would it not follow that if a *psychotic* is in a 'coincident love-hate' state of feeling he experiences a deep conviction that the analyst is also only capable of the same crude and dangerous state of coincident love-hate relationship? Should the analyst show love, he will surely at the same moment kill the patient" (p. 195).

Winnicott is suggesting an "objective" countertransference where the analyst's hatred of the patient replicates what the patient experienced as a child and what he or she evokes in others in the present. To be truly helpful, the therapist must endure a number of "crude" feelings. That is, the therapist must allow the patient to give full expression to the variety of internal affective states, however acceptable or not they seem to the patient. The therapist's ability to withstand the patient's supposedly negative qualities and hostile attacks leads the patient, who introjects the therapist's nonjudgmental stance, toward self-acceptance. In this article, Winnicott is describing psychotic patients, but it is likely that these kinds of countertransference reactions exist with many patients. To deny the reality of the hatred does no good, leading as it does to a false treatment. Patients "know without knowing" that they are hated or should be and will act out that knowledge in some destructive fashion.

One patient, an investment banker, often described incidents where he had clearly taken advantage of others or otherwise showed little regard for them. I found it difficult to work with him, and his narcissism irritated me. Upon reflection, I realized that two things were particularly bothering me. One, conflicts about my own self-centered desires were being activated and reacted against. Two, countertransference was being activated by the projective identification of the patient's experiences with his mother. His need for love and affection had been treated with anger; his mother resented his existence and had not often helped him when he needed her. As an external version of his internal object representation, I was reacting to him in similar fashion. This awareness enabled me to regain my equanimity and to be nonjudgmental and more helpful. It was important for this man to realize how he impacted upon others, and yet it was clear that he was unaware of how others viewed him as self-centered and exploitative. In the treatment, I was able to use my hate experience to clarify his experience with his mother and her dynamics. As he began to understand this, he became able to look to himself and to wonder whether he had similar qualities. This enabled a reappraisal of his relationships with others, and eventually an increase in the quality of his social relationships and a decrease in my discomfort.

The gradual acknowledgement of the "hateful" aspects of self and object reduces splitting, enables mourning, and lets an individual react with others in a more realistic, and therefore more caring and concerned, fashion. The patient, in Winnicott's terms, moves from ruthlessness to concern.

All of us struggle over the denial of contradictory feelings. But the more disconnected patients are from their feelings, be they alexithymic, fragmented, schizoid, or obsessional, the less there is a clear emotional road map for the therapist to understand and interpret. Rather, the therapist must be exquisitely sensitive to the emotional nuances that "leak" from a patient with a strong interest in keeping feelings hidden. When a sense of aliveness is *felt* within the transference/countertransference, it must be followed. There is a *logic* in these disorders, and that too can be followed. That is, if it is known that a patient has internalized certain self- and object representations because of a traumatic experience, it can be expected that these will manifest themselves within problematic relationships. If they are not apparent, the therapist ought to wonder why the usual logic is not being followed. For instance, consider Ms. J. who could never attain that desperately desired perfection. I would become alert to defend against affect when she presented herself in a very calm and collected manner, indicating that she felt "fine." Knowing her internal turbulent state as well as I did allowed me to understand that this unsullied, "perfect" state was designed to hide much more messy and dysphoric feelings. Through time and careful attention, I had become "fluent" in her family language.

Patients who need to disown or deny conflicting emotions, or who do not have the ability to identify them, are sensitive, and it is often best for the therapist to ask questions as opposed to making declarative statements. "Is it possible that you might feel this way?" or "Could you have any other reactions to this situation?" are the kinds of questions that further curiosity. It is far better for the patient to be able to make the interpretation or to identify for him- or herself the other side of the hidden ambivalence than for the therapist to do it.

CONCLUSION

I have emphasized a distinction between healthy ambivalence and indecision, fragmentation, and obsessive meanderings. There are various reasons that it might be hard for an individual to be able to identify their particular feelings about a person or situation. Alexithymics cannot be guided by emotions they do not recognize or feel. In Winnicott"s lexicon, those with "false selves" are not in touch with their true emotions because of the need to hide the potentially damaged and fragile "true self." Others defend against awareness of feelings out of fear that the feelings identify them as "bad." These individuals need to cleanse themselves of any notion of mixed feelings for fear that possession of such leads toward self-condemnation. Some people deny angry feelings for fear that their "good" objects will be contaminated by their "bad" ones.

In all such cases, it is likely that pressing conflicting emotions will become manifest within the transference/countertransference matrix. The clinician needs to be alert to the dangers of too much idealization, because the reacted-against negativity will make its existence known eventually, and its contrast with the idealization may undermine the patient's trust in treatment.

Perhaps Erikson (1963) describes the struggle over ambivalence best. "The personality is engaged with the hazards of existence continuously, even as the body's metabolism copes with decay. As we come to diagnose a state of relative strength and the symptoms of an impaired one, we face only more clearly the paradoxes and tragic potentials of human life" (p. 274).

VIII

---◆---

HATING,
FORGIVING,
AND HEALING

---◆---

*If we have become able, deep in our unconscious minds, to clear
our feelings to some extent towards our parents of grievance, and
have forgiven them for the frustrations we had to bear, then we
can be at peace with ourselves and are able to love others in the
true sense of the word. (Klein, 1937, p. 343.)*

Accepting life's disappointments gracefully is one of life's great challenges.
In this chapter I will consider the processes that enable the partners in
the analytic enterprise to come to grips with these disappointments: over
personal inadequacies and the inadequacies of others, over the limitations of treatment, and over the vagaries of difficult lives. I will focus on
how people work through self-hatred (whether it has been externalized
or not) and *forgive* themselves for their shortcomings—or at least come to
a sufficiently comfortable *accommodation* with them so that *healing* can
occur. These three elements—forgiveness, accommodation, and healing—
are stepping-stones through the painful vicissitudes of life. They are available to patients who have learned how to *soothe* themselves, to find *solace*
in themselves and in the world, and to find what *comfort* they can in their
life situations.

Working through disappointment, failure, and trauma, whether
large or small, requires an accommodation of the self. By this I mean that

individuals must accommodate themselves to the fact that possibilities are limited, both their own and others'. Forgiving usually entails accepting one's limitations and tolerating the distance between the ideal self and the real self. The harshness of the superego determines the success of this endeavor, and successful treatment must result in a modification of superego severity such that self-appraisals result in comfort, not harsh criticism. Accommodation and self-forgiveness can occur only when there is *both* realistic recognition of one's own responsibility for one's situation and a capacity to understand and tolerate it.

I am not talking about a romanticized or promiscuous forgiveness—yet perpetual self-abnegation serves no good end. Furthermore, it is not always possible, or even desirable, to forgive others. Some behavior is so heinous that the concept of forgiveness is not relevant. Still, to live one's life according to one's hatred of others perpetuates the grievance and gives credence to its perpetrator. For those who hold their grievances to their bosoms, making a living out of their rage and mistreatment, it may be more helpful to think in terms of healing, both internal and external, rather than forgiveness.

Many patients (and occasionally most therapists, I sometimes think) believe that psychotherapy can right all wrongs, obliterate the effects of past hurts, and magically undo all faults and inadequacies. These unrealistic aspirations fall away when one focuses on the more reasonable, although still challenging, goal of healing. Healing the splits within one's personality, the effects of trauma (both catastrophic and cumulative), the pain of aspirations unmet, and the recognition of inadequacies and impossibilities allows new development and the establishment and satisfaction of realistic goals.

Just as life disappoints, so does therapy. The fantasy of perfection achieved through treatment must be relinquished and mourned like other idealizations of the process in the course of an optimally successful treatment. Both participants must accept the limitations of their powers to effect change. At the beginning of treatment each has hopes. Even when they make their goals explicit, whether silently or in words, analyst and patient may develop expectations that are semiconscious at best and not clearly articulated. As the treatment progresses and the patient's life is better understood, what can and cannot be achieved gets clearer.

In some ways, the mental health field promises too much. Manufacturers of psychotropic drugs suggest that their pharmaceuticals cure. The "marketing" of psychotherapy cultivates an expectation of quick and inevitable change. But entrenched psychic structures and processes are not so easily altered. Substantial and enduring changes *can* be achieved through competent, intensive psychotherapy, but only with hard work and substantial investments in time, money, and emotion. The more aware the patient is of the deep entrenchment of characterological qualities, the more the intensity of the necessary effort is understandable.

Mourning—of the losses in a painful life story and of the limitations upon any psychotherapeutic treatment—is an essential aspect of the termination process. Patient and therapist must forgive each other and themselves for their inadequacies as the treatment draws to a close. This can happen only if each is able to surrender fantasies of omnipotence. In this chapter I will deal with hatred and omnipotence as they influence the mourning process.

HATRED

Klein (1957) delineates the establishment of hatred in her study of envy. For Klein, envy is a natural and expected affect experienced by all developing infants. The baby envies the feeding breast its ability to provide the sustenance on which the baby depends. "If we consider that deprivation increases greed and persecutory anxiety, and that there is in the infant's mind a phantasy of an inexhaustible breast which is his greatest desire, it becomes understandable how envy arises even if the baby is inadequately fed. The infant's feelings seem to be that when the breast deprives him, it becomes bad because it keeps the milk, love, and care associated with the good breast all to itself. He *hates* and envies what he feels to be the mean and grudging breast" (p. 183, emphasis added).

In one common scenario of the negative therapeutic reaction, the patient envies the therapist's ability to provide and attempts to derail the treatment to decrease those envious feelings. Envy is a sufficiently dysphoric experience that its sufferers feel despoiled of goodness, and this further increases resentment and hatred. The patient faces the infant's quandary: the wish to destroy what is needed for survival (or, in psychotherapy, the help needed to feel worthy of survival).

As Kernberg (1995) points out, when one person hates another, the hated one often possesses an attribute that the hater feels lacking within him- or herself. A person who feels purposefully deprived experiences an enraged sense of entitlement and bitterness. From a Kleinian perspective, in the intense internal world, the hated object is experienced as willfully sadistic, and the urge to destroy this sadistic object is infiltrated with sadistic and violent feelings; the object is perceived as persecutory and deserving of destruction. The individual wishes to destroy the persecutor; the one who is hated has no sense of goodness and deserves to be destroyed.

In "good enough" situations, the capacity of mother or caregiver to absorb these projections enables the young child to introject a relatively benign imago. The buildup of good feelings contributes to the establishment of a positive self-image, which includes internal senses of strength, flexibility, and capability. Aggression becomes manageable because the mother can tolerate and detoxify the infant's aggression. When the caregiver does not have sufficient ego strength for this task, however, unmodulated aggression overwhelms the child and contributes to a split between libidinal and aggressive affects. A parent who cannot absorb a child's aggression leaves the child at sea with intense and overwhelming affects.

The Effects of Cruelty and Hatred

People consumed with hostility and rage often lose the ability to think about alternatives cogently. Moreover, enraged patients may cause so much disruption in the therapeutic atmosphere that their therapists have difficulty thinking clearly too. Bion (1957) and Brenman (1985) describe the cognitive effects of too much hatred and cruelty. Bion suggests that cognitive functioning compromises and results in arrogance, curiosity, and "pseudostupidity." As I discussed in the previous chapter on ambivalence, links between internal objects may be destroyed by the intensity of the aggression. The resulting lack of connection among internalized aspects of the self results in a diminished sense of certainty about the nature of cause and effect and a sense of befuddlement about the workings of the world results. Arrogance may be a result of this narrowing of perception because the patient has little ability to consider data contradictory to strongly held beliefs. The patient holds to beliefs tenaciously, sometimes exceptionally pridefully, as ideologues sometimes do to eliminate any indecision within themselves.

Empathy is also limited by the projection of hostile intent and by the creation of dehumanized projections. Brenman (1985) points to the narrow-mindedness of cruelty. Some people who struggle with feelings of hatred seem to be massively oblivious to their own hostility. They see their anger as justified and so rationalize any hostile or violent behavior.

"Good" and "bad" remain separate; their internal objects are not integrated and any hurt is seen as persecutory and its perpetrator worthy of destruction. Vision and thought are narrowed to the perceived threat, and careful consideration is destroyed by the experienced need to protect the self from assault, whether it be physical or an assault on identity or the sense of self. Galdston (1987) suggests that superego pressures (that is, the desire to project internal feelings of self-loathing) create a scapegoat that once established requires continued maintenance to bolster the ego weakened by self-hate. "The scapegoat becomes a valued object, a 'pet peeve,' 'the one you love to hate,' 'someone to kick around'" (p. 372).

A history of trauma greatly intensifies this problem, as the patient is forced to face not only self-generated persecutory objects but also real and overwhelming external ones. Furthermore, when the perpetrator is the parent, the child is doubly condemned; he or she must work out catastrophic affects without help from a benign parent. The victim-victimizer relationship between self and object is internalized, which perpetuates the need to victimize others so as to not be forced again into the victim role. Sadomasochistic rules define these interactions. As Akhtar (1999) points out, these hating relationships maintain the object tie; there is no possibility of resolution or of "moving on" because the hatred binds the participants. Hatred and hostility, when nothing better is available, serve as an interpersonal connection for those who too greatly fear isolation and loneliness.

Akhtar suggests that the relationship is maintained by the wish for alleviation of the distress. "Hatred offers the hope of reversal of suffering and thus acquires an *addictive quality*" (p. 108, emphasis added). This phenomenon is often seen in marriage counseling; there is a vested interest in maintaining the sadomasochistic relationship, although each participant hopes to be vindicated and feel purified. This is possible, of course, only if the spouse is identified as being totally at fault.

I had a couple in marriage counseling who fit this dynamic. They were young people, surprisingly entrenched in a relationship infused with negativity. The husband had been discovered in a flirtation with another woman; this seems not to have been consummated. The wife was enraged, however, and heaped blame and derision on him, never acknowledging any positive qualities at all in her spouse. The husband acknowledged his shortcomings readily—too readily. His *mea culpas* were self-indulgent—designed to beat himself masochistically and provide him the satisfaction of self-disgust. His wife's refusal to acknowledge any faults of her own apparently caused him great distress but in some ways it really pleased him, because he could feel virtuous for acknowledging his guilt and secretly satisfied by causing her suffering. The wife's sadistic attacks provided her gratification, because she believed her husband's "philandering" exonerated her from any responsibility for personal or marital problems. She no longer had to face her own perceived inadequacy, only that of her husband. The husband paid lip service to his contribution to their difficulties but nothing really changed, and he continued to undercut and undermine her while she continued to maintain her own absolute innocence and savage him. Frustrated by my refusal to buy into this sadomasochistic dynamic, they eventually found their way to another psychologist's office. This therapist eventually contacted me, with their permission, because of *his* frustration. Every so often I get phone calls from the husband, keeping me updated on their situation—and what therapist they are currently working with.

An understanding of the family dynamics provides some perspective. The wife's family had overvalued her brothers and demeaned and denigrated her for being female. Her self-hatred for being female, and her envy of her husband's maleness, were unremitting and resulted in endless attacks upon him. Unconsciously she saw him as the representation of everything she admired yet felt that she lacked. At the same time, of course, her husband did treat her badly, and his refusal to acknowledge this authentically re-created the denial and abuse she had experienced as a child.

The husband's family of origin had negatively valued aggression, particularly "male" aggression. Men were seen as too aggressive; this left him with a negative sense of self as a man and a need to deny his own hostile behavior. At one point he told me that he wished that he were a gay woman, which would eliminate any need for maleness. This fantasy exemplified his conviction that his aggression was derived from his maleness not from his personhood. Each of these spouses envied the other's gender, an impasse that prevented any meaningful change; their unconscious fantasies were stronger and more desirable than anything that reality had to offer.

These unfortunate people could not release themselves from the pathological tie that bound them together. Marriage counseling did not offer me enough transferential leverage to help them see their contributions to their predicament. Their need to externalize their own sense of badness was too intense. Furthermore, the absence of a transferential therapeutic relationship meant that they had no opportunity to internalize a more benign introject. They each had fears of being left alone with their own desperation and that prevented them from ending the relationship. In essence they maintained their embattled marriage for fear of ending up alone, anguished, and filled with self-hatred.

Self-Hatred

In any discussion of self-hatred, self-loathing, and other intensely self-critical feelings, it is important to remember that we all struggle to maintain a reasonable self-concept and a positive self-appraisal. When we, in our therapeutic role, find ourselves horrified by the intense self-hatred and its externalized manifestations (hatred and unbridled hostility) of some individuals, it is hard not to distance ourselves from their, and consequently our own, intense self-critical and intense hating feelings. The countertransference need to cleanse ourselves of our unacceptable attributes may make it difficult to be empathic with those who hate themselves and others so intensely.

   As children develop, they internalize, for good or for ill, a sense of their value. This is shaped by the way they are treated by their caregivers. A "good enough" parent who responds appropriately to the child's needs lessens the likelihood that overwhelming frustration will leave the child with an overwhelming sense of badness. Severe and depriving or otherwise ill-attuned parents, however, leave a legacy of self-hatred and self-disgust.

   A parent's overreaction to normal and expectable childhood behavior creates in the child both a conviction of badness and an unrealistic and unattainable ideal self. This overreaction results in a split within the child's self-appraisal with the ideal being glorified while the less than acceptable denigrated. Thus, the ideal self is further idealized as hostility causes splitting, resulting in the child, by contrast, to feel even more a failure, with all the accumulated resentments and hostilities that go with such feelings. The sense of badness is externalized, and the child experiences the world as malevolent and persecutory. Furthermore, children who cannot metabolize such intense affects, and feel helpless in their grip, may defend against them with fantasies of a compensatory grandiosity. These dynamics give rise to a dilemma–they are driven by the need to prove their essential goodness, yet the intensity and unmodulated quality of their aggression may cause them to act out in ways that contribute to a negative self-concept.

It is helpful for people with issues of self-criticism to understand, even if only intellectually at first, how their own too-severe superegos operate and the reasons for this severity. These patients also need to experience a sufficiently safe containing environment so they can discuss real and imagined transgressions without fear of punishment or humiliation. This kind of experience allows for internalization of a more benign and realistic superego.

The patient described in the previous chapter and in chapter V, who had to endure her mother's hatred, provides good examples of these issues. Her mother's externalization of her own shortcomings was expressed, although never directly, in her hatred of her daughter and in the implication that the daughter was inadequate and undeserving of love. The daughter intuitively understood this but could not accept the horror of knowing that she was hated. Consequently, she developed a compensatory fantasy that she would gain love and acceptance once she became perfect. Any failure or disappointment created extremely negative self-hating percepts. The patient felt disgusted by her needs and by her dependency–that is, as she saw it, by her inadequacy. As she spoke about herself and her basic human needs for love and connection, I could sense the distaste she had for herself. I thought in contrast about parents I knew who were madly in love with their children, who loved their essence, their smells, and the way they tasted. I felt great sadness for what this woman had missed. As the patient began to appreciate the enormity of the pain of her situation, she was able to begin to accept her own inadequacies more realistically and without needing to attack herself. Gradually, the sadness also became hers, and over time I could sense that her distaste became a *taste* for herself.

Hatred and Trauma

Many aspects of hatred reflect internalized self- and object relationships, which are externalized and then experienced as persecutory. People who hate malevolently have often experienced significant degrees of trauma, abuse, or, at the very least, serious misattunements. In other words, sufferers from cruelty and viciousness hate for comprehensible reasons. We can understand how hard it is for them to move beyond hatred. Still, it would be better if those who have already suffered so much could find ways to live out their lives that do not continue to give power to their tormentors.

Trauma on the scale of the Holocaust, for example, may have such catastrophic effects on the psyche that significant accommodation or integration is not possible. Laub (1998) speaks of the psychic disaster ("the empty circle") that can result from such trauma. Similarly, Krystal (1988) says soberly, "There seems to be an absolute limit to how much an individual is able to give up through grieving. The limitation is twofold: First a person can grieve over only so much at *one time*. Second there is an absolute or lifetime limit to what people can absorb in terms of either loss or accepting negative qualities in themselves" (p. 235). Survivor guilt, shame, rage, and humiliation may become too intense to integrate. Furthermore, these affects over time become organizers, protecting the psyche against dissolution. Perhaps the greatest terror is the fear of being trapped in an objectless state; feelings even of rage and shame may feel preferable. It is important to appreciate the level of despair that underlies hatred in trauma victims; to do otherwise risks retraumatization.

Therapeutic Strategies

Kernberg (1995) suggests that there are three steps in working with malevolent hatred. First, the patient must become aware of the intensity of the hatred and envy. Second, the patient must become aware of his or her own sadistic aspects. Third, the patient must become able to tolerate feelings of guilt.

Although his points are well taken, Kernberg leaves out the libidinal side of the dynamics of hatred. These patients have natural and normal needs for attachment, assertion, individuation, and general hedonism that have been denied and perverted by misattuned, misunderstanding, and sometimes cruel parents. Hatred is a desire for attachment, even if part of that desire is to destroy the object. Individuals growing up in such dire circumstances do not develop whole object representations, and often aggressive solutions are the only ones they can find to maintain connection. All patients must understand that behavior is motivated by *combinations* of wishes: the more "positive" ones of love and attachment and the more "negative" ones of hostility and destruction. The manifest appearance of thoughts, feelings, and behavior is not always congruent with the less conscious wishes that underlie them.

Hatred and the Transference

Intense hatred does of course become manifest in the transference. Experience has taught me that I, like most therapists, am more comfortable working with positive or erotic transferences than with negative ones, and it can almost be said that transference is deemed "positive" or "negative" according to whether the clinician experiences it as "pleasant" or "unpleasant." Yet as Brenner (1982) has pointed out, all transferences are ambivalent. The manifest presentation of a particular transference reaction is only its opening gambit. Layers of meaning accrue to behaviors or feelings, and it is often surprising to discover the myriad affects associated with seemingly straightforward transferences. A hostile transference may obscure basic needs for love and affection, while an apparently positive one may be a defense against intensely hostile feelings. Furthermore, the complexity of affects are not given their due when reduced to the categories of "positive" or "negative."

Individuals who hate tend to believe that their feelings are justified. As far as they are concerned, their enemies are worthless and deserve their ill regard. Yet even when there has been clear-cut and terrible trauma inflicted by unthinkable enemies, the belief in the enemy's worthlessness may become very confused with the patient's own self-concept. This makes it hard to gain perspective on a hatred that is closely linked with very painful self-accusations. Moreover, because hatred often serves as a psychic stabilizer, inquisitive or insensitive questioning of the patient's dearly held beliefs may feel undermining. Further still, hatred organizes and defines identity and internal self- and object representations. Consequently, the hating feelings are based upon rigid percepts that gain strength by their continuous self-esteem regulating function. When patient and therapist develop a good working alliance, the foundations for the unpleasant percepts can gradually be chipped away through transference interpretation. How safe and secure the patient feels within the therapeutic relationship will determine what risks can be taken in disassembling a psychic apparatus that offers stability and meaning.

Gabbard (1996) has written at length on the difficulties of working with patients with malignant transference hate. From his perspective (and mine), these patients all too often end up experiencing treatment as unhelpful at best and painful or damaging at worst. They are provocative to a degree that makes countertransferential acting out hard to contain. Gabbard suggests that interpretation of underlying affects and motives should be postponed with patients with malignant hate and that the need to provide a containing function is crucial with these patients. He says, "(1) verbal interpretations may fall on deaf ears when the patient is harboring intense negative feelings toward the analyst, (2) a new set of experiences with a new object is necessary before the patient can accept interpretive interventions, and (3) the traditional role of the analyst as a neutral observer who delivers occasional interpretations from a position of evenly suspended attention is not an adequate characterization of the requirements for the analytic treatment of more disturbed patients" (p. 197).

Patients embroiled in such intense emotions need a safe environment for their expression, where they can begin to understand what they feel without fear of driving the other person crazy. The metabolizing and detoxifying that occur when affects can be expressed openly and without retaliation allow the patient to re-introject projected hostile feelings "cleansed" by interaction with a benevolent therapist, moving the patient toward whole-object percepts and the depressive position. The therapist needs to be able to withstand the attacks; this conveys to the patient that even their most intense emotions can be survived by both of them, and this sense of strength becomes internalized.

Sherby (1989), describing the challenges of working with the rage of borderline patients, says, "As uncomfortable as these attacks are for the analyst, they can be therapeutically invaluable for the patient in that the patient's destructiveness is deflected away from the patient's ego toward the analyst and is diffused in the process (Epstein, 1979). The analyst, by accepting the patient's view of him/her as defective and imperfect, gradually enables the patient's introjected parent to become more tolerant of the patient's own deficiencies. Simultaneously, the analyst's survival in the face of these repeated onslaughts results in the patient's ego coming up against the boundary of the analyst's ego, thereby strengthening the patient's own ego boundaries" (p. 580).

The young law student described in chapter V sought treatment for profound depression. He had seen a number of therapists in the past with no apparent benefit. He had also been tried on multiple medications with little effect. He described a very unpleasant life, feeling alone and out of touch with his peers. He could have relationships, he thought, but only from his own effort; others would go out with him but only if he initiated. His early life had been traumatic; when he was three, his mother had suffered what appears to have been a psychotic depression precipitated by the death of her own mother. Before this he was described as an energetic and fun-loving child; afterward, he was quiet and depressed. His father was a rather schizoid, uninvolved man, but loving in his own way.

The patient described feeling positive with each of his previous therapists at the outset, but he would quickly lose interest and become combative. I fully expected the same to happen with me. I believed that he was reenacting within the transference his painful and perplexing experience with his mother. His loss of interest reflected his experience of his mother's loss of interest in him; his feeling of needing to take the initiative in relationships reflected his desperate attempts to gain his mother's attention; his lack of responsiveness to treatment reflected his mother's refractory course. I also felt that frequent sessions were important to maintain continuity and minimize the trauma of separation, although I knew that he would fight me on this out of his fear of dependency.

I told him all of this, and he listened with non-committal interest. He did agree on three times weekly meetings. He was enraged with me from the beginning and attacked me for incompetence; he did not feel better (although he did), and everything I told him he knew already (although he didn't). I did not dispute any of this, understanding that his protests were about circumstances that had happened many years ago and that remained alive inside him. I knew that it was most important for me to contain his fury to allow him to find the hurt within.

This is not to say that I did not feel frustrated and, at times, enraged with him. I wanted to attack him as he attacked me. When I found myself wanting to point out his shortcomings, I would realize that my countertransference was active. When he noticed that I was frustrated or upset over his attacks, he became even more upset, calling me a wimp and a Milquetoast. This confirmed to me how much he needed me to be able to withstand his fury. I knew that he was desperately afraid of his own shortcomings, which he had identified as the source of his mother's depression. His rage was the rage he imagined his mother felt about his inadequacies.

The treatment centered on elucidating his pain through the transference. His psychic structure had to be brought into the open in all its complexity. Interpretation was much less important than his need to verbalize his pain in a free and secure setting. Gradually, he began to feel less toxic and less depressed and became able to develop relationships.

Most crucial in this treatment was the patient's need to tolerate and metabolize his rage and understand it as a manifestation and reenactment of his early despair. It is important to recognize that his perceptions had some truth to them. That is, I did find him difficult to deal with. I did at times wish he would go away, and I did experience anger toward him. All of these emotions may very well have been what his mother felt toward him when she was struggling with her own depression. The sense of inadequacy that he felt matched the reality of his inability to cheer up his mother, and meet his own needs when his mother could not.

Unlike his mother, however, I could withstand his needs and respond to them in a way that was tolerable. In treatment he became able to comprehend his despair, free himself from his self-punitive and self-attacking perspective, and begin to forgive himself and his mother for their shortcomings.

GUILT, SOLACE, AND FORGIVENESS

Each of us must find a way to maintain a sense of self-worth in spite of our awareness of misdeeds and inadequacies. We all measure ourselves against a standard (the ideal self); the way the measurement takes place, the relative attainableness of the standard, and the meaning ascribed to failures determine self-esteem. People with traumatic backgrounds often do not know how to console or to soothe themselves, and their superegos are rigid and punitive. They tend to have a poorly integrated sense of self and are often condemning and self-persecutory. Misdeeds are viewed as immense failures deserving of real and metaphoric beatings. The sense of self-hate is profound.

People with supportive, nurturing, and consoling backgrounds are more able to maintain a stable equilibrium and sense of self despite occasional misbehavior. We know, of course, that many patients with neurotic disorders can be amazingly guilt-ridden and self-punitive. Yet a qualitative difference exists between the neurotic, who is usually able to maintain function even when "feeling guilty," and the more seriously afflicted, who may become incapacitated or even suicidal when identified as less than perfect.

Forgiving

Schecter (1974) said about forgiveness, "I have found that it is one of the most difficult tasks for the patient to achieve in his therapy: to give up his 'chronic resentment,' his reproachfulness and claim against himself *or* the other as debtor or creditor: in short, to 'forgive'" (p. 114). This task requires, he feels, that patients move away from early symbiotic attachments that carry unrealistic idealizations. This individuation and maturation process leads toward realistic self-evaluation. This crucial step of forgiving or accommodating to disappointment is not always given sufficient attention in analysis. Emphasis in therapy is often focused on underlying desires and wishes, sometimes to the neglect of the quality and ferocity of the judging faculty (superego). It may be that therapists who have not addressed or worked out their own need for forgiveness may be at a loss when this issue comes up in their patients. Accepting one's limitations, "forgiving" oneself, is a complicated task for anyone.

In treatment the patient must first identify the gaps between the idealized and the ideal self; this occurs most effectively when these gaps can be related to a particular behavior, thought, or feeling (in the here and now or in the transference). It is important to differentiate between the *ideal* self, which may potentially be achieved, and the *idealized* self, which is by definition never achievable. Second, the quality of the superego must be delineated. Do failures to achieve the ideal self result in overcritical self-punitiveness, or are individuals able to tolerate realistic disappointments and experience "legitimate" guilt when it is called for? Third, the patient must understand his or her own balance between reparation and destruction. How does a patient work through hostile wishes, both the archaic ones and the more interpersonal? Should or can amends be made for misdeeds? Fourth, grieving and mourning over lost possibilities (including the loss of the ideal self and other disappointments) must be accomplished. The need for pleasure, for life affirming pursuits, is a biological given, according to psychoanalytic thought, and patients must be able to tolerate, even embrace, this hedonistic, pleasure-oriented, biologically determined aspect of their humanity despite disappointments within themselves and toward others and the all too common need to be self-punitive.

Solace

It is clear that all of us must confront disappointments in life, including disappointments with ourselves. How we come to terms with our own inadequacies depends on the standard by which inadequacies are measured: that is, on whether a person has internalized a relatively realistic ideal self or an impossible-to-be-achieved idealized self.

Horton (1981) suggests that the capacity to make use of transitional objects lets a child find solace in difficult times. Similarly, the development of the transitional space in psychoanalytic treatment helps the patient who lacks such abilities develop this needed capacity to find solace. Horton suggests that therapists should help patients create this transitional space, help them find that intermediate space between self and others that enables calm reflection.

Superego Analysis

Sandler and Sandler (1987) make a useful contribution in their distinction between the present and past unconscious. They describe the past unconscious, "'the child within,' as unconscious fantasies which have wish-fulfilling, problem-solving, reassuring and defensive aspects. These include responses to narcissistic injuries and to threats of object loss, as well as to a host of other anxieties, including fears of mutilation. To the inner world which we attribute to the past unconscious we have to allocate *highly developed interactions with the internal representatives of childhood figures*" (p. 334). By contrast, the "present unconscious is concerned with *maintaining equilibrium in the present*, and experiences the peremptory object related wishful fantasies, which we take to echo the past unconscious in the present, as intrusive and upsetting" (p. 335).

The Sandlers view the past unconscious as relatively inaccessible; according to them, elucidation is possible only through reconstruction. They suggest a technique oriented to "construction" of the *present* unconscious by means of here and now associations, particularly transference-related ones. Furthermore, they indicate that because people try to evade or remove awareness of guilt, it is important to identify the maneuvers by which this is attempted.

My feeling is that the best way to accomplish this is to pay close attention to current affectively charged superego-laden material, an approach that parallels ego defense analysis. This enables therapist and patient to work effectively in the present with material that the patient must understand to maintain self-esteem without the use of projection, denial, or other defensive maneuvers. It ties the past in with the present and provides an understanding of the intricate workings of the mind and the underlying fantasies that fuel guilt-driven symptoms. It seems to me that there is much to recommend superego analysis, neglected though it is. As I have just described, a detailed understanding of the superego and its workings are extremely important in helping patients develop peace of mind.

MASOCHISM

Masochism, as psychoanalysis usually defines it, is based in sexual satisfaction. At times, however, the pleasure of masochistic activities is desexualized, resulting in what Freud called "moral masochism" (Freud, 1924). In this sense, therefore, moral masochism is a characterological phenomenon, and its original libidinal basis is obscured. Phenomenologically, moral masochists need to suffer and this need suffuses their very essence.

A patient constantly complained about his wife and her attitude toward him. As we discussed this, it became clear to me that the tone he used to depict his wife's way of speaking to him varied as he described their encounters from cruel and sarcastic to quite benign. When I called this to his attention, he could reconstitute the incidents and provide what appeared to be a more accurate sense of her tone. Rarely was it as severe as he had initially described.

This phenomenon served several purposes. His negative portrayals of his wife certainly provided him with a sense of vengeance. He paid lip service to his wife's criticisms; guilt over real wrongdoings was acknowledged, but true remorse was absent. The most obscure piece of the picture was his general need to suffer. By portraying his wife so negatively, he made his relationship with her, and his life, very unpleasant. Their sexual relationship was nonexistent and they had little pleasure together, while he went about with a hang-dog expression that afforded him significant, but secret, gratification (like the proverbial cat who ate the canary). His character structure demanded obeisance to a strict and unforgiving superego. It gave him *satisfaction* to suffer. To do otherwise felt wrong. He felt uncomfortable and anxious when he experienced pleasure.

This man's moral masochism was intractable, and he was very difficult to treat. To his own mind, he was a responsible man wearied by the pressures of life. To give up his masochistic mindset opened him to the dangers of rampant pleasure and to more severe punishment than he experienced in the status quo; he referred to this possibility as "opening Pandora's box." Certainly, his need to suffer provided him with relief from past guiltworthy actions, but it also provided him with a satisfaction that was very well hidden and difficult to give up. Furthermore, the blanket need to suffer obscured many more dynamic issues that we eventually delineated, including his envy of others for their ability to experience pleasure. His maintenance of the masochistic position also thwarted my efforts, again resulting in his triumphant satisfaction.

Another patient with somewhat similar dynamics feared being "caught by the pleasure police." She presented herself as needing to suffer, but her suffering was once removed. That is, she would talk about situations and suggest that she felt guilty when, in fact, she did not. She thought she *should* feel bad and she talked as though she did, but in reality she was not much troubled by her actions. She presented herself to me as she did for fear that I would judge her if she were not self-condemning. This process alienated her from herself. Close attention to the affective quality of her presentation enabled me to identify this dynamic, which led to a fruitful exploration of its origins and then of her true feelings about situations and whether she felt truly comfortable or not.

This patient also suffered from a variant of moral masochism. She suffered from her self-alienation and to protect herself from criticism. She was proactive in her defense. Her masochism also obscured other behaviors, thoughts, and feelings representing a hostility from which she derived secret pleasure.

Anna Freud's (1946) dictum about the advisability of the analyst maintaining equal distance from ego, id, and superego is sometimes ignored in reference to matters of the superego. Some analysts look upon the superego as a condemning agency alone, but a realistic judging capacity based on a benign standard also offers structure and comfort. Without it archaic part-object persecutory images come to the fore; these do not permit either soothing or solace. Additionally, guilt is an appropriate response to some actions, and in those cases discomfort for misbehavior may itself be comforting.

It is not healthy, however, for individuals to castigate themselves. Schecter (1979) indicates that modification of the superego is of paramount importance in treatment. He describes the "loving and persecuting superego," and suggests that successful treatment results in "(1) a mellowing and taming of the harshness of the persecuting superego combined with more realistic standards; and (2) a growth and development of the loving superego in the direction of greater strength and protectiveness, especially in relation to the persecuting superego" (p. 361).

Deigh (1984) suggests that disappointments result in a strengthening of the ego, and a reduction in self-esteem (as long as it is moderate) can result in a sense of strength and an increased ability to deal with disappointment. He commented, "In particular, [Freud] observed that when a young child forms an erotic attachment to one of his parents and consequently comes to regard the other as a rival, he will, when the time comes to give up that attachment, frequently identify (or identify more strongly) with and then introject the latter parent rather than the former. This too is a way of defending against the blow of the loss of love causes, for it preserves something of that love through an identification with a *successful* rival" (pp. 210–211).

REPARATION

Klein (1937) introduced to psychoanalysis the notion of reparation. In her view, children are beset with a combination of loving and hating feelings toward their mothers. "It is important to realize that the child's development depends on, and to a large extent is formed by, his capacity to find the way to bear inevitable and necessary frustrations and conflicts of love and hate which are in part caused by them: that is, to find his way between his hate which is increased by frustrations, and his love and wish for reparation which bring in their train the sufferings of remorse. The way the child adapts himself to these problems in his mind forms the foundation for all his later social relationships, his adult capacity for love and cultural development. He can be immensely helped in childhood by the love and understanding of those around him, but these deep problems can neither be solved for him nor abolished" (p. 316).

The child's wish to undo or make up for aggressive and destructive desires impels the child toward making good in the world. The child needs to prove to the mother his or her praiseworthiness. When the mother has been restored, in the infant's mind, to the loving person that she was, the child feels safe in feeding and being held (neither mother nor child is viewed as a threat). The mother survives the aggressive assault. Gradually, in Winnicott's words, "Ruthlessness gives way to ruth, un-concern to concern" (1958, pp. 23–24). The child incorporates these feelings of concern for others and is relieved that hostility has not been damaging.

Klein suggests that children who have had benign and understanding parents and have not been swamped by aggressive and destructive wishes are more able to integrate these feelings and find healthy means of reparation. Children with more destructive affects and harsh and punitive parents tend to make reparation by hurting themselves. In the first case, the child makes reparation by life-affirming activities; in the latter, by self-negating ones.

Patients, too, try to make reparation for past misdeeds, real or fantasized, in many ways. Self-punitive and suicidal behaviors are one gross manifestation, but there are many much more subtle maneuvers that patients adopt, often without awareness, to make amends. Certainly, the common thwarting of success and ambition may point toward pathological solutions to Oedipal conflicts. Patients throw themselves into self-defeating situations, into bad relationships, into substance abuse and/or eating disorders; all of these may be efforts to satisfy a voracious judging faculty. Bodily mutilation and other self-destructive actions have unconscious derivatives and are associated with fantasies that need to be explicated. As I have said, it is important to examine all three aspects of such dynamics: the underlying desires (drives and wishes), the defenses against them (ego), and the characteristic quality of the punishing agency.

Also, it is important to keep in mind that all people find ways to punish themselves for wrongdoing. Analysts are on quite comfortable territory in the fantasy realm, when the "crimes" are not "real." But people also *act* in ways that are contrary to their values, and they do feel a sense of responsibility over their shortcomings. It is possible to help them understand that they may have other options open to them for making amends besides self-punishment. We are comfortable identifying behavior as reaction-formation against hostile intent. There are also times when positive, life-affirming activities are designed not to cover up hostility, however, but to make amends for wrongdoing. Out of fear of their faults being identified, patients may tend to obscure their more positive activities.

One patient was extraordinarily helpful and giving to others in need, and his behavior seemed quite genuine and based on real concern. He tended to minimize his contribution, however, because his behavior was motivated *in part* by a wish to make amends for hidden delinquent behavior in the past. Identifying this helped him take more pleasure in his activities and feel more pride in his giving. Furthermore, he was a genuinely kind and caring person—also a real aspect of himself that needed to be identified and accepted. Optimal helpfulness to our patients does not just mean identifying defended-against impulses but also making sense out of reparative desires.

One more example: A man who had terminated treatment ten years before called and left a message requesting a return call. When I spoke with him he said that he had often thought of me in the years since then and about how the treatment had helped him. His present situation was very pleasing to him; he owned a successful business, had married, and was raising two children. He indicated that he attributed his success to my assistance. He was not, however, calling just to tell me that. When he terminated, we had known that it was a bit premature, but it was necessary because of an out-of-state business opportunity. During the course of treatment, it had become apparent that he was racist and anti-Semitic. My confrontation of these issues, particularly as he was aware that I was Jewish, had been difficult and painful to him, but it had been necessary to help him address his hatred—the result of externalizations of his own despised aspects. His phone call to me was an apology for expressing his anti-Semitic feelings all those years ago. It was reparative in the sense that he felt he had righted a wrong and any hostility I felt would be alleviated by the apology. He was relieved by my forgiveness, which was easily granted, and I certainly appreciated the phone call.

HEALING

The Search for Pleasure

Humans are driven by the need to find satisfaction in life. The wish for pleasure is fundamental. "What do they (men) demand of life and wish to achieve in it? The answer to this can hardly be in doubt. They strive after happiness; they want to become happy and to remain so . . . As we see, what decides the purpose of life is simply the programme of the pleasure principle" (Freud, 1930, p. 76). Freud points to sexual pleasure as the ultimate one and considered the development and maintenance of symptoms to be fueled by the desire to gain some satisfaction, some solution to an apparently insoluble psychic problem. Ego needs, for achievement and self-actualization for example, also propel toward great accomplishments. Winnicott (1958) makes a case for *ego orgasm,* ecstatic feelings that operate outside the realm of instinctual gratification via sublimation. Freud (1930) points out the impossibility of achieving happiness, suggesting that it is the *quest* for it that impels. Each person must decide for him- or herself the direction of their efforts. "There is no golden rule which applies to everyone: Every man must find out for himself in what particular fashion he can be saved" (p. 83). It is this drive for satisfaction and pleasure that provides the necessary link between hurt and healing.

Many patients who have suffered trauma find themselves living lives of little satisfaction, with little ability to experience pleasure and joy. They feel bound up with anger and negativity. Other pleasurable affective responses are typically muted also, and a major task of the treatment is to identify and differentiate affects and release strangulated emotions, thus helping the patient gain greater satisfaction in life. Patients with past grievances tend to perpetuate these hurts in their present-day relationships, sometimes reenacting them with others, other times reversing the roles. But they still end up feeling hurt and bewildered, having hoped for a better result from the new rendition. Through the transference relationship, patients can move beyond negating and hurtful internalized self- and object representations and the resulting painful relationships. This requires that the patient learn to recognize the compensatory grandiose and omnipotent structures and fantasies that provided comfort in tough times. It means releasing the idealized expectations that drive masochistic self-denial and self-punishment. It means moving beyond sadomasochistic relationships to where sadness resides, rather than fury and betrayal. It means recapturing split-off and denied painful affects that open the self to profound hurt. It means grieving and mourning over lost possibilities that will never be recaptured. There is great sadness in the recognition of mistakes that might have been avoided, relationships that might have turned out differently and potentials that might have been realized. The implacability of time must be accepted and appreciated.

As I listen to patients express their outrage against those who have damaged them, I sometimes wonder whether these past relationships had anything positive to offer. I imagine that they must have had, for how could my patient have survived as well as he or she did without some caregiving? It is not always necessary or advisable to forgive those who have done great damage, but it can be helpful for patients to reconnect with the sense of attachment that they felt toward their parents. Rarely are people so evil that they have no redeeming qualities.

On the other hand, it's another idealization to think that any individual must be so divinely compassionate as always to be able to see redeeming qualities, no matter how bad the circumstances. Coming to grips with disappointments—accepting the "good enough" or the inability to move beyond one's own grievances—helps the patient accept as well his or her own unfortunate imperfections. Those patients who remain at war with the internal or external parent cannot come to peace with themselves.

It is important to remember that loss can be present only once attachment has occurred. A sense of loss, therefore, represents a positive prognosis; if attachment has occurred, the patient presumably has the capability to maintain a transferential relationship that provides potent opportunities for growth. Empty feelings are far more ominous than feelings of loss, indicating as they do a lack of prior attachment. In this case the transference will be more difficult to establish, and this, in fact, may be the first and primary order of business.

Some people, whatever hurts have been inflicted on them, believe themselves to be at fault. Belief in their own inadequacy and incompetence is their response to overwhelming and confusing experience. The inability to cope effectively in very difficult situations creates shameful feelings of ineptitude. The fantasy of potentially perfect control deludes the patient, even while it provides some solace. To forgive themselves, these people must recognize and accept their (relative) inadequacy and incompetence without *excessive* self-criticism. This requires a realistic recognition and acceptance of their admirable as well as less than admirable qualities; these tend to be denied and minimized. The pleasures of self-denial and self-punishment need to be relinquished in favor of the more life-affirming and lasting pleasures of competence and self-affirmation.

Ms. S. felt herself overmatched in life because of her childhood experience of always being on the short end of competition with her siblings. She endlessly compared herself with others, always feeling inadequate and different. One day as she compared herself, again invidiously, with a co-worker, I pointed out to her that her "deficiency model" neglected her real accomplishments. She did not value the diversity that she brought to the organization; the ways she was unlike every one else to her meant only inadequacy. She *was* different from the others, in a way, but as a friend had pointed out to her, she was "a breath of fresh air." This was a concept that she had never considered.

Much of her treatment centered on the sadomasochistic qualities that caused her to react toward others with hurt and rage. Pointing out to her a lacuna in her reasoning—her neglect of her positive side—fed her self-esteem and resulted in a diminution of her rageful response. The extreme competitiveness that she felt obscured her genuine accomplishments, negated her individuality, and diminished her pleasure in life.

It is the hedonic potential in being human that saves us all. The hardwired need to live, love, and experience pleasure is the thing that impels us through the despairing passages of life. The acceptable expectation of a fulfilling life of pleasure and satisfaction is communicated by parental love. Parental love gives permission to live and prosper despite the parents' aging and eventual death. It conveys a relatively unambiguous desire for the child to survive and surpass. Loving parents can be aware of their own mortality and at times of their own unhappiness, yet they are able often enough to transcend their own narcissistic injuries and act lovingly to their children. It requires maturity to not envy the youth, health, and potential of one's children, but these are the life-affirming feelings that must be recaptured in effective treatment. "How can it be done? All we really need to do is demonstrate to the patients who have alexithymic, "disaffected" patterns that *love is real and that it works"*(Krystal, 1988, p. 331). We do this by demonstrating to them, over and over, that we find them worthwhile, that we value and respect them, and that we appreciate the pursuit of happiness and pleasure.

IX

♦

TRANSFORMATION

♦

My patients always surprise me. Because they drive the therapy—often in unanticipated directions—the course of treatment is never quite as I expect. This is usually exciting and interesting. It demonstrates at the same time the increased creative capacities of the patient and the limited ability of any therapist to know for certain what goes on in another person's mind. It is humbling, too, to contemplate the woeful misapprehensions that I manage to achieve of patients I think I understand so well!

Some surprises are discouraging, however, and so I would like to conclude this endeavor by addressing some issues that are germane to every treatment. They influence the level of success that can be achieved and account for some unfortunate but inevitable disappointments. Character structure exists for good reasons, and it yields with great difficulty. The changes that occur in psychodynamic therapy come with considerable pain and effort. Most patients and therapists find the trouble worthwhile, but not all psychotherapy goes smoothly, and we are all familiar with treatments that blow up or end precipitously. It is grandiose to expect that all patients will react favorably to any individual therapist's particular brand of treatment. Sometimes we can't help—and our response should be thoughtful consideration, without self-accusation, of the possible reasons. I am certainly aware of treatments that have not gone as well as I wished, and in some cases I unhappily attribute these to my own shortcomings. But just as our patients need to forgive and accommodate, so do we. One common problem is premature termination—premature according to the therapist, at least, and precipitous, unexpected, and very perplexing, sometimes to the patient as well as to the therapist. This may reflect unanalyzed negative transference, issues that the patient feels cannot be brought out, or not-quite-concious concerns that neither party can articulate. Oftentimes, for example, patients get discouraged, and this may reflect an unarticulated belief that they are beyond salvation, beyond hope. Sometimes patients just feel that they have gone as far as they can; their decision must be respected, of course, although not necessarily agreed with.

Once people have set their minds upon a course of action, dissuasion is rarely successful. A firm and solid therapeutic alliance, however, may carry the day. Conflict may occur when the therapist feels rejected by the patient's wish to stop, especially when the patient is dissatisfied, but it is best to avoid confrontation. It goes without saying that these situations should be handled just like any other material—sensitively, objectively, and by means of the analyzing function. It is easy for a therapist distraught by a (presumably) premature desire to terminate to alienate a patient. Maintaining the analytic stance, however, disables the projected hostility and enables the patient to consider his or her ambivalence. Maintaining the reflective function creates transitional space for the free investigation of mixed feelings. Many patients who interrupt treatment while maintaining a positive relationship with the therapist return once their imagined or fantasized solutions do not pan out.

HOPE AND DESPAIR

Successful treatment requires that patients be able to confront despair, and then move beyond it to the experience of hope. Despair varies in intensity among patients, but it is a common reaction as they become aware of the complexity of their predicaments—the intricate characterological solutions with which they struggle and the psychic pain that underlies them. This, however, is a different kind of despair than the kind that people present as a symptom. It is realistic and appropriate to feel saddened by lost opportunities in life and by the rigors of intensive change. Most patients have made life choices that are regrettable in retrospect but that still must be lived with; this is one of the most potent arguments for child analysis—to provide the treatment *before* important life choices need to be made.

Despair and depression related to unresolved mourning, or to abusive or traumatic experiences, are effects that need to be worked out and resolved in treatment. The despair of this "vale of tears" is ever-present. It is tolerable when combined with realistic hope, but it can take on a life of its own (and then becomes itself subject to analysis and interpretation) when the patient uses it to fuel self-loathing and masochistic needs. It is important that any unresolved mourning be identified lest treatment be stymied in its final days.

Both patient and therapist must relinquish grandiose and omnipotent expectations, and accommodate to accomplishments that may differ from the ones they had hoped for. Both may have had unrealistic expectations of what treatment can deliver. If this is not addressed in some fashion, an inauthentic pact may be established between them, with both parties acting as if something has transpired that in fact has not. Authentic treatments are emotional ones, with both participants actively engaged. They are lively. An intellectualized treatment is stagnant and boring, and masks the necessary sadness that accompanies every treatment, successful or otherwise.

This acceptance of inevitable disappointments—in treatment and in life—develops out of a recapitulation of the goals identified in the beginning of the therapy. As the patient nears the end of treatment, patient and therapist must explore, implicitly or explicitly, to what extent these goals have been achieved. Ideally their origins will now be better understood than they were, their underlying dynamic motivating elements having been exposed and elaborated. Once-hidden goals will now be more conscious and perhaps transformed into more realistic and achievable ones. Omnipotent and fantasy-based hopes may be less imperious in the new and more inclusive context. Implicit goals will also be clearer, and the individual's life will be altered in ways that make the meeting of these heretofore barely articulated needs possible. Explicit goals may be met or abandoned depending on the patient's new self-understanding and on a new view of how these goals fit into the picture.

When Dr. R. first entered treatment, she expressed a wish to be less "depressed." On a less accessible although still conscious level, she wanted a new personality, so hopeless did she feel of ever being able to accept herself. As our evaluation work progressed, she became aware of implicit character issues involving an essential sense of emotional isolation and emptiness. Unconsciously, she hoped for a magical gender change that would alleviate her despair.

The treatment focused on helping her fill in this essential emptiness, and understanding and appreciating her own needs and desires. Working through her primary identifications—with a schizoid and detached mother and an abusive and domineering father—freed her to consider new possibilities. She became more passionate and more involved in life, and her life in turn became more fulfilling and pleasurable. The explicit goal of being "less depressed" was achieved as her life began to feel meaningful and pleasurable, and she no longer felt so listless. As she felt more and more comfortable in her own skin, she no longer felt the need for a new "personality." The feelings of emptiness and isolation diminished as she came to grips with all she missed from her mother. Her need to re-create the sadomasochistic dynamic of her family lessened, allowing her to establish new relationships that could provide nurturance and more fulfilling identifications. The need for gender choice diminished as she understood its origins in relation to her grandiose identifications with her father and his denigration of her mother.

Despair leads to hope. In the beginning of treatment, the therapist is often the one who must carry the hope and see the buried potential in the patient. As the work progresses and the patient, aware now of the stubbornness and pervasiveness of character problems, despairs of ever being free, hope still needs to be held by the clinician. As change occurs, the patient begins to hope that freedom may be possible after all. As treatment closes, however, a different kind of despair emerges: the recognition of the impossibility of a return to perfect union with an untrammeled, always available mother. These stages of alternating hope and despair must be experienced and acknowledged so that such grandiose fantasies may be relinquished and satisfaction with more ordinary (as opposed to extraordinary) pursuits may be achieved.

PERSISTENCE

Persistence and stubbornness are related to hope, and in the analyst they can both further treatment and impede it.

Mr. K. wasn't aware of it, but he was constantly testing my belief in his right to live a fruitful and enjoyable life. Both his parents had abused him, and he had come to the conclusion, perhaps with reason, that his existence was not valued. In subtle ways he made choices that seemed to reflect a desire to further himself, but were actually self-punitive and denying of his own needs. It took years of interpretation before he could hold in his mind any understanding of his self-negating self-concept. Time and again issues came up that demonstrated his rock-solid belief in his own worthlessness. At times he described a desire to "squeeze the life out of himself."

He had an obsessive-compulsive style and valued a sense of competence and perfection. Unconsciously, he desired the fantasized state of idealized, smooth, and untrammeled connection with the fabricated mother that Chasseguet-Smirgel (1988) has described. At the times that he felt he had attained this, it was very difficult to keep him in treatment, because he imagined himself to be totally self-sufficient and capable. This defensive position obscured his great need for me and his corresponding fear of rejection. I experienced his repeated provocations about terminating treatment and related threats to cut down on his sessions, as crucial tests, but over his long tenure with me I never wavered in my resolve that he needed to remain in treatment, with me, and at the frequency of five times weekly.

My persistence was essential to him; it gave him the protracted opportunity he needed to internalize my belief in his worth, and so to reduce his self-hatred. He had had a sister who had been killed by a car after running out into the street. I experienced his desires to quit and cut down as renditions of that event, and I was determined that I would be a better parent than his own had been, in the sense of not letting him "run out into the street." Patients who have experienced neglect do not often know, in an organic sense, what it means to have needs met. Like their parents, they can get close but miss the mark. This is frustrating to them, when an experience that should be pleasurable turns disappointing. Yet the need to replicate is operational as is the need to maintain the early parent-child tie. Consequently, such patients will fight the therapeutic relationship because this kind of gratification feels wrong and disloyal, and it may take time and great steadiness on the therapist's part to loosen this bind.

On the other hand, persistence can become willful stubbornness and an insistence on being right. When I have a particular agenda in mind—a point to prove—it sometimes interferes with my ability to hear the patient properly. I get embroiled in enactments, replicating for the patient the experience of being misunderstood and perhaps dominated, and for myself, a fear of being discounted and minimized. The practice of psychoanalysis can be lonely and depriving, and the therapist's need for satisfaction can create a sense of urgency or become manifest in a need to be seen as omnipotent and omniscient.

EROTICISM

The ability to experience sensual pleasure is one of the major markers of a successful treatment. Many patients seek treatment feeling alienated from themselves and from their affects. Pleasure is seldom experienced in a direct, body-focused way. Sexual pleasure may be limited or inhibited, or may be achieved only in ways that do not feel life-enhancing. Alcohol or other substances may be used more to control dysphoric affects than in the service of pleasure. Neurotic patients are constrained by childhood hurts and anxieties. Patients who have been sexually abused are arrested in their development by that abuse. But the patient approaching the termination of an ideal treatment develops a sense of the sensual. Activities are enjoyed for their own sake, for the pleasure that they provide. Competitive conflicts diminish and the patient is able to achieve and enjoy success. Creativity increases, and new avenues for enjoyment are found. Strangulated affects find expression.

Some patients are never able to achieve these levels of pleasure, however. People who have been severely traumatized may never really be able to experience pleasure. The closest they may be able to get is a greater sense of peace, or perhaps a lessening of terror. Maybe inner turmoil will be less disruptive, or the world will seem less persecutory. It may be possible to establish relationships where it had not been before. For some patients the ability to establish a therapeutic relationship is an accomplishment in itself. The transitional space of the transference can provide security to such patients in their struggles. To severely disturbed and traumatized patients, such accomplishments are major successes. People dependent upon sadomasochistic defenses must struggle greatly to allow themselves pleasure.

Despite these potential limitations, most patients who accomplish a successful termination have become able to enjoy their lives more fully. The ability to live with pleasure and to take satisfaction in achievements is a surprisingly major accomplishment for many, but both therapist and patient find the therapeutic process more enjoyable as the patient's ability to enjoy increases.

SELF-REFLECTION

To be able to think about oneself, to understand the workings of one's mind, to establish links between past and present, to consider consequences before acting, to be able to solve problems effectively, to be free to explore new avenues of thought—all these are desired outcomes of psychoanalytic treatment. This contemplative ability is hard to come by, the press of impulsivity and thoughtless gratification being as compelling as it is.

One patient told me that she was not prepared to pay me on the last day of the month as she customarily did because she had gotten confused about the date. When I inquired about this confusion, she told me that she had her checkbook with her, but she absolutely refused to consider paying me that day because she had made up her mind that this day was not the correct one. She went on to other matters but came back to her compelling need to act upon her beliefs, even when they were erroneous.

As she considered this, similar situations came to mind, throwing light on a propensity to cling to a preferred version of reality even when this was not in her best interest. She became intense in relationships, for example, feeling panicky if she thought a relationship with a man would not work out, even if he were not particularly suitable.

Over the next week of sessions, she continued to think about these issues and was able to understand in a meaningful way how her compelling and determined need related to childhood anxieties and fears. She was able to talk about her intensity, which had multiple determinants. It represented, in part, anxiety about her sense of attachment. Her mother had been seriously ill with cancer when the patient was a child, and although she eventually recovered, her survival was in question for quite a while. Behind the patient's tenacity lurked a sense of panic. Her mother's hospitalization had intensified Oedipal wishes, representing as it did a feared and wished for victory. Her compulsivity was a defense against a fear of abandonment for her hostile wishes toward her mother and also represented her family's characteristic way of disavowing painful affects and forbidden wishes. Just as she had decided not to write me the check, many things in her family were decided by fiat and not available for discussion. Slowly a new-found ability to *consider* her behavior took the place of her usual disavowal. I thought that this new capacity for contemplation was quite an improvement over the peremptory brushing aside that she had favored before.

This achievement represented the culmination of years of intensive work with her need to disavow, and the underlying affects and fantasies against which it defended. A solid therapeutic alliance felt sufficiently safe that she could consider her behavior in previously unavailable ways. The work of the analysis enabled her to make links between past and present behavior, to understand her mind's characteristic way of working, and to recognize that at times this characteristic style created great difficulty for her.

When we look back on a treatment at the end of it, it is easy to forget how different the current person is from the one who first entered the consulting room. The patient feels better and more in control of life, and is able to think in ways that were impossible before. Even more arresting is the realization that these thoughts were not even *conceivable* before—that the patient never even knew that such ways of thinking existed. That is how the influence of the treatment spreads: first as the patient works with ideas within the transference, then in other psychological venues, and finally in the outside world, each expansion increasing possibilities for family, career, and friendship.

CHARACTER CHANGE AND THE "IMPLICIT"

Throughout this work I have tried to show how the underlying character issues that I see as the implicit dimension of behavior determine the flow and meaningfulness of a person's life. I have also tried to demonstrate that it is attention to these implicit issues that brings vigor and depth to the treatment. Concentration on the patient's internalized self- and object representations–to their "language," as I call it–facilitates access to the dynamics of inner life. It smooths the path from conscious to preconscious to unconscious discovery, as does attention to the preconscious and an orientation to the here-and-now, with forays into the past for context and when unresolved historical matters must be addressed. I have also tried to show how the other-than-instinctual needs of patients are best worked through at the implicit level of character structure. Conflict and defense struggles are important, but are best viewed within the context of the patient's life and character.

Experience has convinced me that patients want to develop a narrative of their lives; they want to understand how they function the way they do and why, and to find ways to represent ineffable experience consciously, through language. I also believe that many characterological constellations commonly ascribed only to the more seriously disturbed can be much more widely found, and at many levels of psychopathology. The need to adjust to painful aspects of reality, to accommodate to disappointments and failures, to deal with imperfections, and to achieve forgiveness (or at least reconciliation) are life tasks that we all struggle with and find their way into every patient's therapy.

TRANSFORMATIONS

As the patient changes, the therapeutic situation does too. The relationship between patient and therapist changes. The patient does more of the analytic work; the analyst recedes a bit. Things feel more equal, and the sense of collaboration increases. The patient's need for the therapist lessens, and correspondingly so does the analyst's need for the patient; I have frequently felt distressed by premature terminations, but never by terminations where this sense of completion has unfolded.

The feeling tone is different, becoming at the same time more emotionally charged, more varied, and more modulated. Complexity of affect and thought increase, and so does creativity, as ideas are put together in new ways. The patient uses the treatment more effectively, feeling less of a need to dispose defensively of uncomfortable affects. Aspects of the self that were once criticized or disavowed may be seen from a different perspective that enhances pride and self-esteem instead of embarrassment and shame. Yet a certain sadness and resignation become evident, too, in appreciation of the limits that life imposes. This disillusionment is very liberating, as it frees the patient from having to accomplish the impossible. Still, the siren song of grandiosity and omnipotence is a powerful one. To appreciate that life is capricious and control illusory brings with it peace, but also disappointment. And it requires that patient and analyst tackle their own deficiencies.

Psychoanalytic treatment accomplishes a great deal—paradoxically both more and less than we expect of it. On one hand, patients don't expect to change in the ways that they do. Often they could never even have conceived of becoming so different. On the other hand, they don't change in the ways they expect, and the grandiose fantasies, infantile desires, past traumas, and secret revenges that have unconsciously guided them must be relinquished. The analyst, too, must come to grips with hopes realized and hopes disappointed. Grandiose beliefs about one's own efficacy must be relinquished, and it can be hard to appreciate the progress that has in fact been made if the therapist had hoped for much more, either from the patient or from him- or herself. Consequently, there is disappointment for both participants. The limitations of self and, by corollary, of the treatment must be acknowledged.

Psychoanalytic work is both humbling and exhilarating. By the time an adult patient reaches an analyst's consulting room, much has happened in his or her life. Major decisions have been made; paths have been chosen that do not allow for return. The past life experiences that have led to psychopathological choices cannot be undone, and neither can some psychopathological structures. But the psychoanalytic encounter gives the patient a chance to fashion new opportunities out of old structures. One patient of mine, at the beginning of treatment, dreamed often of a burnt-out house, charred and unlivable. As the treatment progressed, she still dreamed of the same house, but it was no longer charred and uninhabitable. The analytic relationship offers a respite, a transitional space, in which the patient can gather strength, reconstitute, and investigate and explore areas of the mind never before glimpsed. The resulting transformations paradoxically are both more than expected and less than desired, but they are always impressive and deeply moving.

REFERENCES

Abraham, K. (1924) A short study of the development of the libido, viewed in the light of mental disorders, in *Selected Papers on Psychoanalysis,* pp. 418–501, New York: Brunner/Mazel, 1927.

Akhtar, S. (1997) Someday and if only fantasies, *Journal of the American Psychoanalytic Association,* 44:723–753.

——. (1999) *Inner Torment: Living between Conflict and Fragmentation,* Northvale, N.J.: Jason Aronson Press.

Anderson, M. (1999) The pressure toward enactment, *Journal of the American Psychoanalytic Association,* 47:503–518.

Appelfeld, A. (1998) Buried homeland, *The New Yorker,* November 23, 48–61.

Altschul, S. (1968) Denial and ego arrest, *Journal of the American Psychoanalytic Association,* 16:301–318.

Badaracco, J. Garcia (1992) Psychic change and its clinical evaluation, *International Journal of Psychoanalysis,* 73:209–220.

Bader, M. (1994), The tendency to neglect therapeutic aims in psychoanalysis, *Psychoanalytic Quarterly,* 63:246–270.

Baudry, F. (1989) Character, character type, and character organization, *Journal of the American Psychoanalytic Association,* 37:655–686.

Bion, W. (1957) On arrogance. In *Second Thoughts: Selected Papers on Psychoanalysis,* pp. 86–92, New York: Basic Books, 1967.

——. (1967) Notes on memory and desire, *Psychoanalytic Forum,* 2:272–273.

Bluhm, H. (1999) How did they survive? Mechanisms of defense in Nazi concentration camps, *American Journal of Psychotherapy,* 53:96–

122; originally published in *American Journal of Psychotherapy*, (1948), 2:3–32.

Blum, H. (1974) The concept of erotized transference, *International Journal of Psychoanalysis*, 21:61–76.

Bohm, T. (1999) The difficult freedom from a plan, *International Journal of Psychoanalysis*, 80:493–506.

Bollas, C. (1987). *The Shadow of the Object: Psychoanalysis of the Unthought Thought*, London: Free Association Books.

Brenman, E. (1985) Cruelty and narrowmindedness, *International Journal of Psychoanalysis*, 66:273–281.

Brenneis, C. B. (1997) On the relationship of dream content, trauma, and mind: A view from inside out or outside in? In Shapiro, E., (ed), *The Inner World in the Outer World: Psychoanalytic Perspective*, New Haven: Yale University Press.

Brenner, C. (1981) Defense and defense mechanisms, *Psychoanalytic Quarterly*, 50:557–569.

——. (1982) *The Mind in Conflict*, New York: International Universities Press.

——. (1996) The nature of knowledge and the limits of authority in psychoanalysis, *Psychoanalytic Quarterly*, 65:21–31.

Britton, R. (1995) Psychic reality and unconscious belief, *International Journal of Psychoanalysis*, 76:19–24.

Busch, F. (1995) *The Ego at the Center of Technique*, Northvale, N.J: Jason Aronson Press.

Busch, F. (1997) The patient's use of free association, *Journal of the American Psychoanalytic Association*, 45:407–423.

Carnigan, L. (1999) The secret: study of a perverse transference, *International Journal of Psychoanalysis*, 80:909–920.

Chasseguet-Smirgel, J. (1974) Perversion, idealization, and sublimation, *International Journal of Psychoanalysis*, 55:349–357.

——. (1978), Reflections on the connections between perversion and sadism, *International Journal of Psychoanalysis*, 59:27–35.

——. (1984) *Creativity and Perversion*, New York: W. W. Norton & Co.

——. (1988) From the archaic matrix of the oedipus complex to the fully developed oedipus complex: theoretical perspective in relation to clinical experience and technique, *The Psychoanalytic Quarterly*, 57:505–527.

Chused, J. (1991) The evocative power of enactments, *Journal of the American Psychoanalytic Association*, 39:615–640.

Coen, S. (1998) Perverse defenses in neurotic patients, *Journal of the American Psychoanalytic Association*, 46:1169–1194.

Cohen, J. (1980) Structural consequences of psychic trauma: a new look at "Beyond the Pleasure Principle," *International Journal of Psychoanalysis*, 61:421–432.

Deigh, J. (1984) Remarks on some difficulties in Freud's theory of moral development, *International Review of Psychoanalysis*, 11:207–225.

Epstein, L. (1979) The therapeutic function of hate in the countertransference. In *Countertransference*. (Eds.) Lawrence Epstein and Arthur Feiner, New York: Jason Aronson Press, (1979), pp. 213–234.

Erikson, E. (1963) *Childhood and Society*, New York: W. W. Norton & Co.

Feinsilver, D. (1999) Counteridentification, comprehensive countertransference and therapeutic action: Toward resolving the intrapsychic and interactional dichotomy, *Psychoanalytic Quarterly*, 68:264–303.

Fenichel, O. (1945) *The Psychoanalytic Theory of Neurosis*, New York: W. W. Norton and Co.

Fonagy, P. (1991) Thinking about thinking, *International Journal of Psychoanalysis*, 72:639–657.

——. (1999) Memory and therapeutic action, *International Journal of Psychoanalysis*, 80:215–224.

Fonagy, P. and Moran, G. (1991) Understanding psychic change in child psychoanalysis, *International Journal of Psychoanalysis*, 72:15–22.

Fonagy P. and Target, M. (1996) Playing with reality; I. theory of mind and the normal development of psychic reality, *International Journal of Psychoanalysis*, 77:217–233.

Freedman, R. and Natterson, J. (1999) Enactments: An intersubjective perspective, *The Psychoanalytic Quarterly*, 68:220–247.

Freud, A. (1946) *The Ego and Mechanisms of Defense*, New York: International Universities Press.

Freud, S. (1905a) Three Essays on Sexuality, *Standard Edition*, 7: 123–243.

Freud, S.(1909) Analysis of a phobia in a five-year-old boy, *Standard Edition*, 10:1–150.

——. (1914) Remembering, repeating and working through (further recommendations on the technique of psycho-analysis,) *Standard Edition*, 12:145–156).

——. (1917a) Mourning and melancholia, *Standard Edition*, 14:239–258.

——. (1917b) On Transformations of instinct as exemplified in anal erotism, *Standard Edition*, 17:127–133.

——. (1919) A child is being beaten: A contribution to the study of the origin of sexual perversions, *Standard Edition*, 17:174–204.

——. (1924) The unconscious problem of masochism, *Collected Papers 2*, 225–268, London: Hogarth Press.

——. (1925) Negation, *Standard Edition*, 19:235–239.

——. (1926) Inhibitions, symptoms and anxiety, *Standard Edition*, 20: 77–175.

——. (1927) Fetishism, *Standard Edition*, 21:152–157.

——. (1930) Civilization and its discontents, *Standard Edition*, 21:57–145.

——. (1938) Splitting of the ego in the process of defense, *Standard Edition*, 23: 271–278.

——. (1940) An outline of psychoanalysis, *Standard Edition*, 23:139–207.

Gabbard, G. O. (1996) *Love and Hate in the Analytic Setting*, Northvale, N.J: Jason Aronson Press.

Green, A. (1997) The Negative in Winnicott's work, *International Journal of Psychoanalysis*, 78:1071–1084.

Greenacre, P. (1967) The Influence of infantile trauma on genetic patterns, in, Furst, S. S. (ed), *Psychic Trauma*, pp. 108–153, New York: International Universities Press.

Grey, P. (1994) *The Ego and the Analysis of Defense*, Northvale, N.J.: Jason Aronson Press.

Grossman, L. (1993) The Perverse attitude toward reality, *Psychoanalytic Quarterly*, 62:422–436.

——. (1996) Psychic reality and reality testing in the analysis of perverse defense, *International Journal of Psychoanalysis*, 77:505–518.

Grossman, W. (1991) Pain, aggression, fantasy, and concepts of sadomasochism, *Psychoanalytic Quarterly*, 60:22–61.

Guntrip, H. (1969) S*chizoid Phenomena, Object Relations and the Self*, New York: International Universities Press.

Hartmann, H. (1952) The Mutual influences in the development of ego and id, *Psychoanalytic Study of the Child*, 7:9–30.

Hoffman, I. Z. (1996) The Intimate and ironic authority of the psychoanalyst's presence, *Psychoanalytic Quarterly*, 65:102–136.

Holder, A. (1975) Theoretical and clinical aspects of ambivalence, *Psychoanalytic Study of the Child*, 30:197–220.

Hooberman, R. and Hooberman, B. (1998) *Managing the Difficult Patient*, Madison, Conn.: International Universities Press.

Hopkins, L. (1998) D. W. Winnicott's analysis of Masud Khan: A preliminary study of failures of object usage, *Contemporary Psychoanalysis*, 34:5–47.

Horton, P. C. (1981) *Solace: The Hidden Dimension in Psychiatry*, Chicago: University of Chicago Press.

Jacobs, T. (1986) On Countertransference enactments, *Journal of the American Psychoanalytic Association, 34:289–308*.

Joffe, W. and Sandler, J. (1987) Adaptation, affects and the representational world, in Sandler, J. *From Safety and Superego,* New York: Guilford Press.

Joseph, B. (1992) Psychic change: some perspectives, *International Journal of Psychoanalysis,* 73:237–243.

Kaplan, H. (1991) *Female Perversion,* Northvale, N.J.: Jason Aronson Press.

Kernberg, O. (1995) Hatred as a core affect of aggression, in, *The Birth of Hatred: Developmental, Clinical and Technical Aspects of Intense Aggression,* pp. 53–82, edited by, Akhtar, S., Kramer, S., and Parens, H., Northvale, N.J.: Jason Aronson Press.

——. (1996) The analyst's authority in the psychoanalytic situation, *Psychoanalytic Quarterly,* 65:137–157.

Khan, M. (1963) The concept of cumulative trauma, *Psychoanalytic Study of the Child,* 18:286–306.

——. (1979) *Alienation in Perversions,* Madison, Conn.: International Universities Press.

Killingmo, B. (1989) Confict and deficit: implications for technique, *International Journal of Psychoanalysis,* 70:65–79.

——. (1995) Affirmation in psychoanalysis, *International Journal of Psychoanalysis,* 76:503–518.

Kinston, W. (1980) A theoretical and technical approach to narcissistic disturbance, *International Journal of Psychoanalysis,* 61:383–394.

Klein, D. (1998) Organizing Strands in the Treatment of Adolescents, paper given at the Michigan Psychoanalytic Council, November, East Lansing, Michigan.

Klein, M. (1935) A contribution to the psychogenesis of manic-depressive states, in *Love, Guilt and Reparation and Other Works, 1921–1945,* pp. 262–289, New York: The Free Press.

——. (1937) Love, guilt and reparation, in *Love, Guilt and Reparation and Other Works, 1921–1945,* pp. 306–343, New York: The Free Press, 1975.

——. (1940) Mourning and its relation to manic-depressive states, in *Love, Guilt and Reparation and Other Works, 1921–1945,* pp. 344–369, New York: The Free Press.

——. (1957) Envy and gratitude, in *Envy and Gratitude and Other Works 1946–1963,* pp. 176–235, London: Hogarth Press.

Kohut, H. (1971) *The Analysis of Self,* New York: International Universities Press.

——. (1984) *How Does Analysis Cure,* Chicago: University of Chicago Press.

Krystal, H. (1978) Trauma and affects, *Psychoanalytic Study of the Child,* 33:81–116.

——. (1988) *Integration and Self-Healing: Affect, Trauma, Alexithymia,* Hillsdale, N.J.: The Analytic Press.

Kumin, I. (1996) *Pre-Object Relatedness: Early Attachment and the Psychoanalytic Situation,* New York: Guilford Press.

Langs, R. (1976) *Bi-Personal Field,* Northvale, N.J.: Jason Aronson Press.

Laub, D. (1998) The empty circle, *Journal of the American Psychoanalytic Association,* 46:507–529.

Laub, D. and Auerhahn, N. (1993) Knowing and not knowing massive psychic trauma: forms of traumatic memory, *International Journal of Psychoanalysis,* 74:287–301.

Lepisto, B. (1999) Personal Communication.

Loewald, H. (1960). On the therapeutic interaction of psychoanalysis, *International Journal of Psychoanalysis,* 41:16–33.

Markson, E. (1993) Depression and moral masochism, *International Journal of Psychoanalysis,* 74:931–940.

Maroda, K. (1998) Enactment: When patient's and analyst's past converge, *Psychoanalytic Psychology,* 15:517–535.

McDougall, J. (1995) *The Many Faces of Eros: Psychoanalytic Exploration of Human Sexuality,* New York: Norton Press.

Mitchell, S. (1998), The analyst's knowledge and authority, *Psychoanalytic Quarterly,* 67:1–31.

Novick, J. and Novick, K. K. (1996) *Fearful Symmetry: The Development and Treatment of Sadomasochism,* Northvale, N.J: Jason Aronson Press.

Ogden, T. (1996a) Reconsidering three aspects of psychoanalytic technique, *International Journal of Psychoanalysis,* 77:883–900.

——. (1996b) The perverse subject of analysis, *Journal of the American Psychoanalytic Association,* 44:1121–1146.

Parker, R. (1995) *Mother Love/Mother Hate: The Power of Maternal Ambivalence,* New York: Basic Books.

Perelberg, R. J. (1999) The interplay between identifications and identity in the analysis of a violent young man: issues of technique, *International Journal of Psychoanalysis,* 80:31–45.

Pine, F. (1990) *Drive, Ego, Object and Self: A Synthesis for Clincial Work,* New York: Basic Books.

Racker, H. (1957) The meanings and uses of countertransference, *Psychoanalytic Quarterly*, 26:303–357.

Reed, G. (1997) The analyst's interpretation as fetish, *Journal of the American Psychoanalytic Association*, 45:1153–1181.

Renik, O. (1992) The interpretation as fetish, *Psychoanalytic Quarterly*, 61:542–563.

——. (1995) The analyst's expectations, *Journal of the American Psychoanalytic Association*, 43:83–94.

——. (1998) Getting real in analysis, *Psychoanalytic Quarterly*, 67:566–593.

Rosenfeld, H. (1971) A clinical approach to the psychoanalytic theory of the life and death instincts: An investigation into the aggressive aspects of narcissism, *International Journal of Psychoanalysis*, 52: 169–178.

Rothstein, A. (1995) *Psychoanalytic Technique and the Creation of Analytic Patients*, Madison, Conn.: International Universities Press.

Sandler, J. (1960) The background of safety, *International Journal of Psychoanalysis*, 41:352–365.

——. (1974) Psychological conflict and the structural model: some clinical and theoretical implications, *International Journal of Psychoanalysis*, 55:53–62.

——. (1976) Countertransference and role-responsiveness, *International Review of Psychoanalysis*, 3:43–47.

——. (1981) Character traits and object relationships, *Psychoanalytic Quarterly*, 50:694–708.

——. (1992) Reflections on developments in the theory of psychoanalytic technique, *International Journal of Psychoanalysis*, 73:189–198.

Sandler, J. and Sandler, A. M. (1978) On the development of object relationships and affects, *International Journal of Psychoanalysis*, 59:285–296.

——. (1987) The past unconscious, the present unconscious and the vicissitudes of guilt, *International Journal of Psychoanalysis*, 68: 331–341.

Schafer, R. (1983). *The Analytic Attitude*, New York: Basic Books.

Schecter, D. E. (1974) The ideal self and other, *Contemporary Psychoanalysis*, 10:103–115.

——. (1979) The loving and persecuting superego, *Contemporary Psychoanalysis*, 15:361–378.

Shabad, P. (1993) Repetition and incomplete mourning: The intergenerational transmission of traumatic themes, *Psychoanalytic Psychology*, 10:61–76.

Shengold, L. (1985) Defensive anality and anal narcissism, *International Journal of Psychoanalysis,* 66:47–73.

——. (1989) *Soul Murder: The Effects of Childhood Abuse and Deprivation,* New Haven: Yale University Press.

——. (1992) *Halos in the Sky: Observations on Anality and Defense,* New Haven: Yale University Press.

Sherby, L. B. (1989) Love and hate in the treatment of borderline patients, *Contemporary Psychoanalysis,* 25:574–591.

Stern, D. (1985). *The Interpersonal World of the Infant.* New York: Basic Books.

Stoller, R. (1975) *Perversion: The Erotic Form of Hatred,* New York: Dell Publishing.

Stolorow, R. (1975) The narcissistic function of masochism (and sadism), *International Journal of Psychoanalysis,* 56:441–448.

Strachey, J. (1934), The Nature of the therapeutic action of psychoanalysis, *International Journal of Psychoanalysis,* 15:127–159.

Target, M. and Fonagy, P. (1996) Playing with reality; II. the development of psychic reality from a theoretical perspective, *International Journal of Psychoanalysis,* 77:459–479.

Wallerstein, R. (1965) The goals of psychoanalysis: a survey of analytic viewpoints, *Journal of the American Psychoanalytic Association,* 13: 748–770.

Welles, J. and Wrye, H. (1991) The maternal erotic countertransference, *International Journal of Psychoanalysis,* 72:93–106.

Winnicott, D. (1949) Hate in the countertransference, *International Journal of Psychoanalysis,* 30:69–74.

——. (1950) Aggression in relation to emotional development, in *Through Paediatrics to Psychoanalysis: Collected Papers,* pp. 204–219, New York: Brunner/Mazel.

——. (1953) Transitional objects and transitional phenomena, *International Journal of Psychoanalysis,* 34:89–97.

——. (1958) The sense of guilt, in *The Maturational Processes and the Facilitating Environment,* pp. 15–28, London: Hogarth Press, 1985.

——. (1963) From dependence towards independence in the development of the individual, in, *The Maturational Processes and the Facilitating Environment,* pp. 83–92. London: Hogarth Press, 1985.

——. (1963) The development of the capacity for concern, in *The Maturational Processes and the Facilitating Environment,* pp. 73–82, London: Hogarth Press, 1985.

——. (1963), Psychiatric disorder in terms of infantile maturational processes, in *The Maturational Processes and the Facilitating Environment,* pp. 230–241, London: Hogarth Press, 1985.

——. (1963b) Communicating and not communicating leading to a study of certain opposites. In *The Maturational Processes and the Facilitating Environment,* pp. 179–193, London: Hogarth Press, 1985.

——. (1969) The use of an object, *International Journal of Psychoanalysis,* 50:711–716.

Wrye, H. and Welles, J. (1989) The maternal erotic transference, *International Journal of Psychoanalysis,* 70:673–684.

INDEX

ABOUT THE AUTHOR

Robert E. Hooberman, Ph.D., is a psychologist and psychoanalyst practicing in Ann Arbor, Michigan, where he works with adolescents, adults, and couples. As President of the Michigan Psychoanalytic Council, he is involved in psychoanalytic education and program development. He was formerly Chief Psychologist within the State of Michigan Prison system, and has a special interest in working with difficult patients and those suffering from severe personality disorders. He has presented at numerous conferences, including the Spring 2001 meeting of the Division of Psychoanalysis of the APA. Dr. Hooberman has published *Managing the Difficult Patient* (1998) with his wife, Barbara Hooberman, M.D.